ESTᴰ 1879

EDMONDS

SURE TO RISE

COOKERY BOOK

Revised Edition

69th Edition, 2016

Containing a collection of approximately
400 Everyday Recipes and Cooking Hints

Published by
Goodman Fielder Ltd

The Edmonds Cookery Book

The *Edmonds Cookery Book* has been a constant, reliable companion in Kiwi kitchens for over 100 years. We've grown up with it, learned to cook with it and fed our families from it, as well as prepared picnics, birthday cakes and holiday feasts from it. We've taken it flatting, packed it for our OEs, moved into new homes with it, made notes in it and spilled things all over its pages. What we haven't done is outgrow it.

Every Edmonds recipe is special because each is a classic in its own way, perfected over time and passed on for another generation to enjoy all over again. The edition you're holding now includes more of the favourite recipes you've come to know and love. We've tested, tasted and tried them all again to make sure they are at their best. We've also done a little housekeeping, like adding descriptions and rewriting instructions, so they're a bit easier to follow. We've brought back some gems that got lost along the way and replaced a few recipes that haven't kept pace with modern tastes.

If any of your favourite recipes haven't made the book then don't panic. All the original Cookery Book recipes are available on the Edmonds website, edmondscooking.co.nz. We're pleased to be able to share this new edition with you, and hope you have many joyful years of cooking together.

The Edmonds Story

And the man behind the collection of recipes that is still the biggest selling New Zealand book ever published? Thomas Edmonds, a Christchurch grocery store owner, began making his own baking powder out the back of his store in 1879. When questioned over the superiority of his product he responded 'It is sure to rise, madam' and so the famous Edmonds promise was born. His confidence was well founded. Thomas' 'Sure To Rise' baking powder was immediately popular, selling one million tins by 1912. Today the Edmonds range has grown to include yeast, flour, cake mixes, pastry, mayonnaises and salad dressings.

The first edition of the *Edmonds Cookery Book* was introduced in 1908, as a thank you for the support his business had received from Kiwi households, a lovely gesture that has become a Kiwi classic. Thank you, Thomas.

Contents

Excellence with Edmonds

The Edmonds Cookery Book was created to make cooking simple for new and experienced cooks. This revised edition has been designed to make the recipes easier to follow in a step-by-step format.

Using the Recipes

- Read through a recipe carefully before starting. Check that you have all the ingredients you require before preparing the recipe.
- Recipes are arranged alphabetically in each section for easy reference.
- Helpful hints – found at the beginning of some sections and at the bottom of recipe pages. Read these before starting to make a recipe from that section.
- Ingredients are listed in the order of use in a recipe.
- Preheat the oven before you start cooking. Remember to check the oven rack positions (page 9).
- Prepare tins, dishes or trays before cooking.
- Cooking temperatures and times, and number of serves or quantities made are given at the start of each recipe. Note, though, that oven temperatures may vary in individual ovens so they are a guide only.

We welcome feedback on our recipes. If you would like to share your experiences, make comments or ask questions about the recipes in this book, please contact us via our Consumer Advisory Centre on **0800 805 255** or visit our website **edmondscooking.co.nz**.

Weights and Measures

- New Zealand standard metric cup and spoon measures are used in all recipes.
- All measurements are level.
- Use measuring cups or jugs for liquid measures and sets of 1 cup, ½ cup, ⅓ cup and ¼ cup measures for dry ingredients.
- Brown sugar measurements are firmly packed, so that the sugar will hold the shape of the cup when tipped out.
- Size 6 eggs (53g) are used as the standard size unless otherwise stated.

Abbreviations

tsp	= teaspoon
Tbsp	= tablespoon
L	= litre
ml	= millilitre
cm	= centimetre
mm	= millimetre
g	= gram
kg	= kilogram
°C	= degrees Celsius

Standard Measures

1 cup	= 250ml
1 litre	= 4 cups
1 Tbsp	= 15ml (note an Australian Tbsp is 20ml)
1 dessertspoon	= 10ml
1 tsp	= 5ml
½ tsp	= 2.5ml
¼ tsp	= 1.25ml

Metric/Imperial Conversions in Common Cooking Use

WEIGHT		VOLUME		MEASUREMENTS	
30g	= 1 ounce	1kg	= 2¼ pounds	2.5cm	= 1 inch
120g	= 4 ounces	1L	= 1¾ pints	20cm	= 8 inches
240g	= 8 ounces			30cm	= 12 inches
450g	= 1 pound				

Weights and Measures: Approximate Equivalents

ITEM	MEASURE	WEIGHT
breadcrumbs (fresh)	1 cup	50g
butter	2 Tbsp	30g
cheese (grated, firmly packed)	1 cup	100g
cocoa	4 Tbsp	25g
coconut	1 cup	75g
cornflour	4 Tbsp	25g
cream	½ pint	300ml
dried fruit (sultanas, raisins, dates)	1 cup	150–175g
egg, standard size 6		about 53g
flour	1 cup	125g
flour, wholemeal	1 cup	150g
gelatine	4 Tbsp	25g
golden syrup	1 Tbsp	25g
milk	1 cup	250ml
nuts	1 cup	125–150g
oil	1 Tbsp	15ml
rice, sago	2 Tbsp	25g
	1 cup	200g
salt	2 Tbsp	25g
sour cream	1 cup	250g
sugar, brown	1 cup (firmly packed)	200g
	1 cup (loosely packed)	125–150g
sugar, icing	1 cup	150g
sugar, white	2 Tbsp	30g
	1 cup	225g

Before and After Equivalent Measures

Approximate amounts needed to give measures:

⅓ cup uncooked rice = 1 cup cooked rice

⅓ cup uncooked pasta = 1 cup cooked pasta

2–3 chicken pieces = 1 cup cooked chicken

100g cheese = 1 cup grated cheese

75g mushrooms = 1 cup sliced = ½ cup cooked

4 toast slices bread = 1 cup fresh breadcrumbs

200g (two) potatoes = 1 cup mashed potato

A Guide to Oven Temperatures and Use

PRODUCT	°C	DESCRIPTION
meringues, pavlova	110–140	slow
custards, milk puddings, shortbread, rich fruit cakes, casseroles, slow roasting	150–160	moderately slow
biscuits, large and small cakes roasting, sponges, muffins,	180–190	moderate
short pastry	190–220	moderately hot
flaky pastry, scones, browning toppings	220–230	hot
puff pastry	250–260	very hot

Oven Temperature Conversions

165°C = 325°F
175°C = 350°F
190°C = 375°F
200°C = 400°F

Oven Hints

- Position your oven racks before turning oven on.
- Oven positions in general
    - Bottom of oven: use for slow cooking and low-temperature cooking
    - Middle of oven: for moderate-temperature cooking
    - Above middle: for quick cooking and high-temperature cooking
    - Check your oven manual as it may have specific guidelines for your oven.
- Fan-forced ovens: refer to the manufacturer's directions as the models vary. As a guide, subtract 20°C from recommended temperature for conventional ovens.
- Preheat oven to required temperature before food preparation.
- Cooking temperatures and times are a guide only, as oven temperatures may vary.

Breads & Buns

The miracle of dough rising, the delicious aroma in the kitchen as the bread bakes, the sound of the crust cracking as it cools and the golden beauty of a loaf – these are almost as significant as the flavour and texture of the bread when you eat it. Baking bread at home is one of life's pleasures, so don't miss out! A plain loaf has just four ingredients, flour, yeast, water and salt, and is not at all difficult to make. Your task as the baker is to do some enjoyable mixing and kneading and then sit back while the yeast does its work.

How to make great bread:

Before you start, read through these notes on the ingredients used and the processes of making bread.

Yeast

Yeast is a living plant which needs gentle warmth, food and liquid to make it grow. As it grows it gives off carbon dioxide, which creates the bubbles that make the dough rise, and it also produces alcohol. The alcohol is driven off when you bake the bread and this is what makes freshly baked bread smell so good.

There are two readily available types of yeast:

- Edmonds active yeast is dried yeast granules which become active when mixed with warm water. It can be used in homebrewing.
- Edmonds Surebake yeast is a mixture of active yeast and bread improvers which give homemade bread a soft, fine crumb. We recommend using Surebake in bread-making machines.

Yeast works best at 37°C, which is body temperature. A higher temperature will kill the yeast, whereas a low temperature will retard its activity, but not kill it. By leaving bread dough to rise at room temperature, or even in the fridge, you will produce a better-flavoured loaf which will stay fresh for longer.

To use Edmonds active yeast, begin by mixing the yeast with some warm liquid to reactivate it, then after about 15 minutes add it to the flour with the remaining ingredients.

To use Edmonds Surebake yeast, mix the yeast with all of the measured dry ingredients, and then add all of the required liquid. Stir to a smooth paste.

Replacements

- 1 tablespoon Edmonds active yeast is equivalent to 2 tablespoons Edmonds Surebake yeast.
- One 12g Edmonds instant dried yeast sachet is equivalent to 1½ tablespoons of Edmonds active yeast or 3 tablespoons of Edmonds Surebake yeast.

Flour

- Edmonds high grade flour is best for bread making since its high protein (gluten) content gives the bread good volume and texture. You can also use Edmonds wholemeal flour, and sweet, cake-like breads are made with Edmonds standard flour.

Other bread ingredients

- A small amount of sugar helps feed the yeast and gives bread its golden crust. You can use white or brown sugar, honey, golden syrup, treacle, molasses or malt extract.
- Milk and butter make bread softer and help it stay fresh.
- Add any spices, seeds, herbs, oats or grated cheese with the butter before kneading the dough. Add dried fruits or nuts towards the end of kneading.

Kneading

- Kneading develops the gluten in the dough which helps it rise and gives the baked loaf an even texture.
- Knead dough by folding it towards you and then pushing it down and away, using the palms of your hands. Rotate the dough a quarter turn and repeat the process for 8–10 minutes, until it feels firm and springy and is no longer sticky.
- Use as little extra flour as you can.

Proving bread dough

Using the oven:
- Preheat the oven to 50°C with a dish of hot water on the bottom rack. Turn the oven off. Brush the top of the dough with oil or melted butter and cover with a cloth. Leave the dough to prove for 30 minutes to 1 hour, until it has doubled in volume, then take it out and shape as required.

Using the microwave:
- Brush the top of the dough with oil or melted butter and cover loosely with plastic wrap. Microwave for 10 minutes on 10% power. Stand for 10 minutes, then repeat until the dough has doubled in size.

At room temperature:
- Cover the dough with a damp cloth and put a large plate or lid over the cloth. Leave on the kitchen bench to prove overnight. Shape and bake the next day.

In the refrigerator:
- Cover the bread dough with a damp cloth and a lid and refrigerate overnight. Allow it to return to room temperature – about 1 hour – before proceeding with the recipe.

Crumpets

2 HOURS 14 MAKES

Freshly made crumpets are a revelation! You will need crumpet or egg rings – metal circles about 2cm deep and 7.5–10cm in diameter – to keep them circular. These crumpets are tender, delicious and fun to make.

450g Edmonds standard flour	*2 tsp sugar*
1 tsp salt	*2 tsp Edmonds active yeast*
250ml milk	*¼ tsp Edmonds baking soda*
300ml hot water	*100ml warm water*

1. Sift the flour and salt into a bowl. Mix together the milk and hot water, add the sugar and stir to dissolve.

2. Sprinkle the yeast over the warm liquid and set aside for 10 minutes, until the mixture is frothy.

3. Add the yeast mixture to the flour and mix to a smooth batter, then beat hard for about 5 minutes with a wooden spoon or an electric mixer.

4. Cover the bowl with a damp cloth and leave in a warm place until the batter has doubled in volume – about 1 hour.

5. Dissolve the baking soda in the warm water and beat into the risen batter until smooth. Cover and leave for 10 minutes.

6. While the batter is resting, gently heat a heavy-based frying pan or griddle and oil it lightly. Oil the insides of the crumpet rings using a paper towel, and set them on the griddle.

7. The batter should now be pourable, like thick cream. If it is too thick you won't get the essential honeycomb of holes, and if too thin it will run out from under the rings. Cook a small spoonful of batter to test it then thin with a little warm water or add more flour if you need to.

8. Pour 3–4 tablespoons of batter into each ring until half full, and cook gently until the crumpets rise up, the tops are covered with small holes and they are almost dry to the touch. This will take 6–8 minutes. Using a spatula, turn them over carefully, still in the rings, and cook for another 2 minutes. Place on a wire rack to cool and remove the rings after about 5 minutes. Wipe the rings clean, lightly oil them again and make another batch.

9. Toast the crumpets, spread them generously with butter and serve hot with jam or honey or golden syrup. They will keep for a week in the fridge untoasted.

Cheese Loaf

1 HOUR 2 LOAVES

Based on a recipe in the 1986 Edmonds Cookery Book, this is a quick and tasty bread to which you could add a little chilli powder, some rosemary or other herbs, or some finely chopped celery or spring onion.

3 cups Edmonds standard flour	*2 tsp butter*
3 tsp Edmonds baking powder	*1½ cups grated cheese*
½ tsp salt	*1 cup milk, approximately*
½ tsp dry mustard powder	*extra cheese and paprika*

1. Preheat the oven to 200°C. Butter two 23cm loaf tins and line the bases with baking paper.

2. Sift together the flour, baking powder, salt and mustard powder, rub in the butter, then mix in the grated cheese.

3. Mix with the milk to make a soft, moist dough. Spoon into the loaf tins and top with a little extra grated cheese and a sprinkle of paprika. Bake for 30–40 minutes and place on a wire rack to cool.

Chelsea Buns

3 HOURS   9 MAKES

Spicy, fruity, spiral buns, baked originally at the old Chelsea Bun House in London's Pimlico and enjoyed by thousands of Londoners since the early 18th century. Bake the Chelsea Buns close together to achieve the traditional square shape then pull them apart to eat.

DOUGH
225g Edmonds high grade flour
1½ tsp Edmonds active yeast
1 tsp caster sugar
100ml warm milk

½ tsp salt
75g butter
1 egg, beaten
2 Tbsp extra caster sugar

FILLING
50g butter, softened
100g mixed dried fruit
25g mixed peel

50g brown sugar
½ tsp mixed spice
½ tsp cinnamon

GLAZE
2 Tbsp sugar

2 Tbsp milk

1. In a small bowl mix 2 tablespoons of the flour with the yeast, sugar and warm milk. Leave in a warm place for 10–15 minutes until frothy.

2. Sift the remaining flour and the salt into a large bowl and rub in the butter with your fingers. Pour the yeast mixture and the beaten egg into the flour and mix well to form a soft dough. Knead on a floured board for about 5 minutes, until smooth and elastic.

3. Shape the dough into a ball and leave to rise for about 1½ hours in a lightly buttered bowl, covered with a damp cloth.

4. Grease an 18cm square tin. On a floured surface, roll the risen dough out to a 30cm x 23cm rectangle. Spread evenly with the butter, then mix together the fruit, peel, brown sugar and spices, and sprinkle over the dough.

5. Roll up from a long edge to form an even roll, and cut into 9 pieces. Place cut side down in the prepared tin, not quite touching, cover with a cloth and leave for about 30 minutes until risen and springy.

6. While the buns are rising, preheat the oven to 200°C. Sprinkle the tops of the buns with the extra caster sugar.

7. Bake for 15–20 minutes until golden brown and firm to the touch.

8. Dissolve the sugar in the milk and simmer together to form a glaze. Brush over the buns while they are hot. Pull apart and serve warm.

Cinnamon Scrolls

OVERNIGHT

HOURS

MAKES

Also known as Scandinavian coffee breads, these are deliciously soft and tender and often flavoured with cardamom. The dough rises overnight in the fridge and is easy to shape. You can also use this dough for a brioche-style loaf or sweet rolls.

DOUGH
1 cup warm water
4 tsp Edmonds active yeast
½ cup sugar
115g butter, melted

3 eggs, lightly beaten
½ tsp salt
4½ cups Edmonds standard flour
½ tsp ground cardamom (optional)

FILLING
115g butter, softened
3 tsp cinnamon

½ cup brown sugar

GLAZE
1 egg, beaten
2 Tbsp milk

icing sugar

1. Put the water into a large bowl and sprinkle over the yeast and 1 teaspoon of the sugar. Set aside for 15 minutes.

2. Stir in the remaining sugar, melted butter, beaten eggs and salt, and combine well. Then mix in the flour and cardamom and beat well with a wooden spoon until smooth. It will look more like a biscuit mixture than a bread dough. Cover and put in the fridge for at least 2 hours or overnight.

3. After 2 hours or the next day, lightly grease two 20cm round tins. Turn the chilled dough out onto a floured board and divide it in half.

4. Roll each half out to a 30cm square and spread each with a thin layer of the softened butter, taking the butter right to the edges of the dough. Then sprinkle over the cinnamon and brown sugar evenly.

5. Roll up fairly firmly, press the edges to seal and smooth each roll out with your hands so it is as even as possible. They should now be about 45cm long.

6. Use a sharp serrated knife to cut each roll into about 9 pieces and place cut side down in the prepared tins. Cover with a cloth and leave to rise for 1 hour. They will almost double in size and become soft and puffy.

7. Preheat the oven to 180°C. Mix together the egg and milk for the glaze. When the rolls have risen, brush with the glaze.

8. Bake for about 30 minutes or until a dark golden brown and a skewer inserted into the centre of the bread comes out clean. Leave in the tin for 5 minutes before turning out to cool on a wire rack. Dust lightly with icing sugar and serve warm if possible.

VARIATION

Sticky Cinnamon Scrolls (Schnecken)
You could also bake the spirals of dough in large muffin tins with a layer of butter, sugar, syrup and nuts in the base.

FOR THE STICKY LAYER

200g butter, softened
¾ cup soft brown or Demerara sugar
4 Tbsp honey or maple syrup

3 Tbsp golden syrup
1 cup chopped walnuts

1. Beat together the butter, sugar, honey and syrup and spoon into a large 18-hole muffin tin.
2. Divide the nuts among the tins. After you cut the scrolls, place them in the muffin tins.
3. Cover with a cloth and leave to rise for 1 hour.
4. Place the muffin tin on a baking tray in case the buttery syrup bubbles over.
5. Bake as above and be careful removing the scrolls from the tins as the syrup will be hot.

Flour Tortillas

HOUR

MAKES

Fresh tortillas taste far better than bought ones, and they are simple and satisfying to make. Try them and we guarantee you'll be a fresh tortilla fan.

2 cups Edmonds high grade flour
½ tsp salt

3 Tbsp oil
¾ cup warm water, approximately

1. Sift the flour and salt into a bowl. Stir in the oil and add enough water to form a soft dough.
2. Turn the dough onto a floured board and knead for 3 minutes or until smooth and elastic, adding a little more flour if you need to. Place the ball of dough in a lightly oiled bowl, cover with a damp cloth and leave at room temperature for 30 minutes.
3. Turn out the dough, knead it lightly and divide into 8 pieces. Form each piece into a ball, then flatten into a disc about 7.5cm in diameter and cover with a cloth to keep the dough soft.
4. Heat a heavy-based frying pan. Roll out a portion of dough to a 20cm circle on a lightly floured board, turning the dough over frequently.
5. Cook the first tortilla for about 45 seconds or until golden, then flip over and cook the other side for another 45 seconds. While the first tortilla is cooking, roll out the next one.
6. As the tortillas are cooked, pile them on a warm plate covered with a bowl or another plate to keep them soft. Serve warm with any savoury dish, or use them to make Quesadillas (see below) or Chicken Enchiladas (page 154).

Quesadillas

Spread a tortilla with grated cheese and chopped herbs, then fold in half and cook on a hot griddle until the cheese melts and the tortilla is toasted. Keep pressing the quesadilla down with a spatula as it cooks. Serve 2–3 per person.

Focaccia

1½ HOURS **1 LOAF**

A quick and easy recipe for this delicious Italian flatbread. It's great plain but you can also personalise the topping. There are no rules!

500ml warm water
1½ Tbsp Edmonds active yeast
1½ tsp salt
1 tsp sugar

570g Edmonds high grade flour
olive oil and flaky salt
a few sprigs of rosemary and some
    thinly sliced garlic (optional)

1. Put the water, yeast, salt, sugar and 1 tablespoon of the flour into a large mixing bowl. Stir together, cover and leave for 10 minutes.
2. Add the remaining flour and mix until smooth. Cover the bowl with a damp cloth and set aside for at least 45 minutes, or up to 2½ hours to rise.
3. Preheat the oven to 220˚C. Oil a large, shallow roasting dish.
4. Scrape the risen dough into the dish and, with oiled hands, spread it out evenly. Dimple the top with your fingers and sprinkle with salt. Add small sprigs of rosemary and scatter with the garlic if you like.
5. Bake for 15 minutes until risen and golden brown. Brush with more oil if you wish and serve warm.

Hot Cross Buns

OVERNIGHT **1½ HOURS** **16 MAKES**

Fresh, warm buns are amazing on Good Friday morning – but getting up at 3am to start making them isn't. Mix the dough the night before.

DOUGH
300ml milk
3 tsp Edmonds active yeast
510g Edmonds high grade flour
55g brown sugar
1 tsp salt

3 tsp mixed spice
55g butter
2 eggs, beaten
115g currants
115g mixed peel

CROSSES
2 Tbsp Edmonds self raising flour

2 Tbsp cold water

GLAZE
3 Tbsp sugar

3 Tbsp milk

1. Warm the milk slightly, sprinkle over the yeast and set aside for 10–15 minutes.
2. Put the flour, sugar, salt and spice in a large bowl and mix to combine, then rub in the butter with your fingertips.
3. Pour in the yeast mixture and the beaten eggs and mix until smooth with a wooden spoon or an electric mixer fitted with a dough hook. Finally, stir in the currants and peel. The dough will be sticky. Cover with a damp cloth and a lid (you can use a dinner plate) and leave on the bench overnight.
4. In the morning, grease a shallow tin. Turn the dough out onto a floured board, knead a little and divide into 16 pieces. Roll each piece into a ball and place in the prepared tin about 1cm apart. Cover with a cloth and leave to rise for about 45 minutes.
5. Preheat the oven to 200˚C.
6. For the crosses, make a soft batter with the flour and water and put it into a small

forcing bag or a plastic bag with the corner cut off. Pipe the crosses onto the buns.

7. Bake for about 25 minutes until well risen and golden brown.

8. Dissolve the sugar in the milk and simmer together to form a glaze. Once the buns are cooked, brush the glaze over them, twice.

Pizza

3 HOURS 2 MAKES

The best way to mimic a traditional brick pizza oven is to use a pizza stone and set your oven to its maximum temperature. Allow at least 45 minutes to heat the stone and once the pizza is in, turn on the grill to cook the topping as quickly as possible.

500g Edmonds high grade flour
150g Edmonds wholemeal flour
1 tsp Edmonds active yeast

1 tsp salt
100ml boiling water
200ml cool water

1. Mix together the flours and the yeast in a large bowl.

2. Dissolve the salt in the boiling water, then add the cool water and pour this into the flours. Mix with a wooden spoon, adding more warm water as needed to make a smooth dough. Knead for a few minutes.

3. Put the dough into a warmed, oiled bowl, cover with a damp cloth and leave to rise for 2 hours at room temperature. You can also use the dough straight away if you wish, but the flavour will be less developed.

4. Preheat the oven to its maximum temperature – at least 220˚C – preferably with a pizza stone in it. Lightly oil a 25cm pizza pan if using.

5. When the dough has risen, turn out and knead lightly again. Divide in half and roll each half out into a circle on a floured board or press into the pizza pan.

6. Spread with toppings of your choice. If you are not using a pan, slide the pizza directly onto the pizza stone using a flat baking tray to make the transfer.

7. Cook each pizza for 10–15 minutes or until well risen and golden.

Potato Bread

1½ HOURS 1 LOAF

Mashed potato added to white bread dough makes the bread lighter and helps keep it moist. Kiwis have known this trick since at least 1930, when it first appeared in this book. Since it's a 'quick bread' made with baking powder instead of yeast, you will need to work quickly. Make sure the oven is hot before you start.

500g Edmonds standard flour
1 tsp sugar
1 tsp salt

4 tsp Edmonds baking powder
125g warm mashed potato
150ml each milk and water, mixed

1. Preheat the oven to 200˚C. Grease a 25cm x 11cm loaf tin and line the base with baking paper.

2. Sift together the flour, sugar, salt and baking powder and then rub in the mashed potato with your fingertips.

3. Mix quickly to a soft dough with the milk and water and spoon at once into the prepared tin. Smooth the top with a knife dipped in melted butter.

4. Bake for 45 mintues to 1 hour, until risen and golden on top.

5. Remove from the tin after a few minutes and wrap in a clean cloth until the bread is cold. This prevents a tough crust from developing.

White Bread

625g Edmonds high grade flour	*5g (1 tsp) sugar*
400ml water	*10g (1¼ tsp) salt*
20g Edmonds Surebake yeast	*35ml (20g) vegetable oil*

1. Put all the ingredients into the mixing bowl of an electric mixer fitted with a dough hook. Mix on slow until the dough becomes smooth and elastic. This is the easy way.

2. If kneading by hand, mix all the ingredients together until they form a dough. Knead on a lightly floured surface until the dough becomes smooth and elastic. This may take 15 minutes and will be a real workout.

3. Divide the dough into 4 even pieces and mould into rounds. Cover with a clean tea towel and set aside for 15 minutes.

4. Grease two 25cm loaf tins.

5. Lightly remould each piece of dough into rounds, bringing them back to their original size and knocking back the gases formed in the process. Place 2 rounds of dough into each tin. Cover with the tea towel and leave in a warm place until doubled in size.

6. Preheat the oven to 200°C.

7. Bake for 30 minutes or until the crust is golden brown.

Wholegrain Brown Bread

155g kibbled (cracked) wheat	*25g Edmonds Surebake yeast*
200ml boiling water	*17g salt*
465g Edmonds high grade flour	*5g (1 tsp) sugar*
280g Edmonds wholemeal flour	*35ml (20g) vegetable oil*

1. Put the kibbled wheat into a bowl, pour in the boiling water and give the mixture a good stir. Set aside to cool for 30 minutes.

2. Place the cooled kibbled wheat and water and the remaining ingredients into the bowl of an electric mixer fitted with a dough hook. Mix on slow until the dough becomes smooth and elastic. This is the easy way.

3. If kneading by hand, mix all the ingredients together until they form a dough. Knead on a lightly floured surface until the dough becomes smooth and elastic. This may take 15 minutes and will be a real workout.

4. Divide the dough into 4 even pieces and mould into rounds. Cover with a clean tea towel and set aside for 15 minutes.

5. Grease two 25cm loaf tins.

6. Lightly remould each piece of dough into rounds, bringing them back to their original size and knocking back the gases formed in the process. Place 2 rounds of dough into each tin. Cover with the tea towel and leave in a warm place until doubled in size.

7. Preheat the oven to 200°C.

8. Bake for 30 minutes or until the crust is golden brown.

Crumpets page 12, Chelsea Buns page 13

Potato Bread page 17, Wholegrain Brown Bread page 18

Wholemeal Bread

2 HOURS 2 LOAVES

600g Edmonds wholemeal flour
250g Edmonds high grade flour
540ml water
25g Edmonds Surebake yeast

5g (1 tsp) sugar
17g salt
35ml (20g) vegetable oil

1. Put all the ingredients into the bowl of an electric mixer fitted with a dough hook. Mix on slow until the dough becomes smooth and elastic. This is the easy way.
2. If kneading by hand, mix all the ingredients together until they form a dough. Knead on a lightly floured surface until the dough becomes smooth and elastic. This may take 15 minutes and will be a real workout.
3. Divide the dough into 4 even pieces and mould into rounds. Cover with a clean tea towel and set aside for 15 minutes.
4. Grease two 25cm loaf tins.
5. Lightly remould each piece of dough into rounds, bringing them back to their original size and knocking back the gases formed in the process. Place 2 rounds of dough into each tin. Cover with the tea towel and leave in a warm place until doubled in size.
6. Preheat the oven to 200°C.
7. Bake for 30 minutes or until the crust is golden brown.

Make a 'warm place' for the dough to rise by placing the bowl inside a larger bowl half-filled with hot water. Cover with a cloth.

Scones, Muffins & Loaves

Scones and muffins have always been popular with
Kiwi home bakers, probably because they're unfussy,
relatively simple to make and delicious. The same can be
said for their tasty but equally humble cousin, the loaf.

Banana Loaf

1½ HOURS   1 MAKES

A classic recipe to use up those over-ripe bananas. Slice and serve with butter.

1¾ cups Edmonds self raising flour
¼ tsp Edmonds baking soda
¼ tsp salt
½ cup sugar
2 eggs

¼ cup milk
75g butter, melted
1 cup mashed banana (about 2 large
  bananas)

1. Preheat the oven to 180°C. Grease a 22cm loaf tin and line the base with baking paper.
2. Sift the flour, baking soda and salt into a bowl and mix in the sugar.
3. In another bowl, beat the eggs and stir in the milk, melted butter and mashed banana. Mix quickly into the dry ingredients, stirring until just combined. Spoon into the prepared tin.
4. Bake for 45–55 minutes until well risen and golden. Leave in the tin for 10 minutes before turning out onto a wire rack to cool.

Banana Muffins – Gluten Free

45 MINS   12 MAKES

Banana is delicious but also holds these muffins together really well and keeps them moist.

110g butter, softened
110g caster sugar
2 eggs, size 7
3 large ripe bananas
225g Edmonds gluten free plain flour

1 tsp Edmonds baking powder
½ tsp salt
75g sultanas
gluten free icing sugar

1. Preheat the oven to 200°C. Line a standard 12-hole muffin tin with paper cases.
2. Cream the butter and sugar together in a large bowl until light and fluffy.
3. Add the eggs one at a time, beating well after each addition, until you have a smooth, light, airy mixture.
4. Mash the bananas and add them one at a time. Mix well between each banana until they disappear into the mixture.

5. Mix the flour, baking powder and salt together in a separate bowl. Sift the dry ingredients into the butter and egg mixture in three additions, mixing in each addition until you have a thick but even consistency and all the dry ingredients have disappeared into the wet mixture. Fold in the sultanas gently.

6. Spoon into the paper cases, filling no more than three-quarters full. The baking powder will make them rise so don't overfill.

7. Bake for 25–30 minutes until golden brown. Allow to cool for 5 minutes in the tin then place on a wire rack to cool. Sift over some gluten free icing sugar before serving.

Basic Muffins

30 MINS   12 MAKES

¾ cup Edmonds wholemeal flour
¾ cup Edmonds standard flour
1 tsp Edmonds baking powder
pinch of salt
½ cup brown sugar

50g butter, melted
1 egg
½ tsp Edmonds baking soda
¾ cup milk

1. Preheat the oven to 200°C. Grease a standard 12-hole muffin tin.

2. Sift together the flours, baking powder and salt. Add the wheat husks back to the bowl and stir in the sugar.

3. Mix together the cooled melted butter and the egg, then separately dissolve the baking soda in the milk.

4. Tip both wet mixtures into the dry ingredients and mix quickly with a round-bladed table knife. Don't over-mix; just stir until the ingredients are almost combined. Spoon the mixture into the prepared muffin tins.

5. Bake for 12–15 minutes until risen and golden. Place on a wire rack to cool.

VARIATIONS

Apricot Muffins
Add ½ cup chopped apricots to sifted ingredients.

Spiced Muffins
Add ½ teaspoon cinnamon and ½ teaspoon mixed spice to sifted ingredients.

Chocolate Muffins
Add ½ cup chocolate chips to sifted ingredients.

Banana Muffins
Add ½ cup mashed banana after sifted ingredients.

Berry Muffins
Add ½ cup frozen or fresh berries after sifted ingredients.

Avoid over-mixing muffins and gems as this produces peaked instead of rounded tops and a tunnelled rather than an even texture.

Bran Muffins

30 MINS · 12 MAKES

These are the classic, nubbly brown muffins – thought to be particularly health-giving, and known to be delicious, especially when spread with butter.

1 cup Edmonds standard flour	1 Tbsp butter
1 tsp Edmonds baking powder	1 Tbsp golden syrup
½ tsp salt	1 tsp Edmonds baking soda
¼ cup sugar	1 cup milk
1½ cups Edmonds wheat bran	1 egg, beaten

1. Preheat the oven to 220°C. Grease a standard 12-hole muffin tin.
2. Sift together the flour, baking powder and salt and stir in the sugar and wheat bran.
3. Melt the butter and golden syrup together and separately dissolve the baking soda in the milk.
4. Tip both the wet mixtures and the beaten egg into the dry ingredients and mix quickly with a round-bladed knife. Don't over-mix; just stir until the ingredients are almost combined. Spoon the mixture into the prepared muffin tins.
5. Bake for 12–15 minutes until risen and golden. Place on a wire rack to cool.

Cheese Muffins

30 MINS · 12 MAKES

Sublimely simple. A pinch of cayenne pepper adds a little kick to these savoury beauties.

¾ cup grated tasty cheese	¼ tsp salt
2 cups Edmonds standard flour	50g butter, melted
4 tsp Edmonds baking powder	1 egg, beaten
pinch of cayenne pepper	1½ cups milk

1. Preheat the oven to 200°C. Grease a standard 12-hole muffin tin.
2. Put the cheese into a bowl and sift over the flour, baking powder, cayenne pepper and salt. Stir to combine.
3. Quickly stir in the melted butter, egg and milk using a round-bladed table knife. Don't over-mix; just stir until the ingredients are almost combined. Spoon the mixture into the prepared muffin tins.
4. Bake for 12–15 minutes until risen and golden. Place on a wire rack to cool.

VARIATION
Add 1 tablespoon chopped red or green pepper to the cheese.

Coconut Loaf

1½ HOURS · 1 MAKES

A very popular recipe from the 1957 Edmonds Cookery Book. This creamy-coloured loaf has a golden crust, tastes delicious, keeps well and makes excellent toast.

3 cups Edmonds standard flour	1 cup sugar
3 tsp Edmonds baking powder	1 egg, beaten
¼ tsp salt	1½ cups milk
1 cup fine desiccated coconut	1 Tbsp butter, melted

1. Preheat the oven to 200°C. Grease a 26cm loaf tin and line the base with baking paper.

2. Sift together the flour, baking powder and salt and stir in the coconut and sugar.

3. Add the beaten egg, milk and melted butter and stir to combine. Spoon into the prepared tin.

4. Bake for 45 minutes to 1 hour or until the loaf is golden and springs back when lightly touched.

5. Leave in the tin for 10 minutes before turning out onto a wire rack to cool.

Date Loaf

A simply made, moist and flavoursome loaf. Serve buttered.

1 cup chopped dates	*1 egg, beaten*
1 cup boiling water	*1 cup chopped walnuts*
1 tsp Edmonds baking soda	*¼ tsp vanilla essence*
1 Tbsp butter	*2 cups Edmonds standard flour*
1 cup brown sugar	*1 tsp Edmonds baking powder*

1. Put the dates, boiling water, soda and butter into a bowl and stir until the butter has melted. Set aside for 1 hour.

2. Preheat the oven to 180°C. Grease a 22cm loaf tin and line the base with baking paper.

3. Add the sugar, egg, walnuts and vanilla to the date mixture and beat well.

4. Sift the flour and baking powder onto the date mixture, and gently stir to just combine. Pour the mixture into the prepared tin.

5. Bake for 45 minutes or until the loaf springs back when lightly touched. Leave in the tin for 10 minutes before turning out onto a wire rack to cool.

VARIATION

Apricot Loaf
Replace the dates with dried apricots.

Fruit Loaf

A great loaf for filling the tins and which keeps well. Use whatever dried fruit you have in the pantry.

2 cups Edmonds standard flour	*1 cup dried fruit, e.g. raisins, dates,*
¼ tsp salt	*sultanas*
2 tsp Edmonds baking powder	*1 egg, beaten*
50g butter	*1 cup milk*
½ cup sugar	

1. Preheat the oven to 180°C. Grease a 22cm loaf tin and line the base with baking paper.

2. Sift the flour, salt and baking powder into a bowl and rub in the butter with your fingertips until the mixture resembles coarse breadcrumbs.

3. Stir in the sugar and dried fruit, then pour in the beaten egg and milk. Mix to form a soft dough and scoop the mixture into the loaf tin.
4. Bake for 1 hour or until the loaf springs back when lightly touched. Leave in the tin for 10 minutes before turning out onto a wire rack to cool.

Gingerbread Loaf

1½ HOURS   1 MAKES

A tender and spicy gingerbread which slices well and is traditionally served spread thinly – or generously – with butter.

1 cup Edmonds standard flour	½ cup sugar
pinch of salt	50g butter
1 Tbsp ground ginger	2 Tbsp golden syrup
1 Tbsp cinnamon	1½ tsp Edmonds baking soda
1 cup rolled oats	¾ cup natural unsweetened yoghurt
2 eggs	½ cup sultanas

1. Preheat the oven to 180°C. Grease a 26cm loaf tin and line the base with baking paper.
2. Sift the flour, salt, ginger and cinnamon into a bowl and stir through the rolled oats. In a separate bowl, whisk the eggs and sugar until thick and fluffy.
3. Melt the butter and golden syrup together then add to the egg mixture and fold in the dry ingredients.
4. Dissolve the baking soda in the yoghurt and stir into the mixture with the sultanas until well combined. Scoop into the prepared tin.
5. Bake for 55 minutes or until the loaf springs back when lightly touched. Leave in the tin for 10 minutes before turning out onto a wire rack to cool.

Ginger Gems

20 MINS   16 MAKES

These are a New Zealand classic and were once essential on a well-stocked afternoon tea table. Crusty and tender, they are served split and buttered. You will need a tray of cast iron gem irons to make them properly.

1 cup Edmonds standard flour	1 tsp Edmonds baking soda
1½ tsp ground ginger	½ cup milk
¼ cup sugar	1 egg, beaten
50g butter	extra butter
2 Tbsp golden syrup	

1. Preheat the oven and gem irons to 200°C.
2. Sift the flour and ground ginger into a bowl and stir in the sugar. Melt together the butter and golden syrup. Dissolve the soda in the milk.
3. Add the beaten egg and melted butter mixture to the dry ingredients and mix quickly. Pour in the combined milk and soda, then mix again.
4. Take the heated gem irons from the oven and drop a little butter into each hole. The butter should sizzle gently. You don't need to spread the butter around; it will move up the sides of the gem iron when the mixture goes in. Drop in the gem mixture from the side of a large tablespoon.
5. Bake for 10 minutes or until well risen and golden brown. After a minute, turn the gems out onto a wire rack to cool.

Girdle or Griddle Scones

20 MINS · 8 MAKES

Way back when domestic ovens were rare, scones were usually cooked over the fire on a heated cast iron plate. In Ireland this plate was called a griddle, in Scotland, a girdle and in Wales, a bake stone. They should be baked slowly so that they are tender and have a thin crust.

1 cup Edmonds standard flour
2 tsp Edmonds baking powder
pinch of salt

1 Tbsp butter
½ cup milk, approximately

1. Place a heavy-based frying pan or griddle over a low to medium heat.
2. Sift the flour, baking powder and salt together in a bowl. Rub in the butter with your fingertips until the mixture resembles fine breadcrumbs.
3. Add enough milk to make a fairly soft dough, mixing with a round-bladed table knife. Roll out to a 1cm thick round on a lightly floured board.
4. Cut the dough into 8 wedges. Butter the pan or griddle very lightly and cook the scones for about 5 minutes on each side. They should be dark golden brown and well risen, and the sides should be dry to the touch.
5. Place on a wire rack to cool, covered with a cloth.

Pancakes

1½ HOURS · 8 MAKES

These crepes – very thin, French-style pancakes – are perfect for eating with lemon juice, sugar and cream.

1 cup Edmonds standard flour
⅛ tsp salt
1 egg, beaten

¾ cup milk
water, to mix

1. Sift the flour and salt into a bowl. Add the beaten egg, mixing to combine.
2. Gradually beat in the milk until you have a smooth batter and chill for 1 hour. The batter will thicken on standing.
3. Stir the batter and add a little water if necessary to bring it back to a pouring consistency.
4. Heat a greased pancake pan or small frying pan and pour in just enough batter to cover the base of the pan. Cook until golden underneath.
5. Release with a knife around the edge. Flip or turn and cook the other side. Stack the pancakes on a plate as you cook them.

Edmonds baking powder provides a double raising action – it activates as soon as moisture is added and continues on in the early cooking. This is why you should preheat your oven as it is generally not a good idea to let your batter stand for too long before baking.

Pikelets

20 MINS | 18 MAKES

Pikelets are delicious with butter and jam, or with jam and whipped cream – you can even go savoury with sour cream, smoked salmon and dill. To make American-style pancakes, double this recipe and make them larger. Serve in a stack with maple syrup, bacon and blueberries.

1 cup Edmonds standard flour	*1 egg*
1 tsp Edmonds baking powder	*¼ cup sugar*
¼ tsp salt	*¾ cup milk, approximately*

1. Sift the flour, baking powder and salt into a bowl.
2. In another bowl beat the egg and sugar with a whisk until pale and thick.
3. Add the egg mixture and the milk to the dry ingredients and mix until just combined.
4. Gently heat a non-stick frying pan and drop tablespoonfuls of the mixture from the point of the spoon onto the surface.
5. When bubbles start to burst on the top of the pikelets, turn them over and cook the second side until golden. Place in a clean tea towel to cool.

Pikelets – Gluten Free

20 MINS | 20 MAKES

1 cup Edmonds gluten free self raising flour	*1 egg*
½ tsp salt	*¼ cup caster sugar*
	¾ cup milk

1. Sift the flour and salt into a bowl. Beat the egg and sugar together with a whisk or fork until thick, then add to the dry ingredients along with the milk. Mix until well combined.
2. Heat a greased frying pan to hot and place tablespoonfuls of batter in the pan.
3. Turn the pikelets when bubbles start to burst on the top surface. Cook the second side until golden brown. Place on a clean tea towel to cool.

Pinwheel Scones

25 MINS | 20 MAKES

In many early editions of the Edmonds Cookery Book, these scones were called Chelsea Buns. There is now a recipe for yeast-raised Chelsea Buns (page 13) so these are a quicker, more scone-like version from the 1986 edition.

DOUGH

3 cups Edmonds standard flour	*50g butter*
4½ tsp Edmonds baking powder	*1–1½ cups milk*
¼ tsp salt	

FILLING

2 Tbsp melted butter	*1½ tsp cinnamon*
½ cup white or brown sugar	*½ cup mixed peel or mixed dried fruit*

Over-mixing pikelet batter produces tough pikelets. If pikelets brown unevenly, wipe the cooking surface with a paper towel to remove excess butter.

1. Preheat the oven to 200°C. Line a baking tray with baking paper or grease it lightly.
2. Sift the flour, baking powder and salt into a bowl. Rub in the butter with your fingertips until the mixture resembles fine breadcrumbs.
3. Add the milk and mix quickly with a round-bladed table knife to a soft dough. Scrape the dough onto the prepared tray and flour the top.
4. Roll the dough into a 30cm square and brush with the melted butter. Sprinkle over the sugar, cinnamon and mixed peel or dried fruit, leaving a bare strip along one edge.
5. Roll up into a log, finishing at the bare edge, and press to seal. Cut into 20 slices and place them on the baking tray, cut side down.
6. Bake for about 12 minutes until risen and golden. Place on a wire rack to cool.

Scones

These scones are an Edmonds and a Kiwi staple and this will possibly be the most visited page in the whole book.

3 cups Edmonds standard flour
5 tsp Edmonds baking powder
¼ tsp salt

75g butter
1¼ cups milk
extra milk for glazing

1. Preheat the oven to 220°C. Grease or flour a baking tray.
2. Sift the flour, baking powder and salt into a bowl. Rub in the butter with your fingertips until the mixture resembles fine breadcrumbs.
3. Add the milk and quickly mix with a round-bladed table knife to a soft dough. For light and tender scones the mixture should be quite soft and a little sticky. Scrape the dough onto the floured baking tray and flour the top.
4. Working quickly, pat the dough out to 2cm thickness. With a floured knife, cut it into 12 even-sized pieces, then separate the scones to allow 2cm space between them. Brush the tops with milk.
5. Bake for 10 minutes or until golden brown. Place on a wire rack to cool, wrapped in a clean tea towel to keep them soft.

VARIATIONS

Cheese Scones
Add ¾ cup grated cheese, ¼ teaspoon cayenne pepper and ¼ teaspoon mustard powder to the flour. Before baking, top each scone with more grated cheese.

Date Scones
Add ¾ cup chopped dates, 1 tablespoon sugar and ½ teaspoon cinnamon to the flour. Before baking, sprinkle the scones with a mixture of cinnamon and sugar.

Sultana Scones
Add ¾–1 cup sultanas to the flour.

Ginger Scones
Add 1 teaspoon sugar and 1 teaspoon ground ginger to the flour and use only 1 cup of milk to mix. Roll out the dough to 1cm thickness on a floured board, cover half of the dough with 50g sliced crystallised ginger and fold the other half on top. Cut into squares and brush with milk before baking. Delicious spread with butter.

Scones – Gluten Free

30 MINS · 12 MAKES

A light and fluffy scone, best eaten on the day they are made.

3 cups Edmonds gluten free self
 raising flour
1 tsp xanthan gum
½ tsp salt

250ml cold lemonade (for sweet) or
 soda water (for savoury)
250ml cold cream
1 egg, beaten (optional)

1. Preheat the oven to 200˚C.

2. Sift the flour, xanthan gum and salt into a bowl, and mix with a whisk.

3. Mix the lemonade or soda water and cream in a jug, pour over the dry ingredients and mix to a soft dough.

4. Turn out onto a surface floured with gluten free flour and pat or roll out to 2cm thickness.

5. Cut and place close together on a cold baking tray.

6. Brush the tops with beaten egg if desired, then let stand for 10 minutes.

7. Bake for 15 minutes or until golden brown. Place on a wire rack to cool, wrapped in a clean tea towel to keep them soft.

Biscuits

Who doesn't love fresh, homemade biscuits with a cup of tea? These simple, time-tested favourites have been filling Kiwi family biscuit tins for generations.

How to make perfect biscuits:

- Always preheat the oven and put the biscuit mixture onto cold baking trays, lined with baking paper or lightly greased.
- If the recipe calls for creaming the butter and sugar, and you want to use a food processor, put the eggs and sugar in first. Process until smooth, then add the softened butter a little at a time, pulsing to mix.
- Try to have all the biscuits the same size for even baking, and space them evenly on the baking sheets.
- Once they are cooked, allow the biscuits to cool on the trays for a minute or two, then move them with a spatula to a wire cooling rack.
- Store in an airtight container to keep them crisp.
- Don't store biscuits in the same container as cakes or they will soften.
- Iced biscuits should be eaten within a week, but un-iced biscuits will keep for a month in an airtight tin or jar.

Afghans

30 MINS — 24 MAKES

The origin of the biscuit may be debated but Kiwis are proud to call this chocolatey, crunchy classic their own.

200g butter, softened
½ cup sugar
1¼ cups Edmonds standard flour
¼ cup cocoa

2 cups cornflakes
Chocolate Icing (page 99)
24 walnut halves

1. Preheat the oven to 180°C and line a baking tray with baking paper.
2. Cream the butter and sugar until light and fluffy. Sift together the flour and cocoa and stir into the creamed mixture. Fold in cornflakes.
3. Spoon small mounds of mixture onto the prepared tray, gently press the mixture together and flatten slightly.
4. Bake for 15 minutes or until set. Leave on the tray for 1–2 minutes then place on a wire rack to cool. When cold, ice with Chocolate Icing and decorate with a walnut half.

VARIATION
Afghan Slice
Press the Afghan mixture into a 20cm x 30cm slice tin. Bake at 180°C for 25 minutes or until set. When cold, ice with Chocolate Icing.

Almond Biscuits

Crisp golden biscuits topped with a toasted almond.

125g butter, softened
½ cup sugar
1 egg
½ tsp almond essence

1½ cups Edmonds standard flour
1 tsp Edmonds baking powder
12–15 blanched almonds

1. Preheat the oven to 180˚C. Line a baking tray with baking paper.
2. Cream the butter and sugar until light and fluffy, then beat in the egg and almond essence.
3. Sift in the flour and baking powder and mix to a firm dough.
4. Roll teaspoonfuls of the dough into balls, place on the prepared tray and press lightly with a floured fork. Press half a blanched almond onto each biscuit.
5. Bake for 15 minutes or until golden. Leave on the tray for 1–2 minutes then place on a wire rack to cool.

Anzac Biscuits

Contrary to legend, Anzac biscuits weren't sent to our troops serving overseas in WW1. However they were commonly sold at church fetes and galas to raise funds for the war effort. They didn't get their name until peacetime, with the first Anzac recipe appearing about 1919.

¾ cup Edmonds standard flour
1 cup rolled oats
1 cup coconut
¾ cup sugar

115g butter
2 Tbsp golden syrup
1 tsp Edmonds baking soda
2 Tbsp boiling water

1. Preheat the oven to 180˚C. Line two baking trays with baking paper.
2. In a large bowl, mix together the flour, rolled oats, coconut and sugar.
3. Melt the butter and golden syrup together, then put the baking soda in a cup and pour in the boiling water. Stir to dissolve the soda then pour it onto the butter mixture.
4. Stir the wet ingredients into the dry ingredients and mix to a crumbly paste.
5. Drop heaped teaspoonfuls of the mixture onto the prepared trays. Leave at least 2cm space around each biscuit as they will spread.
6. Bake for about 15 minutes or until golden brown. Leave on the trays for 5 minutes then place on a wire rack to cool.

Basic (Refrigerator) Biscuits

Make one simple dough and you can ring the changes with many different flavourings.

125g butter, softened
¾ cup sugar
1 tsp vanilla essence

1 egg
2 cups Edmonds standard flour
1 tsp Edmonds baking powder

For crisper biscuits, flatten, with a floured fork to 5–8mm thickness.

1. Preheat the oven to 190°C. Line a baking tray with baking paper.
2. Cream the butter, sugar and vanilla together until light and fluffy. Add the egg, beating well. Sift the flour and baking powder together and mix into the creamed mixture.
3. Roll heaped teaspoonfuls of mixture into balls and place on the prepared tray. Flatten slightly with a floured fork.
4. Bake for about 12 minutes or until pale golden. Leave on the tray for 1–2 minutes then place on a wire rack to cool.

NOTE
You can also shape the biscuit dough into a log, wrap it in waxed paper or tinfoil and chill it for an hour or so, then slice into discs for baking. The dough will also keep in the freezer for 1 month.

VARIATIONS
Chocolate Biscuits
Add 2 tablespoons cocoa when sifting flour.
Orange Biscuits
Replace vanilla essence with 1 tablespoon grated orange rind in creamed mixture.
Lemon Biscuits
Replace vanilla essence with 2 teaspoons finely grated lemon zest in creamed mixture.
Spice Biscuits
Add 2 teaspoons mixed spice when sifting flour.
Sultana Biscuits
Fold ½ cup sultanas into creamed mixture.

Belgian Biscuits

90 MINS · 18 MAKES

These spicy, jam-filled treats used to be called German biscuits. Then WW1 happened and asking for German biscuits didn't seem like such a good idea in many parts of the world. The name change began in Britain and spread through the Commonwealth.

150g butter, softened
½ cup brown sugar
1 egg
2 cups Edmonds standard flour
1 tsp Edmonds baking powder

1 tsp cinnamon
1 tsp ground ginger
1 tsp mixed spice
1 tsp cocoa

ICING
1 cup icing sugar
1 Tbsp lemon juice

a few drops red food colouring
red jelly crystals

FILLING
½ cup raspberry or plum jam

1. Preheat the oven to 180°C. Line a baking tray with baking paper.
2. Cream the butter and sugar until light and fluffy, then add the egg and beat well.
3. Sift all the dry ingredients together, add to the creamed mixture and combine to make a firm dough. Wrap the dough in greaseproof paper and chill for about 30 minutes for easier rolling.
4. On a lightly floured board, roll out the dough to 3mm thickness. Cut out rounds using a 6.5cm cutter and place on the baking tray. Reroll the scraps of dough, chilling

the dough again if it becomes too soft.

5. Bake for 12–15 minutes or until firm on top and slightly brown underneath. Leave on the tray for 1–2 minutes then place on a wire rack to cool.

6. Sift the icing sugar and mix to icing consistency with lemon juice, then add the red food colouring.

7. When cold, ice half the biscuits and sprinkle with some jelly crystals. Spread the other halves with raspberry or plum jam and place the iced biscuits on top.

Bran Biscuits

MINS · MAKES

Based on a recipe in the 1930 edition of the Edmonds Cookery Book, these are simple, crisp, spicy and very good with a cup of tea. Serve plain or buttered.

125g butter, softened	*1 cup Edmonds standard flour*
¼ cup sugar	*1 tsp Edmonds baking powder*
1 egg	*½ tsp mixed spice*
1½ cups Edmonds wheat bran	*pinch of salt*

1. Preheat the oven to 180˚C. Line a baking tray with baking paper.

2. Cream the butter and sugar until light and fluffy, then add the egg and beat well.

3. Add the bran and then sift the remaining dry ingredients together and mix into the creamed mixture. Combine to form a firm dough.

4. Turn out onto a floured board and push the dough together with your hands to complete the mixing and make the dough smooth.

5. Divide the dough into quarters. Sprinkle the bench with extra bran and roll out the dough, one piece at a time, to 5–7mm thickness. Cut the dough into squares or rectangles and place on the prepared tray.

6. Bake for 20 minutes or until set and lightly golden. Leave on the tray for 1–2 minutes then place on a wire rack to cool.

Cheese Biscuits

MINS · MAKES

Light and tasty. Try them plain, buttered or with a little apricot jam.

1 cup Edmonds standard flour	*pinch of cayenne pepper*
1 Tbsp icing sugar	*50g butter*
1 tsp Edmonds baking powder	*½ cup grated cheese*
pinch of salt	*3 Tbsp milk, approximately*

1. Preheat the oven to 200˚C. Line a baking tray with baking paper.

2. Sift the flour, icing sugar, baking powder, salt and cayenne pepper into a bowl. Rub the butter into the flour mixture until it resembles fine breadcrumbs, then mix in the cheese. Add just enough milk to form a stiff dough.

3. Knead lightly and roll out to 2mm thickness. Cut into 4cm squares and place on the prepared tray. Prick each biscuit with a fork.

4. Bake for 10 minutes or until lightly golden. Leave on the tray for 1–2 minutes then place on a wire rack to cool.

Chocolate Chip (Santé) Biscuits

35 MINS 25 MAKES

Dark chocolate Santé bars have been made in England since the 1860s. Before the invention of chocolate chips, Santé bars were chopped into the biscuit dough.

125g butter, softened	1½ cups Edmonds standard flour
¼ cup sugar	1 tsp Edmonds baking powder
3 Tbsp sweetened condensed milk	½ cup chocolate chips
few drops of vanilla essence	

1. Preheat the oven to 180°C. Line a baking tray with baking paper.

2. Cream the butter, sugar, condensed milk and vanilla until light and fluffy. Sift the flour and baking powder together and mix into the creamed mixture, followed by the chocolate chips.

3. Roll tablespoonfuls of the mixture into balls, place on the prepared tray and flatten with a floured fork.

4. Bake for 20 minutes until golden. Leave on the tray for 1–2 minutes then place on a wire rack to cool.

Chocolate Crackles

1 HOUR 24 MAKES

These biscuits have been children's party essentials through the decades. Make them with rice bubbles or cornflakes.

250g vegetable shortening	4 cups puffed rice breakfast cereal
1 cup icing sugar	or cornflakes
¼ cup cocoa	1 cup fine desiccated coconut

1. Melt the vegetable shortening in a saucepan.

2. Sift together the icing sugar and cocoa and add to the pan. Mix well, then tip in the rice bubbles or cornflakes and coconut.

3. Stir everything together, then put spoonfuls into paper cupcake cases. Set in the fridge for 30 minutes.

Chocolate Cream Biscuits

1 HOUR 16 MAKES

Cocoa and spice make these biscuits special – and the chocolate filling adds charm and a contrasting creamy texture. A favourite from the 1952 Edmonds Cookery Book.

75g butter	1 tsp mixed spice
125g sugar	2 Tbsp cocoa
1 egg	Chocolate Buttercream Icing or
175g Edmonds standard flour	Chocolate Ganache (page 98)
1 tsp Edmonds baking powder	

1. Preheat the oven to 190°C. Line a baking tray with baking paper.

2. Cream the butter and sugar until light and fluffy then beat in the egg. Sift the dry ingredients together and combine with the creamed mixture until you have a firm dough. Wrap in greaseproof paper and chill for at least 10 minutes.

3. Roll out on a floured surface to 4mm thick and cut out rounds.

4. Bake for 12 minutes until firm. Leave on the tray for 1–2 minutes then place on a wire rack to cool.

5. When cold, sandwich together with Chocolate Buttercream Icing or Chocolate Ganache (page 98).

Coconut Whispers

These golden biscuits are crunchy at first, with a slightly chewy centre. Use only fine desiccated coconut or they won't hold together.

55g butter	*1 egg*
115g sugar	*2 cups fine desiccated coconut*
½ tsp vanilla essence	

1. Preheat the oven to 160°C. Line two baking trays with baking paper.

2. Cream the butter and sugar until light and fluffy then add the vanilla and egg and mix well. Fold in the coconut and combine well.

3. Put teaspoonfuls on the prepared trays, leaving a little space for spreading, and flatten with a wet fork.

4. Bake for about 25 minutes until golden. Leave on the tray for 1–2 minutes then place on a wire rack to cool.

Duskies

These classics from the 1957 Edmonds Cookery Book are similar to Afghans in taste and texture.

125g butter	*2 Tbsp cocoa*
1 cup icing sugar	*½ cup fine desiccated coconut*
1 egg	*½ cup chopped walnuts*
150g Edmonds standard flour	*Chocolate Icing (page 99)*
1 tsp Edmonds baking powder	*shredded coconut*

1. Preheat the oven to 200°C. Line a baking tray with baking paper.

2. Cream the butter and sugar until light and fluffy, then add the egg and beat again.

3. Sift the flour, baking powder and cocoa together and add to the creamed mixture. Lastly add the coconut and walnuts and place small spoonfuls on the prepared tray.

4. Bake for 12–15 minutes until firm and well risen. Leave on the tray for 1–2 minutes then place on a wire rack to cool.

5. When cold, ice with Chocolate Icing and decorate with shredded coconut.

Easter Biscuits

This very old English recipe for flaky golden biscuits flavoured with spicy currants and lemon zest first appeared in the Edmonds Cookery Book in the 1950s.

2 cups Edmonds standard flour	*¼ cup currants*
1 tsp Edmonds baking powder	*¼ tsp cinnamon*
140g butter	*½ tsp finely grated lemon zest*
½ cup caster sugar	*1 egg, lightly beaten*

Coconut Loaf page 24
Gingerbread Loaf page 26

1. Preheat the oven to 180°C. Line two baking trays with baking paper.
2. Sift the flour and baking powder into a bowl. Rub in the butter until it resembles fine breadcrumbs then add the sugar, currants, cinnamon and lemon zest.
3. Add the beaten egg to the dry ingredients, mixing to form a stiff dough. Wrap in greaseproof paper and chill for 10 minutes.
4. Turn the dough out onto a lightly floured board and roll out to 4mm thickness. Cut out rounds using a 7–8cm cutter and place the biscuits on the prepared trays.
5. Bake for 15–20 minutes or until golden brown. Leave on the tray for 1–2 minutes then place on a wire rack to cool.

NOTE
For an even lighter result use 2 egg yolks. If you do this, brush the biscuits with lightly beaten egg white and sprinkle them with caster sugar before baking.

Elsie's Fingers

A recipe from the 1923 Edmonds Cookery Book for small buttery biscuits with a crunchy coating. Fun to make and to eat.

125g butter
75g sugar
1 egg
1½ cups Edmonds standard flour

1½ tsp Edmonds baking powder
2 Tbsp sugar
3 Tbsp finely chopped walnuts

1. Preheat the oven to 180°C. Line a baking tray with baking paper.
2. Cream the butter and sugar until light and fluffy and beat in the egg. Then sift the flour and baking powder together and add to the creamed mixture.
3. Mix the sugar and walnuts together. Take tablespoonfuls of the mixture and roll into 6cm fingers, then roll each one in the sugar and walnuts. Place on the prepared tray.
4. Bake for about 15 minutes until golden. Leave on the tray for 1–2 minutes then place on a wire rack to cool.

Florentines

A classic recipe from Europe – a little fiddly perhaps, but worth the effort.

150g butter
¾ cup caster sugar
45g honey
2 Tbsp cream

130g flaked almonds
15g Edmonds standard flour
½ cup chopped glacé cherries
2 Tbsp chopped mixed peel

ICING
150g dark chocolate

1. Preheat the oven to 200°C. Line two baking trays with baking paper.
2. Melt the butter, sugar, honey and cream in a saucepan and bring to the boil, stirring.
3. Reduce the heat to low, add the remaining ingredients and cook for 5 minutes, stirring constantly.
4. Place 4 teaspoonfuls of the mixture on each baking tray and spread each out to a 7cm circle. They will spread out to 10 cm in the oven.
5. Bake the first tray for 8–10 minutes until the Florentines are thin, golden and

bubbling. Watch closely in the last 2 minutes as they burn very easily.

6. Leave for 1 minute to firm up slightly, then carefully nudge the edges of each Florentine with the edge of a knife to form them into neat circles.

7. Slide the sheet of baking paper with the Florentines onto a cooling rack and leave to cool and harden. Bake the next tray in the same way and repeat until all the mixture is used.

8. When they are all cooked turn them over and spread melted chocolate on the underside of each biscuit. Use a fork to make wavy lines in the surface of the chocolate. Leave to set firmly.

Fruit Delights (Bumblebees)

Sweet and chewy little morsels in which fruit and nuts are bound together with sweetened condensed milk. Try any mixture of fruit and nuts that takes your fancy.

1 cup fine desiccated coconut	*1 cup chopped raisins*
¾ cup sweetened condensed milk	*½ cup chopped walnuts*
1 cup chopped dates	*1 Tbsp lemon juice*
½ cup crystallised ginger	*extra fine desiccated coconut*
½ cup chopped dried figs	

1. Preheat the oven to 180°C. Line two baking trays with baking paper.

2. Combine all the ingredients except the extra coconut in a large bowl and mix well. If the mixture is too sticky to handle, add more coconut.

3. Shape tablespoonfuls of the mixture into fingers, roll them in the extra desiccated coconut and place on the prepared tray.

4. Bake for 20 minutes until golden brown and firm. Slide the baking paper onto a wire rack to cool completely.

Gingerbread People

This is the perfect dough for Gingerbread People or Christmas biscuits. Make a small hole in the biscuits before baking, then you can thread through thin ribbon and hang them on the Christmas tree. They keep very well.

150g unsalted butter	*¼ tsp ground cloves*
70g soft brown sugar	*¾ tsp baking soda*
70g white sugar	*1 large egg, size 7, lightly beaten*
200g treacle	*4 cups Edmonds high grade flour*
2 tsp ground ginger	*Royal Icing (page 100)*
2 tsp cinnamon	

1. Preheat the oven to 160°C. Line two baking trays with baking paper.

2. Cut the butter into small lumps and place in a large mixing bowl. Place the sugars, treacle and spices in a heavy-based saucepan and stir with a wooden spoon until melted together and the mixture comes to the boil.

3. Add the baking soda and stir again until the mixture froths up and turns a pale gold.

4. Remove from the heat and pour the treacle mixture onto the butter. Stir well until the butter melts and the mixture is smooth.

5. Mix in the egg, then sift the flour and stir in, one cup at a time.

6. Turn the dough out onto a lightly floured board and knead lightly until smooth.

7. Divide in half and shape each portion into a rectangle. Wrap in greaseproof paper and chill for a few minutes if the dough seems too soft to roll easily.

8. Roll out one piece of the dough at a time to 5mm thickness. Cut out shapes and place on the prepared trays. The dough will be quite soft to begin with and you may need to use a spatula to lift the biscuits. You can re-roll the scraps several times – the dough does not get tough.

9. Bake for 15–20 minutes until firm to the touch and just beginning to brown. Leave on the trays for a 1–2 minutes then place on a wire rack to cool. When cold, ice the Gingerbread People with Royal Icing.

Gingernuts

125g butter, softened
¼ cup brown sugar
3 Tbsp golden syrup
1 tsp Edmonds baking soda

1 Tbsp boiling water
2 cups Edmonds standard flour
pinch of salt
3 tsp ground ginger

1. Preheat the oven to 180°C. Line a baking tray with baking paper.

2. Cream the butter, sugar and golden syrup until light and fluffy.

3. Dissolve the baking soda in the boiling water and add to the creamed mixture. Sift the flour, salt and ginger together and add to the creamed mixture, mixing well.

4. Roll tablespoonfuls of the mixture into balls, place on the prepared tray and flatten with a floured fork.

5. Bake for 20–30 minutes or until golden. Leave on the tray for 1–2 minutes then place on a wire rack to cool.

Hokey Pokey Biscuits

These crisp biscuits fizz slightly on your tongue, thanks to the baking soda and golden syrup.

125g butter
½ cup sugar
1 Tbsp golden syrup

1 Tbsp milk
1½ cups Edmonds standard flour
1 tsp Edmonds baking soda

1. Preheat the oven to 180°C. Line a baking tray with baking paper.

2. Combine the butter, sugar, golden syrup and milk in a saucepan over a medium heat. Heat until the butter is melted and the mixture is almost boiling, stirring constantly.

3. Remove from the heat and allow the mixture to cool to lukewarm. Sift the flour and baking soda together, add to the cooled mixture and stir well.

4. Roll tablespoonfuls of the mixture into balls, place on the prepared tray and press down with a floured fork.

5. Bake for 15–20 minutes or until golden brown. Leave on the tray for 1–2 minutes then place on a wire rack to cool.

Honey Snaps

30 MINS 20 MAKES

Very thin, crisp, golden biscuits.

50g butter	½ cup Edmonds standard flour
2 Tbsp sugar	1 tsp Edmonds baking powder
3 Tbsp honey	½ tsp ground ginger

1. Preheat the oven to 180˚C. Line two baking trays with baking paper.
2. Melt the butter, sugar and honey together in a saucepan over a medium heat.
3. Remove from the heat. Sift the flour, baking powder and ginger together and stir into the melted mixture until smooth.
4. Drop teaspoonfuls onto the prepared trays, leaving enough room for the snaps to spread to double their size.
5. Bake for 10 minutes or until golden. Leave on the trays for 1–2 minutes then place on a wire rack to cool.

Melting Moments

1 HOUR 16 MAKES

A New Zealand baking classic which has remained unchanged in Edmonds Cookery Books since the 1930s. As delicious as ever.

200g butter, softened	½ tsp Edmonds baking powder
¾ cup icing sugar	Buttercream Icing (page 97) or
1 cup Edmonds standard flour	raspberry jam
1 cup Edmonds Fielder's cornflour	

1. Preheat the oven to 180˚C. Line two baking trays with baking paper.
2. Cream the butter and icing sugar until light and fluffy. Sift the flour, cornflour and baking powder together and add to the creamed mixture, working everything together to make a smooth dough.
3. Roll heaped teaspoonfuls of the dough into balls, place on the prepared trays and press down lightly with a floured fork.
4. Bake for 20 minutes or until lightly golden on the base. Leave on the trays for 1–2 minutes then place on a wire rack to cool.
5. When cold, sandwich pairs of biscuits together with Buttercream Icing or raspberry jam.

Peanut Brownies

40 MINS 20 MAKES

125g butter, softened	1 tsp Edmonds baking powder
1 cup sugar	pinch of salt
1 egg	2 Tbsp cocoa
1½ cups Edmonds standard flour	1 cup roasted unsalted peanuts

1. Preheat the oven to 180˚C. Line two baking trays with baking paper.
2. Cream the butter and sugar until light and fluffy. Add the egg and beat well.
3. Sift the flour, baking powder, salt and cocoa together and add to the creamed mixture. Add the peanuts, roughly chopped if you wish, and mix well.

4. Roll tablespoonfuls of the mixture into balls, place on the prepared trays and press down with a floured fork.

5. Bake for 15 minutes or until firm and coloured on the base. Leave on the trays for 1–2 minutes then place on a wire rack to cool.

Shortbread

2 HOURS 30 MAKES

This smooth-textured, buttery shortbread is a New Zealand specialty that keeps well and makes a lovely gift. If you prefer a more crumbly texture, use caster sugar instead of icing sugar.

250g butter, softened
1 cup icing sugar

1 cup Edmonds Fielder's cornflour
2 cups Edmonds standard flour

1. Preheat the oven to 130˚C. Line two baking trays with baking paper.

2. Cream the butter and icing sugar until light and fluffy. Sift the cornflour and flour together and add to the creamed mixture.

3. Turn onto a floured surface and knead well, pushing the mixture with your hands until it forms a smooth dough.

SHAPING – TWO OPTIONS

- Divide the dough in half and roll out each half on a piece of baking paper into a circle about 1cm thick. Mark the dough into wedges and prick the surface all over with a fork. Chill for 20 minutes and then slide the baking paper onto the prepared trays. Bake for about 1 hour until a very pale gold. Cut into wedges for serving.

- Form the dough into a log, wrap in greaseproof paper and chill for 10 minutes. Then cut into 5mm thick biscuits. Place on the prepared trays and prick with a fork. Bake for about 30 minutes or until pale golden.

Shrewsbury Biscuits

45 MINS 20 MAKES

A classic English biscuit, named after a small town in Shropshire. The best possible jam sandwich.

125g butter, softened
½ cup sugar
1 egg
1 Tbsp finely grated lemon zest

2 cups Edmonds standard flour
1 tsp Edmonds baking powder
raspberry jam

1. Preheat the oven to 180˚C. Line two baking trays with baking paper.

2. Cream the butter and sugar until light and fluffy. Add the egg and lemon zest and beat well.

3. Sift the flour and baking powder together and add to the creamed mixture. Turn out and knead well.

4. Roll out the dough on a lightly floured board to 4mm thickness. Cut out rounds using a 7cm cutter then cut a 1cm hole in the centre of half the biscuits. Place on the prepared trays.

5. Bake for 10–15 minutes until pale gold. Leave on the trays for 1–2 minutes then place on a wire rack to cool.

6. When cold, sandwich the biscuits in pairs with raspberry jam. Don't use too much jam, just enough to stick the halves together so it shows through the hole in the top biscuit.

Walnut Wafers

30 MINS 36 MAKES

These crisp and crunchy wafer biscuits are very hard to resist and have been a popular recipe in the Edmonds Cookery Book since the 1930s.

125g butter	125g Edmonds standard flour
125g sugar	1 tsp Edmonds baking powder
125g treacle	75g chopped walnuts

1. Preheat the oven to 175°C. Line two baking trays with baking paper.
2. Cream the butter, sugar and treacle together until light and fluffy. Sift the dry ingredients together and add into the creamed mixture, combining well. Lastly add the walnuts. Put small spoonfuls on the prepared trays, allowing plenty of room for the wafers to spread.
3. Bake for 10–15 minutes until firm to the touch. Leave on the trays for 1–2 minutes then place on a wire rack to cool

Yoyos

1 HOUR 20 MAKES

Just like Melting Moments but with the addition of a sweet custard flavour.

175g butter, softened	1½ cups Edmonds standard flour
¼ cup icing sugar	¼ cup Edmonds custard powder
¼ tsp vanilla essence	
BUTTER FILLING	2 Tbsp Edmonds custard powder
50g butter, softened	½ cup icing sugar
1 Tbsp hot water	

1. Preheat the oven to 180°C. Line two baking trays with baking paper.
2. Cream the butter and icing sugar until light and fluffy, and then add the vanilla.
3. Sift the flour and custard powder together and combine with the creamed mixture to form a soft dough.
4. Roll teaspoonfuls of the mixture into balls, place on the prepared trays and press down with a fork.
5. Bake for 15–20 minutes until golden. Leave on the trays for 1–2 minutes then place on a wire rack to cool.
6. Mix all the filling ingredients together until light and fluffy.
7. When cold, sandwich in pairs with the Butter Filling.

Large Cakes

Everyone loves a piece of cake. This section of the cookbook has probably had more flour spilt on it than any other over the years. Whether you're baking for a birthday, for visitors, or just for everyday, you'll find the perfect recipe here.

How to make the perfect cake:

- Preheat the oven and prepare the cake tins before starting to mix the cake.
- To prepare a cake tin, grease the inside lightly and line the base with a piece of baking paper, cut to fit.
- Have all the ingredients at room temperature, including the eggs and milk, so they will mix in easily.
- Sift the dry ingredients together and stir to combine them well.
- Creaming the butter and sugar is important because it beats air into the mixture, which helps the cake to rise and gives it a light texture. Use a wooden spoon or an electric mixer, and make sure the butter is soft, but not melted. Beat hard for several minutes until the mixture is pale and fluffy.
- Fold in the sifted dry ingredients alternately with liquids, beginning and ending with dry ingredients. Folding means mixing very gently, just turning the mixture over and rotating the bowl as you go. Mix just enough to combine the ingredients. A slotted metal spoon is a good implement to use for folding.
- Don't overfill cake tins – allow room for the mixture to rise. Aim to have the tin two-thirds full.
- When the cake is cooked it should spring back when touched lightly with your finger and the mixture will have pulled slightly away from the sides of the tin.
- Leave large cakes to cool in the tins for 10 minutes before turning them out onto a wire rack to cool. This allows the cake to 'set' and helps to stop it breaking.
- Leave cakes until completely cold before filling and icing.

Arabian Nut Cake

(2) HOURS

A deliciously moist cake from the 1952 Edmonds Cookery Book. Served with whipped cream, this makes a luscious dessert.

¾ cup hot coffee
1 cup chopped dates
125g butter
1 cup brown sugar
1 tsp vanilla essence
2 eggs
1¾ cup Edmonds standard flour
2 tsp Edmonds baking powder

½ tsp Edmonds baking soda
½ tsp salt
½ cup chopped walnuts
icing sugar (optional)
Coffee Buttercream Icing (page 98)
extra chopped walnuts

1. Pour the hot coffee over the dates and set aside to cool.

2. Preheat the oven to 175°C. Grease a 20cm deep round cake tin and line the base with baking paper.

3. Cream the butter and sugar until light and fluffy, then add the vanilla and the eggs one at a time, beating well after each addition.

4. Sift the dry ingredients together and fold through the creamed mixture alternately with the date mixture. Lastly fold in the chopped walnuts until combined. Scoop the mixture into the prepared tin and level the top.

5. Bake for about 1 hour or until the cake springs back when lightly touched. Leave in the tin for 10 minutes before turning out onto a wire rack to cool.

6. Dust with icing sugar or ice with Coffee Buttercream Icing and sprinkle with chopped walnuts around the edge of the cake.

Banana Cake

1½ HOURS

This classic recipe is one of the most popular in the Edmonds Cookery Book and one of the most searched-for Kiwi recipes online.

125g butter, softened
¾ cup sugar
2 eggs
1–1½ cups mashed ripe bananas
  (3–4 bananas)
1 tsp Edmonds baking soda

2 Tbsp hot milk
2 cups Edmonds standard flour
1 tsp Edmonds baking powder
Chocolate Icing or Lemon Icing
  (page 99)
icing sugar (optional)

1. Preheat the oven to 180°C. Grease a 20cm deep round cake tin and line the base with baking paper.

2. Cream the butter and sugar until light and fluffy, then add the eggs one at a time, beating well after each addition.

3. Add the mashed banana and mix well.

4. Stir the baking soda into the hot milk and add to the creamed mixture, then sift the dry ingredients together and fold through the creamed mixture. Scoop the mixture into the prepared tin and level the top.

5. Bake for about 50 minutes or until the cake springs back when lightly touched. Leave in the tin for 10 minutes before turning out onto a wire rack to cool.

6. When cold, ice with Chocolate or Lemon Icing or dust with icing sugar.

VARIATION

You could also bake the mixture in two 20cm round sandwich tins for 25 minutes. Sandwich the cakes together with whipped cream and sliced banana and dust the top with icing sugar.

Mash over-ripe bananas and freeze until you are ready to make banana cake, muffins or loaf.

Carrot Cake

(1½) HOURS

A moist and spicy cake that has been a favourite for decades. Easy to mix, tastes very good, sounds like health food, and – if you can resist the cream cheese icing – it's dairy-free as well.

1 cup Edmonds wholemeal flour
1 tsp Edmonds baking soda
½ tsp cinnamon
1 tsp mixed spice
1 cup sugar
1½ cups grated carrot, lightly packed

1 cup sultanas or mixed dried fruit
¼ cup chopped walnuts
¾ cup oil
2 eggs
Cream Cheese Icing (page 98)

1. Preheat the oven to 180°C. Lightly grease a 20cm square cake tin and line the base and two sides with baking paper, or use a 20cm ring tin, lightly greased and dusted with flour.
2. Put the flour, baking soda and spices in a bowl and mix them thoroughly. A whisk is a good implement for this.
3. Add the sugar, grated carrot, fruit and walnuts and mix again.
4. With a fork, beat together the oil and the eggs and tip them onto the other ingredients. Mix until well combined and pour into the prepared tin.
5. Bake for 40–45 minutes or until the cake springs back when lightly touched. Cool in the tin on a wire rack. When cold, ice with Cream Cheese Icing.

Chocolate Almond Mud Cake

(1) HOUR

A very moist and rich cake made with ground almonds rather than flour, this makes a delicious dessert or special-occasion cake.

175g unsalted butter, softened
¾ cup brown sugar
1 tsp vanilla essence
6 eggs, separated

150g dark chocolate, melted
140g ground almonds
icing sugar, whipped cream, berries

1. Preheat the oven to 190°C. Grease a 20cm round springform tin and line the base with baking paper.
2. Cream the butter, sugar and vanilla until light and fluffy, then beat in the egg yolks. Fold in the melted chocolate and ground almonds.
3. In another bowl, beat the egg whites until soft peaks form. Gently fold the whites into the chocolate mixture. Keep folding until there are no white streaks then scoop into the prepared tin.
4. Bake for 20 minutes then reduce the heat to 150°C for a further 15 minutes or until the cake is firm.
5. Leave in the tin to cool, then release the sides and transfer carefully to a serving plate. Dust with icing sugar and serve warm or cold with cream, and berries if in season.

VARIATION
Chocolate Liqueur Cake
Replace the vanilla essence with 2 teaspoons chocolate, coffee or orange liqueur and fold a little of the same liqueur through the whipped cream when you serve it.

Chocolate Buttermilk Cake

A moist, decadent and delicious gluten free chocolate cake.

125g butter
125g dark chocolate
1 cup caster sugar
1 tsp vanilla extract
1¾ cups buttermilk
3 eggs

1¾ cups Edmonds gluten free
  plain flour
½ tsp baking powder
1 tsp baking soda
½ tsp salt

FROSTING
1½ cups icing sugar
⅓ cup cocoa powder

1½ Tbsp butter, softened
1½ Tbsp milk

1. Preheat oven to 180°C conventional or 160°C fan-forced. Grease a 22cm round cake tin. Dust with cocoa powder.
2. Melt the butter and chocolate carefully in a saucepan over low heat, stirring constantly until smooth. Remove from the heat and add the sugar while the chocolate mixture is still hot.
3. Whisk in the vanilla, buttermilk and eggs, then sift in the dry ingredients and gently whisk until smooth. Pour the mixture into the prepared tin.
4. Bake for 40–45 minutes or until a skewer comes out clean. Leave in the tin for 10 minutes before turning out onto a wire rack to cool.
5. For the frosting: sift the icing sugar and cocoa powder into a bowl and add the softened butter and milk. Mix with a wooden spoon until smooth. Add a few extra drops of milk if required. Spread over cooled cake.

Chocolate Cake

A classic, dark cake made with cocoa, not chocolate.

175g butter, softened
1¾ cups sugar
1 tsp vanilla essence
3 eggs
½ cup cocoa
2 cups Edmonds standard flour

2 tsp Edmonds baking powder
1 cup milk
Chocolate Buttercream Icing
  (page 98)
icing sugar (optional)

1. Preheat the oven to 180°C. Grease a 22cm deep round cake tin and line the base with baking paper.
2. Cream the butter, sugar and vanilla essence until light and fluffy. Add the eggs one at a time, beating well after each addition.
3. Sift the cocoa, flour and baking powder together and add to the creamed mixture alternately with the milk. Pour the mixture into the prepared tin.
4. Bake for 45–55 minutes or until the cake springs back when lightly touched. Leave in the tin for 10 minutes before turning out onto a wire rack to cool.
5. When cold, ice with Chocolate Buttercream Icing or dust with icing sugar.

Spread cake batters to the sides of the tin so the cake rises evenly.

Chocolate Cake – One Egg

40 MINS

An economical cake with a sponge-like texture and also an excellent recipe for beginner bakers.

50g butter
1 Tbsp golden syrup
1 egg
½ cup sugar
few drops of vanilla essence
1 Tbsp cocoa

1 cup Edmonds standard flour
1 tsp Edmonds baking powder
1 tsp Edmonds baking soda
¾ cup milk
Chocolate Buttercream Icing
   (page 98)

1. Preheat the oven to 190°C. Grease two 20cm shallow round cake tins and line the bases with baking paper.
2. Melt the butter and golden syrup in a small saucepan and transfer to a mixing bowl. Add the egg, sugar and vanilla and beat well.
3. Sift the cocoa, flour and baking powder together and dissolve the baking soda in the milk.
4. Fold the dry ingredients into the mixture alternately with the milk. Pour into the prepared tins.
5. Bake for 20 minutes or until the cakes spring back when lightly touched. Leave in the tins for 5 minutes before turning out onto a wire rack to cool.
6. When cold, sandwich together with Chocolate Buttercream Icing.

Coffee Cake

1½ HOURS

A sophisticated and delicious cake, perfect for a special occasion.

2 tsp instant coffee powder
1 Tbsp boiling water
75g butter, softened
¾ cup caster sugar
1 tsp vanilla essence

3 eggs, separated
1¼ cups Edmonds standard flour
¼ cup Edmonds Fielder's cornflour
1½ tsp Edmonds baking powder
3 Tbsp milk

FILLING
150ml cream, whipped

TOPPING
Coffee Buttercream Icing (page 98)
walnut pieces
icing sugar (optional)

1. Preheat the oven to 190°C. Grease two 20cm shallow round cake tins and line the bases with baking paper.
2. Dissolve the instant coffee in the boiling water. Cream the butter, sugar, coffee mixture and vanilla until light and fluffy.
3. Beat in the egg yolks, one at a time.
4. Whip the egg whites in a large bowl until soft peaks form. Sift the flours and baking powder together and fold a little at a time into the creamed mixture alternately with spoonfuls of the beaten egg white. Be gentle.
5. Lastly, stir in the milk then pour the mixture into the prepared tins.
6. Bake for 20–25 minutes or until the cakes spring back when lightly touched. Leave in the tins for 5 minutes before turning out onto a wire rack to cool.

7. When cold, fill with whipped cream, spread Coffee Buttercream Icing over the top and decorate with walnut pieces. Or just sift icing sugar over the top.

Coconut Layer Cake

A very pretty and simple cake from the 1957 Edmonds Cookery Book, with a delightful lemony coconut filling.

125g butter
125g sugar
3 eggs, beaten
125g Edmonds standard flour

1 tsp Edmonds baking powder
50g fine desiccated coconut
2–3 Tbsp warm milk
icing sugar

FILLING
grated zest and juice of 1 lemon
1 cup icing sugar

1 egg, beaten
½ cup fine desiccated coconut

1. Preheat the oven to 190°C. Grease two 20cm shallow round cake tins and line the bases with baking paper.
2. Cream the butter and sugar until light and fluffy then gradually mix in the beaten eggs.
3. Sift the dry ingredients together and fold into the creamed mixture with the coconut. Then add the milk to make a soft cake batter. Pour into the prepared tins.
4. Bake for 20 minutes or until the cakes spring back when lightly touched. Leave in the tins for 5 minutes before turning out onto a wire rack to cool.
5. Put the lemon zest and juice, icing sugar and egg into a saucepan. Cook over a low heat, gently stirring, until the mixture thickens, then stir in the coconut and set aside to cool.
6. When the cakes are cold, sandwich the two layers together with the filling and dust the top with icing sugar.

Ladysmith Cake

In this clever recipe you get a multi-layered, jam-filled cake all baked in one tin. It was named to celebrate the lifting of a four-month siege of the South African town of Ladysmith in February 1900, during the Boer War.

175g butter, softened
¾ cup sugar
1½ cups Edmonds standard flour
1 tsp Edmonds baking powder

3 eggs, beaten
2 tsp cinnamon
¼ cup raspberry jam
¼ cup chopped walnuts

1. Preheat the oven to 180°C. Grease an 20cm square cake tin and line the base with baking paper.
2. Cream the butter and sugar until light and fluffy. Sift the flour and baking powder together and add to the creamed mixture alternately with the beaten eggs.
3. Put just under half the mixture into another bowl and sift on the cinnamon then fold it evenly through. Spread this mixture evenly in the prepared tin.
4. Spread over the raspberry jam and top with the remaining cake mixture. Sprinkle the top with the chopped walnuts.
5. Bake for 50 minutes or until the cake springs back when lightly touched. Leave in the tin for 10 minutes, then turn out carefully onto a wire rack to cool.

Lemon Syrup Cake

A very pretty golden cake with an intense lemony tang and a soft, fine crumb. You could make it in a loaf tin for ease of cutting and transporting.

115g butter, softened
¾ cup sugar
2 tsp finely grated lemon zest
2 eggs

1½ cups Edmonds standard flour
1 tsp Edmonds baking powder
¾ cup milk

SYRUP
¼ cup lemon juice

⅓ cup caster sugar

1. Preheat the oven to 180°C. Grease a 20cm round cake tin or a 22cm loaf tin and line the base with baking paper.
2. Cream the butter and sugar until light and fluffy, then add the lemon zest and the eggs one at a time, beating well after each addition.
3. Sift the dry ingredients together and fold through the creamed mixture in about three lots, alternating with the milk. Scoop the mixture into the prepared tin and level the top.
4. Bake for about 40 minutes or until the cake springs back when lightly touched.
5. While the cake is cooking make the syrup by stirring the lemon juice and sugar together then set aside until the cake is ready.
6. Leave the cake in the tin on a wire rack and spoon over the lemon syrup. It will soak in a little and run down the sides of the cake, leaving a thin crust of sugar on the top. Finish cooling in the tin, then turn out carefully.

Madeira Cake

With its fine golden crumb and buttery lemon flavour, Madeira cake is one of the jewels of the English baking tradition – and a New Zealand favourite too. It is usually a small, deep cake but it also bakes very well in a loaf tin, which makes it easier to slice.

200g butter, softened
200g sugar
½ tsp finely grated lemon zest
3 eggs, beaten

2 cups Edmonds standard flour
1 tsp Edmonds baking powder
1 Tbsp lemon juice
2 tsp caster sugar

1. Preheat the oven to 180°C. Lightly grease a 15cm deep round cake tin or a 20cm loaf tin and line with baking paper.
2. Cream the butter and sugar until light and fluffy then stir in the lemon zest.
3. Add the beaten eggs to the creamed mixture a little at a time, beating well after each addition.
4. Sift the flour and baking powder together and fold in. Lastly fold in the lemon juice. Scoop the mixture into the prepared tin and sprinkle with the caster sugar.
5. Bake for 40 minutes or until the cake springs back when lightly touched. Leave in the tin for 10 minutes before turning out onto a wire rack to cool.

Pour cold syrup on a hot cake or hot syrup on a cooled cake.

VARIATION
Seed Cake
For a traditional seed cake, another English favourite, add 1 teaspoon caraway seeds
with the dry ingredients.

Marble Cake

1
HOUR

*There is something magical about a cake that reveals a multi-coloured interior when
cut. Perfect for a children's birthday party, where you can choose the colours to suit.*

3 eggs
¾ cup caster sugar
1 cup Edmonds standard flour
1 tsp Edmonds baking powder
50g butter

2 Tbsp boiling water
1 Tbsp cocoa
2–3 drops red food colouring
Buttercream Icing (page 97)
icing sugar (optional)

1. Preheat the oven to 180°C. Grease a 20cm round cake tin and line the base with
baking paper.
2. Beat the eggs until frothy then gradually beat in the sugar until the mixture is very
thick and pale.
3. Sift the flour and baking powder together and fold gently into the egg mixture,
followed by the butter melted with the boiling water.
4. Divide the mixture into thirds. Stir the cocoa into one third, and add enough red
food colouring to make a pink mixture with another third. Leave the last third plain.
5. Spoon the three mixtures in diagonal stripes into the tin and use a knife to swirl
together all the mixtures.
6. Bake for 20–25 minutes or until the cake springs back when lightly touched. Leave
in the tin for 10 minutes before turning out onto a wire rack to cool.
7. When cold, ice with Buttercream Icing or dust with icing sugar.

Macaroon Cake

1
HOUR

A simple, buttery vanilla cake with a baked-on coconut macaroon topping.

125g butter, softened
½ cup sugar
3 egg yolks
1 tsp vanilla essence

1½ cups Edmonds standard flour
1 tsp Edmonds baking powder
pinch of salt
2 Tbsp milk

TOPPING
3 egg whites
½ cup sugar

1½ cups fine desiccated coconut

1. Preheat the oven to 180°C. Grease a 23cm shallow square cake tin and line the base
with baking paper.
2. Cream the butter and sugar until light and fluffy, then add the egg yolks and vanilla,
beating well.
3. Sift together the flour, baking powder and salt and add to the creamed mixture
alternately with the milk.

4. Scoop the mixture into the prepared tin and level the top.

5. To make the topping, beat the egg whites until soft peaks form and then fold in the sugar and coconut. Spread evenly over the cake.

6. Bake for 30 minutes or until an inserted skewer comes out clean. Leave in the tin for 10 minutes before turning out carefully onto a wire rack to cool. To protect the topping, reverse again immediately using another rack.

VARIATION

Raspberry Macaroon Cake
Spread 2 tablespoons raspberry jam over the cake before adding the macaroon topping.

Sticky Gingerbread

A rich, moist gingerbread best served in squares with a cup of tea – or even with custard for dessert.

125g butter, softened	*¼ tsp salt*
½ cup sugar	*1½ tsp Edmonds baking soda*
1 cup golden syrup	*1½ tsp ground ginger*
1 egg	*1 tsp cinnamon*
2½ cups Edmonds standard flour	*1 cup water*

1. Preheat the oven to 180˚C. Butter a 20cm square cake tin and line the base with baking paper.

2. Cream the butter and sugar in a bowl until light and fluffy. Warm the golden syrup slightly until runny and beat it into the creamed mixture.

3. Add the egg and beat well. Sift the dry ingredients together and stir into creamed mixture alternately with the water.

4. Pour the mixture into the tin and bake for 50 to 60 minutes. Leave in the tin for 10 minutes before turning out onto a wire rack to cool.

Tosca Cake

A famous Scandinavian cake which is topped with a thick layer of caramelised almonds.

2 eggs	*1 tsp Edmonds baking powder*
½ cup sugar	*75g butter, melted and cooled*
1 tsp vanilla essence	*2 Tbsp milk*
¾ cup Edmonds standard flour	

TOPPING

3 Tbsp butter	*¼ cup sugar*
¼ cup slivered almonds	*2 Tbsp milk*

1. Preheat the oven to 180˚C. Grease a 25cm springform tin, or a tart tin with a removable base. Line the base with baking paper.

2. Beat the eggs until foamy and then gradually add the sugar, beating until the mixture is thick and lemon-coloured. Mix in the vanilla.

3. Sift the flour and baking powder together and carefully fold into the egg mixture. Mix together the melted butter and milk and fold in gently until the mixture is smooth and blended. Scoop into the prepared tin and bake for 30 minutes.

4. Meanwhile, prepare the topping. Melt the butter in a frying pan. Add the almonds and stir over a medium heat until toasted and golden. Stir in the sugar and milk, turn the heat to high and bring to a vigorous boil, stirring constantly. Boil for 2½ minutes or until the mixture begins to darken and thickens slightly.

5. Pour the hot topping over the cake, spreading it out evenly. Now you can put the cake under the grill for a few minutes until the topping is bubbling and lightly browned, or bake the cake for another 10 minutes.

6. Cool completely in the tin on a wire rack.

Soften butter in the microwave for easy creaming.

Chocolate Almond Mud Cake page 47, Lemon Syrup Cake page 51

Classic Sponge Sandwich page 57, Sponge Kisses page 77

Sponges

Sponge cake has been a mainstay of Kiwi households and tearooms for longer than anyone can remember. There are two forms of sponge, one produced by the batter method, the other by the foam method.

How to make a perfect sponge:

- Preheat the oven and prepare the tins before you start mixing.
- Grease the cake tins lightly and dust them with flour. For total peace of mind you can line the base of each tin with a circle of baking paper.
- Always have the eggs at room temperature so they will reach maximum volume when you beat them.
- Sift the dry ingredients together twice to aerate them.
- Beat the eggs and sugar together with a wire whisk, a hand egg-beater or an electric beater. (Do not use a wand blender because it cannot beat air into the eggs.)
- Keep beating until the mixture is very thick and pale – at least 10 minutes. You should be able to draw a figure eight with the mixture falling off the ends of the beater in an unbroken trail.
- Fold in the dry ingredients very gently with a slotted metal spoon. Steady the mixing bowl with one hand. Beginning with the edge of the spoon against the far side of the bowl, cut down through the mixture and pull the spoon gently towards you, scraping against the bottom of the bowl. When the spoon touches the near side of the bowl, rotate it slightly and lift it up, 'folding' the mixture up and onto itself. At the same time, give the bowl a quarter turn towards you. Keep cutting, folding and turning until everything is well combined.
- When making a sponge sandwich, it is a good idea to weigh the mixture in each tin before baking to make sure the layers will be even.
- When the sponge is cooked it will spring back when lightly touched with a finger and the edges will shrink slightly away from the sides of the tin.
- Cool the sponges in sandwich tins for 5 minutes before turning out onto a wire rack to cool.

Classic Sponge Sandwich

This delicate, feather-light sponge is the perfect vehicle for jam and whipped cream and always looks splendid on the afternoon tea table. It first appeared in the 1957 Edmonds Cookery Book.

3 eggs, separated
pinch of salt
½ cup caster sugar
½ cup Edmonds standard flour
¼ cup Edmonds Fielder's cornflour

1 tsp Edmonds baking powder
25g melted butter
jam and whipped cream
icing sugar

1. Preheat the oven to 190°C. Lightly grease two 20cm sandwich tins and line the bases with baking paper. Dust the insides of the tins with flour.

2. Beat the egg whites and salt until foamy, then add the sugar gradually and beat in the egg yolks one at a time. After 10 minutes' beating the sugar will be dissolved and the mixture very pale and fluffy. (Don't skimp on the beating time; it is important for a well-risen sponge.)

3. Sift the flour, cornflour and baking powder together, then sift them again onto the egg mixture and fold them in very gently using a slotted spoon. Lastly fold in the melted butter. Scoop into the prepared tins and spread out evenly.

4. Bake for 15–20 minutes or until the surface is lightly browned and the sponges spring back when lightly touched. Leave in the tins for 5 minutes before turning out onto a wire rack to cool.

5. When cool, fill with jam and whipped cream and dust the top with icing sugar.

Sponge Cake

1 HOUR

A firm sponge, perfect for trifle or lamingtons and unchanged in the Edmonds Cookery Book since the 1930s.

3 eggs
pinch of salt
¾ cup caster sugar

1 cup Edmonds standard flour
1 tsp Edmonds baking powder
50g butter, melted

1. Preheat the oven to 180°C. Lightly grease a 20cm square cake tin and line the base with baking paper. Dust the inside of the tin with flour.

2. Beat the eggs with the salt until very foamy; this will take about 1 minute with an electric beater. Add the sugar gradually, beating very well, then keep beating for about 5 minutes until the mixture is very pale and fluffy.

3. Sift the flour and baking powder together, then sift them again onto the egg mixture. Fold in gently with a slotted spoon and lastly fold through the melted butter until well combined. Scoop into the prepared tin.

4. Bake for 25–30 minutes until the sponge cake is golden, well risen and springs back when lightly touched.

5. Leave in the tin for 5 minutes before turning out onto a wire rack to cool.

Sponge Roll

50 MINS

Often called a Swiss roll, this tender sponge is a good vehicle for jam or lemon honey and lots of whipped cream.

3 eggs
pinch of salt
½ tsp vanilla essence
½ cup caster sugar
5 Tbsp Edmonds standard flour

1 tsp Edmonds baking powder
25g butter, melted
icing or caster sugar
jam or lemon honey and
  whipped cream

1. Preheat the oven to 200°C. Lightly grease a 20cm x 30cm sponge roll tin and line the base and two sides with baking paper.

2. Beat together the eggs and salt until fluffy, about 3 minutes, then add the vanilla and the sugar a little at a time and beat for 7 more minutes, until a pale creamy colour and very thick. After 10 minutes' beating the sugar will all have dissolved.

3. Sift the flour and baking powder together, then sift them again onto the egg mixture and fold them in very gently using a slotted spoon. Lastly fold in the melted butter. Scoop into the prepared tin and spread out evenly.

4. Bake for 8–10 minutes or until the surface is lightly browned and the cake springs back when lightly touched.

5. While the sponge is baking, put a piece of greaseproof paper on a clean cloth on the bench and dust it with icing sugar or caster sugar.

6. Turn the sponge onto the sugared paper, remove the baking paper carefully and trim the edges of the sponge. Cool for 10 minutes.

7. Spread with jam or lemon honey and whipped cream. Roll the sponge carefully from a short side, holding the edges of the paper.

Three Minute Sponge

A very quickly made, one-bowl sponge cake. Serve as a sponge sandwich, or use for a trifle or lamingtons.

1½ cups Edmonds standard flour	*2 Tbsp milk*
1 cup sugar	*2 tsp Edmonds baking powder*
3 eggs	*jam and whipped cream*
50g butter, melted	*icing sugar*

1. Preheat the oven to 190°C. Lightly grease two 20cm sandwich tins and line the bases with baking paper. Dust the sides of the tins with flour.

2. Put the flour and sugar into a large mixing bowl and combine well.

3. Break in the eggs, followed by the melted butter and milk.

4. Beat hard for 3 minutes until the mixture is pale and smooth. Lastly fold in the baking powder. Scoop into the prepared tins.

5. Bake for 15–20 minutes or until the sponges spring back when lightly touched. Leave in the tins for 5 minutes before turning out onto a wire rack to cool.

6. When cool fill with jam and whipped cream and dust the top with icing sugar.

VARIATION
Lemon or Orange Sponge
Add 2 teaspoons finely grated lemon or orange zest and replace the milk with lemon or orange juice.

Use an electric beater if you have one – sponges need to be beaten for a long time.

Fruit Cakes

Kiwis do seem to love their fruit cakes and we bake more per capita than most countries. They're also a delicious way to increase your daily fruit intake.

How to make the perfect fruit cake:

- Since fruit cakes cook for several hours, it is best to line the cake tin with baking paper, then tie two layers of brown paper around the outside of the tin. This helps stop the outside of the cake from becoming dry before the inside is cooked.
- After scooping the cake batter into the tin, wet your hand with cold water and flatten the mixture. This stops any fruit from sticking out of the top and burning.
- Bake fruit cakes in the lower half of the oven at a low temperature – around 140–160°C.
- To test when the cake is cooked, insert a fine metal skewer into the centre of the cake and pull it out. There should be no cake mixture adhering to the skewer and the skewer should feel hot to the touch.
- If the top of the cake seems to be browning too quickly, cover with tinfoil or brown paper.
- When the cake is cooked, place it, in its tin, on a cooling rack and cover it loosely with a clean cloth. Allow the cake to cool in the tin. This can take several hours.
- Once the cake has cooled, you can pour over about ½ cup brandy or rum to keep it moist and improve the flavour. If the top is crusty, make little holes with a skewer or toothpick to help the brandy soak in.
- To store, leave the baking paper on the cake and wrap it securely in tinfoil.
- Keep the cake in a lidded tin in a cool, dark place.
- Allow a rich fruit cake to mature for several weeks before cutting. This helps stop the cake from crumbling as well as improving the flavour. To cut the cake, use a very sharp knife – one with a serrated edge works well.

Boiled Fruit Cake

3 HOURS

A quickly mixed, everyday fruit cake. You can vary the dried fruit to include your favourites.

500g mixed dried fruit
water
250g butter
1½ cups sugar
3 eggs, beaten

3 cups Edmonds standard flour
4 tsp Edmonds baking powder
½ tsp almond essence
½ tsp vanilla essence

1. Grease a 23cm square cake tin and line it with baking paper. Tie a double layer of brown paper around the outside of the tin.
2. Put the mixed dried fruit into a large saucepan and add just enough water to cover the fruit. Cover and bring to the boil then remove from the heat.

3. Stir in the butter and sugar, stirring constantly until the butter has melted. Set aside to cool.
4. Preheat the oven to 160°C.
5. Mix the beaten eggs into the cooled mixture. Sift the flour and baking powder together then add to the fruit mixture and lastly add the essences. Scoop the mixture into the prepared cake tin then wet your hand under the cold tap and smooth the surface.
6. Bake the cake below the centre of the oven for 1–1½ hours or until an inserted skewer comes out clean.
7. Cool in the tin on a wire rack, covered with a clean cloth.

Cathedral Window Cake

3 HOURS

When you cut a thin slice of this rich cake and hold it up to the light, the colours of the glacé fruit will look like panes in a stained-glass cathedral window. Make the cake a few days ahead to allow it to mature.

125g glacé pineapple rings	*3 eggs*
3 glacé pears	*½ cup caster sugar*
½ cup glacé green cherries	*1 tsp vanilla essence*
½ cup glacé red cherries	*2 Tbsp brandy*
125g glacé apricots	*¾ cup Edmonds standard flour*
125g blanched almonds	*½ tsp Edmonds baking powder*
250g whole Brazil nuts	*1 tsp ground nutmeg*
½ cup crystallised ginger	*¼ tsp salt*

1. Preheat the oven to 150°C. Line a 23cm loaf tin with baking paper and tie a double layer of brown paper around the outside of the tin.
2. Chop each of the pineapple rings and pears into six pieces. Halve the green and red cherries. Chop the apricots into quarters. Put the chopped fruits, almonds, Brazil nuts and ginger into a bowl and mix to combine.
3. In a separate bowl, beat the eggs, sugar, vanilla and brandy together with an electric beater or a whisk.
4. Sift the flour, baking powder, nutmeg and salt together and fold into the egg mixture. Pour this onto the fruit and nuts, mixing thoroughly. Scoop the mixture into the prepared tin then wet your hand under the cold tap and smooth the surface.
5. Bake for 2 hours or until an inserted skewer comes out clean.
6. Cool in the tin on a wire rack, covered with a clean cloth. Remove the baking paper and wrap in tinfoil to store. Leave for two days before cutting.
7. Use a very sharp knife to cut the cake into very thin slices.

Baking powder should be stored in a cool, dry place as any moisture will cause it to lose its potency.
Do not store baking powder mixed with flour as flour contains moisture.

Fruit Cake

A dark, spicy, moist fruit cake in mid-20th century style. Keeps well and slices beautifully.

675g mixed dried fruit	1 Tbsp marmalade
¼ cup mixed peel	pinch of salt
3 cups Edmonds high grade flour	1 tsp Edmonds baking powder
225g butter	1 tsp mixed spice
1 cup brown sugar	½ tsp ground nutmeg
2 Tbsp golden syrup	5 eggs, beaten

1. Preheat the oven to 150°C. Line a deep 20cm square cake tin with baking paper and tie a double layer of brown paper around the outside of the tin.

2. Combine the dried fruit and peel in a bowl and dust with 2 tablespoons of the flour to help prevent the fruit from sinking.

3. Cream the butter and brown sugar together then add the golden syrup and marmalade.

4. Sift the remaining flour, salt, baking powder and spices together. Beat the eggs until thick and fluffy and add them to the creamed mixture alternately with the dry ingredients.

5. Scoop the mixture into the prepared tin then wet your hand under the cold tap and smooth the surface.

6. Bake for 2–2½ hours or until an inserted skewer comes out clean. Cool in the tin on a wire rack, covered with a clean cloth.

7. Wrap in tinfoil and a cloth and store in a cool place. Keep for a week before cutting.

Rich Christmas Cake

Our wonderful celebration Christmas fruit cake. Just remember to start your cake by Labour Day in order for the flavours to fully develop for Christmas Day.

1¾ cups orange juice	2 tsp finely grated lemon zest
¾ cup dark rum or brandy	1 cup blanched almonds
2 Tbsp finely grated orange zest	2½ cups Edmonds high grade flour
500g currants	½ tsp Edmonds baking soda
500g raisins	1 tsp cinnamon
2 cups sultanas	1 tsp mixed spice
2 cups chopped dates	½ tsp ground nutmeg
150g crystallised ginger, chopped	250g butter
150g mixed peel	1½ cups brown sugar
150g glacé cherries, halved	2 Tbsp treacle
½ tsp vanilla essence	5 eggs, beaten
¼ tsp almond essence	

1. Place the orange juice, rum and orange zest in a saucepan and bring to the boil. Remove from the heat and add the dried fruit. Cover and leave the fruit to soak overnight.

2. The next day, stir the essences, lemon zest and almonds into the fruit mixture. Sift the flour, baking soda and spices into a bowl.

3. Preheat the oven to 150°C. Line a deep 23cm square cake tin with baking paper and tie a double layer of brown paper around the outside of the tin.
4. Cream the butter, sugar and treacle until light and fluffy and add the eggs a little at a time, beating well after each addition.
5. Fold in the sifted ingredients alternately with the fruit mixture.
6. Scoop the mixture into the prepared tin then wet your hand under the cold tap and smooth the surface.
7. Bake for 4 hours or until an inserted skewer comes out clean. Cool in the tin on a wire rack, covered with a clean cloth
8. Wrap in tinfoil and a cloth and store in a cool place.
9. If you want a more flavoursome cake pour 2–3 tablespoons of brandy or sherry over the cake after it has cooled and before storing it. If the top is crusty, make little holes with a skewer or toothpick to help the alcohol soak in.

Sultana & Lemon Cake

2½ HOURS

A light-coloured, moist cake as an alternative to those dark, heavy fruit cakes.

3 cups sultanas
250g butter, softened
1 cup sugar
3 eggs, beaten
1 tsp finely grated lemon zest

2 cups Edmonds standard flour
1 tsp Edmonds baking powder
¼ cup candied lemon peel
¼ cup lemon juice
¼ cup milk

1. Put the sultanas in a saucepan and cover with water. Bring to the boil and simmer for 10 minutes. Drain well and set aside to cool.
2. Preheat the oven to 160°C. Grease a 20cm round cake tin and line the base with baking paper.
3. Cream the butter and sugar until light and fluffy, then add the beaten eggs a little at a time, followed by the lemon zest.
4. Sift the flour and baking powder together and fold in to the creamed mixture, then stir in the cooled sultanas and lemon peel. Lastly add the lemon juice and milk.
5. Scoop the mixture into the prepared tin then wet your hand under the cold tap and smooth the surface.
6. Bake for 1½ hours or until the cake springs back when lightly touched in the centre. Cool in the tin on a wire rack, covered with a clean cloth.

Small Cakes

They may be small but they have big personalities.
You'll have a lot of fun making and eating these classic little treats.

Chocolate Éclairs

(2) HOURS
(15) MAKES

Forget those behemoths from the supermarket, these éclairs are tiny and delicate so you can eat more than one!

250g Choux Pastry (page 102)

FILLING
whipped cream   **Chocolate Icing (page 99)**

1. Preheat the oven to 200°C. Grease two baking trays.
2. Scoop the choux pastry into a large forcing bag fitted with a 2cm plain nozzle.
3. Pipe 7cm strips of the mixture onto the prepared trays. Use a knife to cut the mixture at the end of each éclair so it doesn't keep trailing out of the forcing bag.
4. Bake for 30 minutes or until the éclairs are puffy and golden, then lower the heat to 120°C and continue baking for about 15 minutes until the éclairs are dry. Place on a wire rack to cool thoroughly.
5. Use a sharp knife to cut a slit in the side of each éclair. If there is any soft mixture inside, scoop it out and discard. Fill with whipped cream and ice the tops with Chocolate Icing.

NOTE
Whipped cream will soften the pastry shell in about an hour, so if you want to keep the éclairs for longer than an hour use Crème Pâtissière (Pastry Cream) (page 99).

Christmas Mince Pies

(1) HOUR
(16) MAKES

Make your own this Christmas – they will be far better than any bought ones . . .

350g Sweet Shortcrust Pastry (page 103) or 3 sheets Edmonds sweet short pastry, thawed

1 cup Christmas Mincemeat (page 65)   **caster sugar**
2–3 Tbsp milk   **icing sugar**

1. Preheat the oven to 180°C.
2. On a lightly floured board, roll out the sweet shortcrust pastry to 3mm thickness or use the ready-rolled pastry sheets. Cut out rounds with a 7cm cutter and the same number of tops with a 6cm cutter. You should get about 16 of each.
3. Fit the larger circles of pastry into patty tins and put about 1 tablespoon of mincemeat into each.

4. Brush the edges of the bases with milk and place the tops on, pressing gently to seal the edges.

5. Brush the tops with milk, sprinkle with a little caster sugar and make a small slit in the tops.

6. Bake for about 20 minutes until lightly browned, then remove from the tins to cool on a rack. Dust with icing sugar.

7. Before serving, reheat in a low 140°C oven for 15 minutes or until warm.

Christmas Mincemeat

Have a go at making your own mincemeat. So much better than store-bought and you can add your favourite flavours.

*2 apples, unpeeled,
  quartered and cored*
1¼ cups currants
1¼ cups sultanas
1¼ cups raisins
1 cup mixed peel

¼ cup blanched almonds
1 cup brown sugar
¼ tsp salt
½ tsp ground nutmeg
275g butter, softened
2 Tbsp brandy or whisky

1. Mince or finely chop the apples, currants, sultanas, raisins, peel and almonds.

2. Add the sugar, salt, nutmeg, softened butter and brandy or whisky, and mix well.

3. Spoon the mixture into clean jars and seal well. Keep for at least 2 weeks before using.

Cinnamon Oysters

These light and delicate cinnamon sponge cakes, generously filled with whipped cream, were created by Mrs Thelma Brown, who was a music teacher at Anderson's Bay in Dunedin. Mrs Brown contributed her recipe to the 1951 League of Mothers Cookery Book and Household Hints. They have become a New Zealand classic.

2 eggs
¼ cup caster sugar
2 tsp golden syrup
60g Edmonds standard flour
1 tsp Edmonds baking powder

½ tsp Edmonds baking soda
1 tsp cinnamon
½ tsp ground ginger
whipped cream
icing sugar

1. Preheat the oven to 200°C. Lightly grease a small, shallow 12-hole patty tin or cinnamon oyster tray and dust with flour.

2. Warm a mixing bowl by running hot water inside it and then dry it thoroughly. Beat the eggs and sugar until pale and thick. This will take about 3 minutes with an electric beater.

3. Add the golden syrup and keep beating for another 5 minutes.

4. Sift the flour, baking powder, baking soda and spices together then fold gently into the egg mixture. Spoon the mixture into the prepared tins.

Cinnamon Oysters can be frozen very successfully, cream and all.

5. Bake for 8–10 minutes. The surface of the cakes should spring back when lightly touched.

6. Leave in the tins for a couple of minutes until the cakes shrink away from the sides a little, then turn out carefully, loosening them with a round-bladed table knife if necessary. Place on a wire rack to cool.

7. When cold, cut a slit into the side of each cake with a small serrated knife and spoon or pipe in some whipped cream. Dust with icing sugar.

Coconut Macaroon Tartlets

40 MINS — 16 MAKES

Small pastry cases filled with a little jam and a layer of golden, slightly chewy coconut macaroon filling. A good way to use up leftover egg whites and some fruity homemade jam.

125g Rough Puff Pastry (page 102) or 2 sheets of Edmonds flaky puff pastry, thawed

FILLING
2 egg whites
½ cup sugar
½ cup fine desiccated coconut
1 tsp finely grated lemon zest

3 Tbsp raspberry, plum or blackcurrant jam
icing sugar

1. Preheat the oven to 215°C.

2. Roll out the rough puff pastry to 3mm thickness or use the ready-rolled pastry sheets. Cut out 6–7cm rounds with a cutter. You should get 16 rounds. Line small shallow patty tins with the circles.

3. Make the macaroon filling by beating the egg whites until stiff, then beat in the sugar a little at a time. Lastly fold in the coconut and lemon zest.

4. Spoon a little jam into each pastry case and top with 1 tablespoon of the filling, sprinkling with a little more coconut.

5. Bake for 10–12 minutes or until lightly golden, then remove from the oven and dust with icing sugar. Place on a wire rack to cool.

VARIATION
Use apricot jam and add ¼ teaspoon almond essence to the macaroon mixture.

Cream Puffs

2 HOURS — 20 MAKES

Fill these with cream or a little custard or Crème Pâtissière for a treat.

250g Choux Pastry (page 102)
FILLING
whipped cream

icing sugar (optional)

Coffee Icing (page 99)

1. Preheat the oven to 200°C. Grease two baking trays.

2. Scoop the choux pastry into a large forcing bag fitted with a 1cm plain nozzle. Pipe out small heaps onto a baking tray. Or just use two spoons to shape the puffs – wet them to stop the mixture from sticking. The puffs will treble in size when they cook so leave plenty of space around them.

3. Bake for 30 minutes or until the puffs are risen and golden, then lower the heat to

120°C and continue baking for about 15 minutes until the puffs are dry. Place on a wire rack to cool thoroughly.
4. Use a sharp knife to cut a slit in the side of each puff. If there is any soft mixture inside, scoop it out and discard. Fill with whipped cream and ice the tops with Coffee Icing or dust with sifted icing sugar.

Cupcakes

A lovely light little cupcake, perfect for decorating.

125g butter, softened
1 tsp vanilla essence
½ cup caster sugar
2 eggs

1 cup Edmonds standard flour
2 tsp Edmonds baking powder
¼ cup milk

1. Preheat the oven to 190°C. Line a 12-hole patty tin or muffin tin with paper cupcake cases.
2. Cream the butter, vanilla essence and sugar together until light and fluffy. Add the eggs one at a time, beating well after each addition.
3. Sift the flour and baking powder together and fold gently into the creamed mixture. Lastly stir in the milk. Spoon the mixture into the paper cases.
4. Bake for 15 minutes or until the cakes spring back when lightly touched. Place on a wire rack to cool and then ice and decorate as you wish.

VARIATIONS
Butterfly Cakes
Cut a slice from the top of each cupcake. Cut the slice in half. Place teaspoonfuls of whipped cream in each cavity. Arrange the 'wings' on the cupcakes. Dust with icing sugar.
Chocolate Cupcakes
Replace 2 tablespoons of the measured flour with 2 tablespoons cocoa. Ice with Chocolate Icing (page 99).
Citrus Cupcakes
Replace the vanilla essence with 2 teaspoons grated orange or lemon zest. Ice with Orange (page 100) or Lemon Icing (page 99).
Queen Cakes
Stir in ½ cup sultanas or currants before adding the milk.

Cupcakes – Gluten Free

You wouldn't even know these little cakes are gluten free.

125g butter, softened
¾ cup caster sugar
1 tsp vanilla essence
3 eggs, size 7

1½ cups Edmonds gluten free self raising flour
½ cup milk

1. Preheat the oven to 160°C. Line a 12-hole patty tin or muffin tin with paper cupcake cases.
2. Cream the butter and sugar together until light and fluffy. Add the vanilla and the eggs, one at a time, beating well after each addition.
3. Sift the flour and fold gently into the creamed mixture. Lastly stir in the milk, making sure not to over-mix. Spoon the mixture into the paper cases.
4. Bake for 20 minutes or until the cakes spring back when lightly touched. Place on a wire rack to cool and then ice and decorate as you wish.

Custard Squares

Two layers of crisp pastry filled with a generous amount of creamy custard.

450g Rough Puff Pastry (page 102) or 2 sheets Edmonds flaky puff pastry, thawed

CUSTARD
4 Tbsp Edmonds custard powder   **50g butter**
3 Tbsp icing sugar   **1 egg, beaten**
2 cups milk

TOPPING
Glacé Icing (page 99)   **icing sugar (optional)**

1. Preheat the oven to 215°C. Dampen two baking trays with a little cold water. Line a 20cm square cake tin.
2. Roll out the rough puff pastry to 3mm thickness or use the ready-rolled pastry sheets. Cut into two 25cm squares. Tidy any rough edges.
3. Place the pastry on the prepared baking trays and prick thoroughly with a fork all over. This will discourage the pastry from rising too much since you want flat, flaky sheets. Chill on the trays for 15 minutes.
4. Bake for about 20 minutes until dark golden brown. Carefully turn each piece of pastry over after 15 minutes to ensure it is cooked right through. Place on a wire rack to cool.
5. In a saucepan, mix the custard powder, icing sugar and ¼ cup milk to a smooth paste. Add the remaining milk, butter and egg and cook, stirring, until the mixture is very thick. Cover with a damp paper towel or plastic wrap pressed onto the custard surface to prevent a skin forming. Leave until cool but still pourable.
6. Trim the cooked pastry sheets to 20cm squares. Fit one in the base of the tin, pour over the cooled custard and top with second square of pastry. Leave to set for 20 minutes and then ice with Glace Icing or dust with icing sugar. Cut into squares with a serrated knife when set.

Eccles Cakes

Small currant-filled cakes originally from the small town of Eccles in Lancashire, where they have been made since the end of the 18th century. The recipe survived transportation to several of Britain's colonies and they remain deservedly popular today.

225g Rough Puff Pastry (page 102) or 3 sheets Edmonds flaky puff pastry,
  thawed
caster sugar

FILLING

50g butter   *½ tsp cinnamon*
50g brown sugar   *a little grated nutmeg*
55g mixed peel   *85g currants*

1. Preheat the oven to 210°C. Line a baking tray with baking paper.
2. Make the filling by melting the butter and mixing it with the other ingredients.
3. Roll out the pastry to 5mm thickness or use the ready-rolled sheets and cut into
10cm rounds with a cutter. Put a large teaspoonful of the filling in the centre of each
round, wet the edges and pinch them together at the top to form a round package.
4. Turn the cakes over and flatten them with a rolling pin until the currants show
through. Place on the prepared tray, slash two or three times across the top, brush with
water and sprinkle with caster sugar.
5. Bake for about 20 minutes until golden brown. Place on a wire rack to cool.

Fruit Squares

1 HOUR 24 MAKES

*Known to generations of children as 'fly cemeteries' these are delicious, despite their
grisly name.*

200g Rough Puff Pastry (page 102) or 2 sheets Edmonds flaky puff pastry,
  thawed
icing sugar

FILLING

50g butter, melted   *¼ tsp finely grated lemon zest*
1 Granny Smith apple, peeled, cored   *1 Tbsp lemon juice*
  and grated   *1 tsp cinnamon*
¼ cup raisins   *¼ cup brown sugar*
¼ cup sultanas   *¼ cup currants*
1 tsp mixed spice

1. Preheat the oven to 200°C. Line a baking tray with baking paper.
2. Make the filling by placing all the ingredients in a bowl and mixing to combine well.
3. Divide the pastry in half and roll out each piece into a large rectangle about 20cm x
30cm and 2mm thick or use the ready-rolled sheets.
4. Lift one sheet onto the prepared tray using a rolling pin and spread with the filling,
leaving a 1cm border around the edge. Brush this edge with water.
5. Place the second sheet of pastry onto the fruit filling and press the edges to seal.
Prick the pastry all over with a fork.
6. Bake for 30–35 minutes or until golden. Cut into squares while hot and dust with
icing sugar.

Fruit Tartlets

1½ HOURS · MAKES 30

The perfect way to celebrate summer berries and stone fruit, and also very pretty on the plate.

350g Sweet Shortcrust Pastry (page 103) or 3 sheets Edmonds sweet short pastry, thawed

FILLING
1 cup full-cream milk
2 egg yolks

2 Tbsp Edmonds custard powder
2 Tbsp sugar

TOPPING
fresh, ripe fruit – e.g. kiwifruit, grapes, strawberries, blueberries, sliced peaches or apricots

GLAZE
¼ cup apricot jam
2 tsp water

icing sugar (optional)

1. Make the filling first by whisking the milk, yolks, custard powder and sugar to a smooth paste in a saucepan. Cook over a low heat, stirring until the mixture thickens. Remove from the heat, pour into a bowl, cover and leave to cool.
2. Preheat the oven to 190°C.
3. On a lightly floured board, roll out the pastry to 2mm thickness or use the ready-rolled sheets. Cut out 7cm rounds with a fluted cutter and use to line patty tins. Prick the bases with a fork.
4. Bake for about 10 minutes until golden brown and cooked through. Place on a wire rack to cool.
5. Fill the cases with the cooled custard and decoratively arrange the fruit of your choice on top.
6. Gently heat the jam and water and push through a strainer. Brush the fruit with the apricot glaze or dust with icing sugar.

Friands

45 MINS · MAKES 12

These delicate almond cakes originated in the financial district of Paris. Originally baked in shallow rectangular tins, the cakes resembled bars of gold, and were called financiers since traders at the stock exchange would eat them with a hasty morning coffee.

⅓ cup Edmonds gluten free plain flour
½ tsp Edmonds baking powder
1 cup icing sugar
1½ cups ground almonds
5 egg whites

170g butter, melted and cooled
1 tsp finely grated lemon zest or vanilla essence
⅓ cup flaked almonds
extra icing sugar

1. Preheat the oven to 180°C. Lightly grease a standard 12-hole friand or muffin tin.
2. Sift the flour, baking powder and icing sugar into a mixing bowl and add the ground almonds. Toss everything together with your fingers to break up any lumps of almonds and to combine well.
3. In another bowl, whisk the egg whites until just foamy but not yet firm.

4. Fold the egg whites into the almond mixture with a large spoon, then gently whisk in the melted butter and lemon zest or vanilla essence.

5. Spoon the mixture into the prepared tins and sprinkle with the flaked almonds.

6. Bake for 20–25 minutes or until the friands are golden and spring back when lightly touched. Use a round-bladed table knife to loosen the friands from the tins and place on a wire rack to cool. Dust with icing sugar before serving.

NOTE

Friands are a good recipe for using leftover frozen egg whites.

Jam Tarts

30 MINS · 18 MAKES

As made by the Queen of Hearts – very simple and always popular. Use your best homemade jam.

350g Sweet Shortcrust Pastry (page 103) or 2 sheets Edmonds sweet short pastry, thawed

FILLING
½ cup tart-flavoured red jam　　　**whipped cream (optional)**

1. Preheat the oven to 200°C.

2. Roll out the pastry to 3mm thickness or use the ready-rolled sheets. Cut out 7cm rounds with a cutter and use them to line shallow patty tins.

3. Prick the bases with a fork and chill the cases for 10 minutes. Place a small teaspoonful of jam into each case.

4. Bake for about 10 minutes. Place on a wire rack to cool and serve plain or with a little whipped cream in each. Too much jam in the tart cases will overflow and burn in the oven, so be frugal with the jam.

Lamingtons

1 HOUR · 20 MAKES

A classic recipe invented around 1902 and quickly adopted by New Zealand home bakers.

200g Three Minute Sponge (page 59)　　**2 cups fine desiccated coconut**
**　or store-bought sponge**　　　　　　**whipped cream (optional)**

CHOCOLATE ICING
2 Tbsp cocoa　　　　　　　　　　　**2¼ cups icing sugar**
6 Tbsp boiling water　　　　　　　　**¼ tsp vanilla essence**
25g butter, melted

1. Make or purchase the sponge the day before you need it.

2. Dissolve the cocoa in the boiling water and mix in the butter.

3. Sift the icing sugar into a bowl and then pour in the cocoa mixture. Add the vanilla and stir until well combined.

4. Cut the sponge into 4cm squares and dip each square into the chocolate icing, then roll in fine desiccated coconut. Leave to dry on a wire rack. Cut a slit along the top of each cake and fill with whipped cream if desired.

VARIATION

Raspberry Lamingtons

Make up a raspberry jelly following the packet instructions. Set aside to cool and thicken slightly. It should be about the consistency of raw egg white. Dip squares of sponge in the jelly, roll them in coconut and leave to dry on a wire rack.

Marmalade Cakes

30 MINS   12 MAKES

Completely delicious, old-fashioned small cakes quickly made with Edmonds frozen flaky puff pastry. Use good-quality marmalade.

250g Rough Puff Pastry (page 102) or 2 sheets Edmonds flaky puff pastry, thawed
icing sugar

FILLING
2 eggs   **55g butter, melted**
2 Tbsp marmalade

1. Preheat the oven to 200°C.
2. Roll out the pastry to 3mm thickness or use the ready-rolled sheets. Cut out 12 rounds of pastry with a 7cm cutter and fit them into a shallow 12-hole patty tin.
3. Beat the eggs until liquid, but not fluffy, then mix in the marmalade and the melted butter. Spoon the filling into the pastry cases.
4. Bake for 15–20 minutes or until the topping is risen and golden and the pastry is cooked. Cool in the tin on a wire rack.
5. Sift a little icing sugar over the marmalade cakes before serving. The filling will be puffy at first, but then sink as it cools. This is normal – they still taste wonderful.

Meringues

3 HOURS   12 MAKES

2 egg whites   **½ cup caster sugar**
pinch of salt   **whipped cream**
pinch of cream of tartar*

1. Preheat the oven to 120°C. Line two baking trays with baking paper.
2. Beat the egg whites with the salt and cream of tartar until stiff but not dry. Beat in about half of the sugar and keep beating until the mixture is shiny – about 2 minutes.
3. Add the remaining sugar in one lot and fold it in with a spoon. This gives a crisper meringue rather than one with a soft centre. Spoon or pipe into mounds on the prepared trays.
4. Bake for 2–3 hours, depending on their size. They should be dry and crisp and a very pale cream colour, but not brown.
5. Place on a wire rack to cool. Sandwich together in pairs with whipped cream and set in large paper cases for serving.

*Cream of tartar is a stabiliser which helps keep the meringue firm, but the recipe will still work without it.

Beat the egg whites just before you use them or they will separate.

Fruit Tartlets page 70, Cinnamon Oysters page 65, Meringues page 72

Ginger Gems page 26, Girdle or Griddle Scones page 27

VARIATIONS
- Use soft brown sugar for slightly chewy, caramel-coloured meringues.
- Make pink marbled meringues by adding a few drops of red food colouring to the mixture and using a knife blade to swirl the colour though the final mixture.
- Make spicy, Christmas-flavoured meringues by mixing ½ teaspoon cinnamon and ¼ teaspoon mixed spice with the sugar.
- Make minty chocolate meringues, by adding a little green food colouring and ¼ teaspoon peppermint essence to the final mixture. Half dip the meringues in melted dark chocolate once they are cool.

Neenish Tarts

2 HOURS   30 MAKES

A cornerstone of a New Zealand afternoon tea. Shortcrust pastry cases filled with a light vanilla cream and distinctively iced with one half chocolate and the other white.

PASTRY
125g butter, softened
½ cup sugar
1 egg
1 tsp Edmonds baking powder

pinch of salt
2 cups Edmonds standard flour
or 400g Edmonds sweet short
*   pastry, thawed*

FILLING
115g butter, softened
55g icing sugar
½ tsp vanilla essence or finely grated lemon zest

1½ tsp gelatine
3 Tbsp boiling water

Glacé Icing (page 99)

1. Make the pastry by creaming the butter and sugar until light and fluffy. Add the egg and beat well.
2. Sift the dry ingredients onto the creamed mixture and combine to form a smooth dough. Turn out onto a floured board and knead lightly. Wrap in greaseproof paper and chill for 15 minutes.
3. Preheat the oven to 180˚C.
4. Make the filling by creaming the butter and icing sugar until light and fluffy then mixing in the vanilla or lemon zest. Dissolve the gelatine in the boiling water and add a little at a time, beating vigorously. Set aside.
5. Roll out the pastry to 2mm thickness. Cut out 30 rounds using a 7cm cutter and use them to line patty tins. Prick the bases.
6. Bake for 12 minutes or until cooked through, then place on a wire rack to cool.
7. Fill the cooled cases with the vanilla cream, level the tops and chill until the filling is firm.
8. Ice one half of each tart with white Glacé Icing and the other half with Chocolate Icing.

Portuguese Custard Tarts

1 HOUR 18 MAKES

A rich and creamy lemon and vanilla custard cooked in flaky pastry cases – a perfect combination of textures and flavours.

200g Rough Puff Pastry (page 102) or 2 sheets Edmonds flaky puff pastry, thawed

FILLING
4 egg yolks
50g caster sugar
2 Tbsp Edmonds Fielder's cornflour
1 cup cream

½ cup water
1 strip of lemon zest
2 tsp vanilla essence

1. Make the filling first. In a saucepan, whisk together the egg yolks, sugar and cornflour until well combined. Add the cream and water and keep whisking until the mixture is smooth.
2. Place over a medium heat, add the strip of lemon zest and stir until the mixture comes to the boil. Remove from the heat immediately, remove the lemon zest, stir in the vanilla essence and set the custard aside to cool, stirring every now and then to prevent a skin from forming.
3. Roll out the pastry on a floured board to about 3mm thickness or use the ready-rolled sheets. Cut out 18 rounds with a 7cm cutter and use them to line patty tins. Chill for 10 minutes.
4. Preheat the oven to 200°C.
5. Spoon the cooled filling into the chilled cases. Bake for 25 minutes, rotating the trays after 10 minutes. When the tarts are done, the custard should have dark brown spots here and there. If they look a little pale you could place them under the grill for a few minutes but watch them closely.
6. Remove from the oven, place on a wire rack to cool a little. For the perfect taste and texture sensation, try to eat them while they are still warm.

Rock Cakes

30 MINS 15 MAKES

A very old-fashioned and delicious addition to a hearty morning tea, Rock Cakes are definitely not rock hard – but they do look like craggy, pebbly rocks. Serve them buttered and with jam if you like.

1 cup Edmonds standard flour
1 tsp Edmonds baking powder
50g butter, cut into small lumps
¼ cup sugar
½ cup currants

¼ cup mixed peel
1 tsp mixed spice (optional)
1 egg, beaten
2 Tbsp milk, approximately

1. Preheat the oven to 200°C. Line a baking tray with baking paper.
2. Sift the flour and baking powder into a bowl and rub in the lumps of butter with your fingertips until the mixture resembles coarse breadcrumbs.
3. Add the sugar, currants, peel and the mixed spice if you wish, and quickly mix in the egg and enough milk to make a stiff dough. Spoon the mixture in small, rocky heaps on the prepared tray.
4. Bake for 10–12 minutes until golden. Place on a wire rack to cool.

Sponge Kisses

5 HOURS · 18 MAKES

You can store these crisp little cakes in an airtight container for up to two weeks, then fill them with jam and cream and let them sit for three hours before serving. They will miraculously soften and have the texture of a freshly baked sponge.

2 eggs
pinch of salt
½ cup caster sugar
¾ cup Edmonds standard flour

1 tsp Edmonds baking powder
4 Tbsp extra caster sugar
jam and whipped cream
icing sugar

1. Preheat the oven to 190°C. Line two baking trays with baking paper.

2. Beat the eggs with the salt until foamy, about 2 minutes, then beat in the sugar, a spoonful at a time. Beat for another 8 minutes to make 10 minutes beating time in all. The sugar will be completely dissolved and the mixture will be a pale, creamy colour and very thick.

3. Sift the flour and baking powder together, then sift them again onto the egg mixture and fold in very gently.

4. Drop or pipe small spoonfuls onto the prepared trays and dust the tops with the extra caster sugar.

5. Bake for 10–12 minutes or until light golden. Leave on the tray to cool for 5 minutes then use a spatula to move them to a wire rack to cool completely.

6. Store in a airtight container until 3–5 hours before you plan to serve them, then sandwich in pairs with a little jam and whipped cream. Set aside to soften and dust with icing sugar to serve.

Slices & Squares

Another very popular section of the Edmonds Cookery Book. Kiwis have always been keen on slices and squares and there are a couple of classics in here that very few could say they haven't tried at least once.

Albert Squares

45 MINS · 24 MAKES

A soft, cake-like slice generously filled with currants and topped with lemon icing and coconut.

BASE
125g butter
¾ cup sugar
2 eggs, beaten
2 tsp golden syrup
½ tsp vanilla essence

1 cup currants
2 cups Edmonds standard flour
2 tsp Edmonds baking powder
pinch of salt
½ cup milk

ICING
1½ cups icing sugar
½ tsp vanilla essence
½ tsp finely grated lemon zest

lemon juice to mix
3 Tbsp fine desiccated coconut

1. Preheat the oven to 180°C. Lightly grease a 20cm x 30cm shallow tin and line the base and two sides with baking paper.
2. Cream the butter and sugar until light and fluffy. Add the eggs a little at a time, beating well after each addition, then beat in the golden syrup and vanilla essence.
3. Fold in the currants, then sift the dry ingredients together and fold in alternately with the milk. Spread into the prepared tin.
4. Bake for 30 minutes or until the centre springs back when lightly touched.
5. Sift the icing sugar into a bowl then stir in the vanilla, lemon zest and sufficient lemon juice to make a spreading consistency.
6. When the base is cold, ice and sprinkle with coconut. Cut into fingers or squares.

Almond Fingers

2 HOURS · 32 MAKES

A delicious shortcake topped with a thin, crisp layer of meringue and sprinkled with shredded almonds. Based on a recipe which first appeared in the Edmonds Cookery Book in 1923.

125g butter, softened
50g sugar
1 egg, separated
¼ tsp almond essence (optional)

1½ cups Edmonds standard flour
½ tsp Edmonds baking powder
½ cup icing sugar
40g flaked or slivered almonds

1. Cream the butter and sugar until light and beat in the egg yolk and the almond essence, if you wish.

2. Sift the flour and baking powder together and add to the creamed mixture. Mix to a firm dough, form into a rough rectangle, cover and chill for 10 minutes.

3. On a floured surface, roll out the chilled dough into a rectangle about 30cm x 20cm and 6mm thick.

4. Beat the egg white until stiff and then sift the icing sugar onto the egg whites and beat to make a spreadable meringue. Scoop onto the shortcake base and spread it out evenly. A small palette knife is good for this. Sprinkle with the almonds and leave for 1 hour to dry slightly.

5. Preheat the oven to 180°C. Line a baking tray with baking paper.

6. Use a sharp knife to cut the shortcake into fingers, wiping the knife blade between each cut. Carefully lift the fingers onto the prepared tray using a palette knife.

7. Bake for 20–25 minutes until the meringue is pale gold and the shortcake is nicely browned underneath. Place on a wire rack to cool.

Apple Shortcake Squares

1½ HOURS 16 MAKES

Pale and fragrant apple between two layers of golden shortcake. Resist adding more flour to the shortcake which would make it doughy. Chill the mixture thoroughly before rolling it out and you will have a sweet and tender result.

FILLING
3 apples, peeled and sliced
2 Tbsp sugar
2 Tbsp water
1 tsp finely grated lemon zest
pinch of cinnamon

SHORTCAKE
1¾ cups Edmonds standard flour
2 tsp Edmonds baking powder
125g butter
¾ cup caster sugar
1 egg, beaten
1 Tbsp milk
1 Tbsp caster sugar
icing sugar

1. Cook the apples slowly in a covered saucepan with the sugar, water, lemon zest and cinnamon. When they are soft, put them in a bowl to cool.

2. Preheat the oven to 180°C. Lightly grease a 22cm square cake tin and line the base and two sides of the tin with baking paper.

3. Sift together the flour and baking powder and rub in the butter with your fingertips until the mixture resembles coarse breadcrumbs, or use a food processor.

4. Add the sugar, beaten egg and milk and mix or process until the shortcake clumps together.

5. Turn out onto a floured board, flour the top and divide in half. Shape each half into a flat disc, put each on a plate and chill for 20 minutes.

6. Roll out one half of the dough and fit into the prepared tin. Spread the cooled apple evenly over the top.

7. Roll out the remaining dough, drape it over the rolling pin and lift it over the apples, or roll out the dough on baking paper, then flip it onto the apples and peel the paper away. Tidy up the edges with dampened fingers. Brush the top with water and sprinkle with the caster sugar.

8. Bake for 25 minutes until risen and golden. Leave in the tin on a wire rack for 15 minutes, and then use the baking paper to lift the shortcake out of the tin. Transfer to a cutting board, dust with icing sugar and cut into squares.

Apricot & Lemon Slice

A quickly mixed no-bake slice. Ideal for the kids to help make.

125g butter
½ cup sweetened condensed milk
250g packet malt biscuits, crushed
1 cup dried apricots, finely chopped
1 tsp finely grated lemon zest

1 cup fine desiccated coconut
Lemon Icing (page 99)
extra 2 Tbsp fine desiccated
  coconut (optional)

1. Lightly grease a 20cm x 30cm shallow tin and line the base and two sides with baking paper.
2. Place the butter and sweetened condensed milk in a small saucepan and stir over a gentle heat until the butter has melted.
3. Mix the crushed biscuits, dried apricots, lemon zest and coconut together.
4. Stir in the butter mixture and combine well. Press into the prepared tin and chill for 1 hour.
5. Finish with Lemon Icing and sprinkle with coconut, if you wish. Cut into squares once the icing has set.

Caramel Date Fingers

A simple shortcake with a delicious baked-in date filling. You could replace the dates with prunes, dried apricots or raisins, or a mixture of fruit if you wish.

FILLING
1 cup dates, chopped
1 cup water
1 Tbsp brown sugar

1 tsp butter
2 tsp cocoa
¼ tsp vanilla essence

BASE
125g butter
½ cup sugar
1 egg

1¾ cups Edmonds standard flour
1 tsp Edmonds baking powder

1. Put the dates into a saucepan with the water, brown sugar, butter and cocoa. Cook gently over a low heat, stirring constantly until the mixture is smooth and paste-like. Add the vanilla essence and set aside to cool.
2. Preheat the oven to 180°C. Lightly grease a 20cm square cake tin and line the base and two sides with baking paper.
3. Cream the butter and sugar until light and fluffy then add the egg and beat well.
4. Sift together the flour and baking powder and mix in well.
5. Press half of the dough into the base of the prepared tin and spread with the cooled date mixture.
6. Pat or roll out the remaining dough on a piece of greaseproof or baking paper. Flip it onto the date filling and press down lightly.

7. Bake for 30 minutes or until lightly browned. Cool in the tin on a wire rack, dust with icing sugar then turn out of the tin and cut into fingers.

VARIATION
For a tender and light wholemeal shortcake, replace the white flour with 1¼ cups wholemeal flour and add 1 tablespoon golden syrup to the dough. This is a soft mixture which you will need to pat out, rather than roll out.

Caramel Meringue Slice

1 HOUR 24 MAKES

A much-loved New Zealand recipe combining a crisp shortcake base, smoothly delicious caramel filling and crisp meringue topping. Always a winner.

BASE
75g butter
1½ Tbsp sugar
1 egg

1 cup Edmonds standard flour
1 tsp Edmonds baking powder
pinch of salt

FILLING
½ x 395g can sweetened
 condensed milk
1 Tbsp butter
1 Tbsp golden syrup

2 egg yolks
1 tsp vanilla essence
½ cup brown sugar
1½ Tbsp Edmonds standard flour

MERINGUE
2 egg whites

4 Tbsp sugar

1. Preheat the oven to 190°C. Lightly grease a 20cm x 30cm shallow tin and line the base and two sides with baking paper.
2. Cream the butter and sugar until light and fluffy then add the egg and beat well.
3. Sift the dry ingredients together and add to the creamed mixture. Form into a stiff dough and press evenly into the prepared tin.
4. Bake for 10–15 minutes until firm and golden.
5. Put all the filling ingredients except the flour into a saucepan and warm gently, stirring to combine. Add the flour and mix it through, then set aside to cool a little.
6. Make the meringue topping by beating the egg whites until stiff, then beating in the sugar.
7. Reduce the oven temperature to 160°C. Pour the cooled caramel filling over the base, then top with the meringue and cook for another 20–25 minutes until the caramel is golden. Cut into squares or fingers while hot and cool in the tin on a wire rack.

Chinese Chews

40 MINS · 24 MAKES

Dates make this chewy and ginger gives it bite, but the cake itself is very tender and light. Simple to make and surprisingly delicious.

2 eggs
1 cup brown sugar
50g butter, melted
1 tsp vanilla essence
1 cup Edmonds standard flour
½ tsp Edmonds baking powder

pinch of salt
1 cup chopped dates
1 cup chopped walnuts
¾ cup crystallised ginger
2 Tbsp milk

1. Preheat the oven to 200°C. Lightly grease a 30cm x 20cm shallow tin and line the base and two sides with baking paper.
2. Whisk the eggs and brown sugar for about 2 minutes until well combined and slightly fluffy.
3. Using a large metal spoon, fold in the melted butter and vanilla essence. Sift the dry ingredients together and then fold in.
4. Lastly add the dates, walnuts, crystallised ginger and milk. Mix to combine well. Scoop the mixture into the prepared tin and spread out evenly.
5. Bake for 15–20 minutes until lightly browned and springy to the touch.
6. Leave in the tin on a wire rack for 5 minutes then, using the edges of the baking paper, lift the whole cake out onto a chopping board. While the cake is still warm cut into squares or fingers using a long-bladed knife. Press the edges back into position if they roughen when you cut them.

VARIATION
Replace half of the ginger with chopped dried apricots for a very bright-tasting slice.

Chocolate Brownie

1½ HOUR · 20 MAKES

A firm and darkly fudgy brownie made with lots of chocolate.

150g butter, melted
1 cup cocoa
4 eggs
2 cups sugar
1 tsp vanilla essence

¾ cup Edmonds standard flour
1 tsp Edmonds baking powder
250g dark chocolate, chopped
icing sugar to dust

1. Preheat oven to 160°C. Lightly grease a 27cm x 18cm shallow tin and line the base and two sides with baking paper.
2. Melt the butter and stir in the cocoa then add the eggs one at a time, beating well after each addition.
3. Add the sugar, vanilla, and sifted flour and baking powder to the mixture and stir until well combined. Then stir through the chopped chocolate and pour the mixture into the prepared tin.
4. Bake for 45-50 minutes or until the mixture is just firm when pressed in the centre. Don't over-bake or the brownies will not have the desired fudgy centre. Leave in the tin for 20 minutes before turning out onto a wire rack to cool. Remove the baking paper and reverse onto another rack.

5. Dust with icing sugar and cut into squares when cold.

VARIATION
Replace ½ the dark chocolate with white chocolate, or add ½ cup frozen raspberries, or
½ cup chopped walnuts at the end of mixing to create different flavours and textures.

Chocolate Caramel Slice

Shortcake topped with a generous layer of golden caramel and chocolate.

BASE
150g butter
1 Tbsp golden syrup
½ cup brown sugar

1 cup rolled oats
1 cup Edmonds standard flour
1 tsp Edmonds baking powder

FILLING
1 cup brown sugar
2 Tbsp sweetened condensed milk
2 Tbsp butter

1 cup icing sugar
1 Tbsp hot water

TOPPING
Chocolate Icing (page 99) or 100g
  dark chocolate, melted

1. Preheat the oven to 180ºC. Lightly grease a 20cm square cake tin and line the base
and two sides with baking paper.
2. Melt the butter, golden syrup and brown sugar in a saucepan large enough to mix all
the ingredients. Add the rolled oats and sifted flour and baking powder mixing to form
a firm dough.
3. Press evenly into the prepared tin and bake for 15 minutes.
4. While the base is baking make the filling by putting the brown sugar, condensed
milk and butter into a saucepan. Heat until bubbling and remove from the heat. Add
the icing sugar and water then beat to combine.
5. Spread the cooked base with the warm caramel filling. Cool in the tin on a wire rack
and when cold spread over the Chocolate Icing or melted chocolate. Cut into slices
when the topping has set.

Chocolate Coconut Rough

*The classic chocolate and coconut combo in a crunchy slice, roughly iced. It's quick
and straightforward to make – no creaming of butter and sugar – and keeps well.*

BASE
1 cup Edmonds standard flour
2 Tbsp cocoa
1 tsp Edmonds baking powder
1 cup fine desiccated coconut

115g butter
115g sugar
2 Tbsp boiling water

ICING
1 cup icing sugar
2 Tbsp cocoa
1 cup fine desiccated coconut

50g butter
1 Tbsp boiling water

1. Preheat the oven to 190°C. Lightly grease a 20cm x 30cm shallow tin and line the base and two sides with baking paper.
2. Sift the flour, cocoa and baking powder into a bowl and add the coconut. Rub in the butter with your fingertips – or use the food processor – then mix in the sugar.
3. Add the boiling water, mix to make a dough and press evenly into the prepared tin.
4. Bake for 25–30 minutes until firm and cooked. Cool in the tin on a wire rack.
5. Sift the icing sugar and cocoa into a bowl, then mix in the coconut. Add the butter and the boiling water and mix to a spreading consistency. Add a little more water if you need to.
6. Spread the icing evenly over the warm base and cut into squares or fingers when cold.

VARIATION
For a fresh-tasting chocolate peppermint version just add ½ tsp peppermint essence to the icing.

Chocolate Fudge Cake

An Antipodean version of a traditional French snack – a piece of dark chocolate eaten with a sweet, dry biscuit. Our approach is to break up the biscuits and fold them through a dark chocolate mixture. In some parts of New Zealand chocolate fudge cake is known as Hedgehog Slice.

250g wine biscuits
125g butter
100g sugar
2 Tbsp cocoa

1 egg, size 7, lightly beaten
½ cup chopped walnuts
½ cup sultanas (optional)
50g dark chocolate, melted

1. Line a shallow 20cm square tin with baking paper.
2. Break the wine biscuits into smallish pieces with your hands – or spread them on the bench and press lightly with a rolling pin to produce a mixture of small pieces and coarse crumbs.
3. Melt the butter in a saucepan over a low heat, then stir in the sugar and cocoa.
4. Remove from the heat and cool for a few minutes, then stir in the beaten egg. Return to the heat and stir until the mixture thickens.
5. Remove from the heat and add the walnuts and sultanas if you wish, followed by the broken biscuits. Mix everything together and press evenly into the prepared tin.
6. Put in the fridge or a cool place to set – about 30 minutes – and then turn out onto a board. Drizzle with the melted dark chocolate before you cut into small bars or squares.

Edmonds baking powder provides a double raising action. It activates as soon as moisture is added and continues on during cooking. This is why you should preheat your oven as it is generally not a good idea to let your batter stand for too long before baking.

Coconut Chocolate Brownies

1 HOUR   15 MAKES

The coconut gives this brownie a lovely chewy texture and the use of cocoa versus chocolate makes it very economical.

125g butter
¼ cup cocoa
1 cup sugar
2 eggs
1 tsp vanilla essence

½ cup fine desiccated coconut
½ cup Edmonds standard flour
½ tsp Edmonds baking powder
icing sugar

1. Preheat the oven to 180°C. Lightly grease a 20cm square cake tin and line the base and two sides with baking paper.
2. Melt the butter in a medium saucepan and sift in the cocoa. Stir over a low heat for 1–2 minutes.
3. Remove from the heat and stir in the sugar, then add the eggs one at a time, beating well after each addition.
4. Mix in the vanilla and coconut, then sift the flour and baking powder and stir in. Pour into the prepared tin
5. Bake for 15–20 minutes. Don't over-bake or it will be dry. Leave the brownie in the tin for 5 minutes before turning out onto a wire rack to cool.
6. Cut into bars when cold and dust the tops with icing sugar.

VARIATION
Add ½ cup chopped dark or white chocolate, or ½ cup chopped walnuts at the end of mixing to create different flavours and textures.

Coconut Dream Bars

1½ HOUR   24 MAKES

A layered slice with a baked-on nutty caramel topping.

BASE
½ cup brown sugar
2 cups Edmonds standard flour

170g butter, softened

TOPPING
3 eggs
1 cup brown sugar
1 Tbsp Edmonds standard flour
1 tsp Edmonds baking powder

1 tsp vanilla essence
1 cup coconut
1 cup coarsely chopped walnuts

1. Preheat the oven to 180°C. Lightly grease a 20cm x 30cm shallow tin and line the base and two sides with baking paper.
2. Combine the sugar and flour for the base and rub in the butter with your fingertips, or use a food processor, stopping when the mixture begins to form clumps.
3. Tip into the prepared tin and press down firmly and evenly.
4. Bake for 15–20 minutes until just beginning to brown at the edges, then remove from the oven and place the tin on a wire rack to cool while you make the topping.

5. Whisk together the eggs and brown sugar with an electric beater until pale and thick – about 2 minutes.

6. Fold in the remaining ingredients and spread the mixture over the warm base. Return to the oven and bake for a further 20–25 minutes until the topping is golden brown. Cool in the tin and cut into fingers when cold.

Energy Bars

1 HOUR 18 MAKES

A quickly made muesli-style bar with plenty of texture, flavour and goodness. Perfect for lunchboxes.

1 cup brown sugar
100g butter
½ cup apricot jam
1 tsp vanilla essence
¼ cup golden syrup
3 cups rolled oats

1 cup dried fruit, chopped
1 tsp mixed spice
½ cup sesame seeds
½ cup shredded coconut
1 cup pumpkin seeds

1. Preheat the oven to 180°C. Lightly grease a 20cm x 30cm shallow tin and line the base and two sides with baking paper.

2. In a saucepan, melt together the sugar, butter, apricot jam, vanilla and golden syrup.

3. Combine the remaining ingredients in a large bowl and mix well.

4. Pour in the melted mixture and stir until thoroughly combined. Press firmly into the prepared tin.

5. Bake for 25 minutes or until golden. Cool slightly in the tin on a wire rack and cut into bars.

Ginger Crunch

45 MINS 24 MAKES

The classic recipe for a crisp, crunchy slice, thinly iced. You could double the icing if you like a thicker layer, but thin is best.

BASE
½ cup sugar
1½ cups Edmonds standard flour
½ tsp Edmonds baking powder

1 tsp ground ginger
125g butter

ICING
55g butter
1 Tbsp golden syrup

2 tsp ground ginger
½ cup icing sugar

1. Preheat the oven to 180°C. Lightly grease a 20cm x 30cm shallow tin and line the base and two sides with baking paper.

2. Put the dry ingredients in a food processor and pulse briefly to combine then drop in the butter in pieces and process just until the mixture forms fine crumbs. If you prefer, you could rub the butter into the dry ingredients by hand.

3. Pour the crumbs into the prepared tin, spread them out evenly and press down firmly with your fingers to compact them slightly. They will stick together properly as they bake.

4. Bake for 20–25 minutes until the mixture is a pale, golden brown and smells cooked.

5. While the base is cooking, put the butter, golden syrup and ginger in a saucepan and heat gently, stirring. When they are melted and combined, sift the icing sugar into the pan. Mix to a fairly runny consistency. Keep mixing until all the melted butter is thoroughly incorporated.

6. Remove the base from the oven and immediately pour on the icing, spreading it out in a thin layer. Cut into fingers immediately and leave to cool in the tin on a wire rack, then break apart along the cuts.

Lemon Bars

2 HOURS • 24 MAKES

Pale, pretty and with a penetrating citrus tang, these slim golden bars combine the delicious texture of lemon honey with a crisply tender biscuit base.

BASE
170g butter
¾ cup icing sugar

1½ cups Edmonds standard flour

TOPPING
200g caster sugar
1½ Tbsp Edmonds standard flour
zest of 2 lemons

juice of 3 lemons
3 eggs
icing sugar

1. Preheat the oven to 180°C. Lightly grease a 20cm x 30cm shallow tin and line the base and two sides with baking paper.

2. Combine the base ingredients in a food processor, or rub the butter into the flour and baking powder and work into a smooth paste with your fingers. It should be fairly soft and malleable. Press the dough evenly into the prepared tin.

3. Bake for 15–20 minutes until lightly golden. Don't overcook as it is going back into the oven later.

4. Combine the topping ingredients in a bowl, mixing with a fork until well amalgamated. (If you make the topping in advance, make sure to mix it again before you pour it on or all the sugar will stay at the bottom of the bowl.)

5. Pour the mixture onto the hot biscuit base and return to the oven for another 30 minutes.

6. Remove from the oven and place the tin on a wire rack to cool. Chill for at least 1 hour then dust the top with icing sugar and cut into bars.

Louise Cake

1 HOUR • 24 MAKES

A biscuit base spread with good red jam and topped with a thin layer of coconut meringue makes a very pretty afternoon tea plate.

BASE
75g butter, softened
55g sugar
2 egg yolks

1 Tbsp lemon juice
1¼ cups Edmonds standard flour
½ tsp Edmonds baking powder

TOPPING
¼ cup raspberry, plum or
  blackcurrant jam
2 egg whites

½ cup sugar
½ cup fine desiccated coconut

1. Preheat the oven to 180˚C. Lightly grease a 20cm x 30cm shallow tin and line the base and two sides with baking paper.

2. Cream the butter and sugar until light and fluffy, then add the egg yolks and mix thoroughly.

3. Add the lemon juice and then sift in the flour and baking powder and mix to a firm dough.

4. Press the dough evenly into the prepared tin, and spread over the jam. You don't need a thick layer.

5. Beat the egg whites until stiff then gently fold in the caster sugar and the coconut using a metal spoon. Spread carefully over the jam, again trying to keep an even thickness. Sprinkle with a little more coconut.

6. Bake for about 25 minutes until the coconut is just turning golden brown. Remove from the oven, and cut into squares or fingers while it is still warm. Cool in the tin on a wire rack.

Marshmallow Shortcake

② HOURS 18 MAKES

Fluffy white marshmallow on a crisp biscuit base, topped with melted dark chocolate. From the 1976 Edmonds Cookery Book.

BASE
125g butter, softened
125g sugar
1 egg

½ tsp vanilla essence
225g Edmonds standard flour
1 tsp Edmonds baking powder

FILLING
1 cup cold water
4 tsp gelatine
1 cup sugar

1 egg white
1 cup icing sugar

TOPPING
finely desiccated coconut (optional)   *Chocolate Icing (page 99) (optional)*

1. Preheat the oven to 180°C. Lightly grease a 20cm x 30cm shallow tin and line the base and two sides with baking paper.

2. To make the base, cream butter and sugar until light, then beat in the egg and vanilla.

3. Sift over the dry ingredients then mix to a firm dough. Press evenly into the prepared tin.

4. Bake for about 25-30 minutes or until golden brown and cooked. Cool in the tin on a wire rack while you make the filling.

5. Place the cold water in a medium saucepan. Sprinkle over the gelatine and add the sugar. Bring to the boil and boil for 8 minutes, then cool. Keep an eye on it as the mixture may overflow if your pan is not big enough. The boiling will remove any of the white scum you may see forming on the surface.

6. Beat egg white until stiff. Beat in the icing sugar a little at a time then slowly pour in the slightly cooled gelatine mixture. Beat until stiff and thick - about 3 minutes.

7. Spread over cooked shortcake immediately. Sprinkle with coconut, or allow to set and ice with Chocolate Icing.

Tan Squares

1 HOUR   32 MAKES

Another caramel-filled shortcake, but in this classic recipe the top layer is mixed with some chopped walnuts and dark chocolate chips and crumbled over the caramel.

BASE AND TOPPING

280g Edmonds standard flour	½ tsp vanilla essence
85g sugar	2 Tbsp chopped walnuts
170g butter	30g dark chocolate, chopped

FILLING

55g butter	½ x 395g can sweetened
1 Tbsp golden syrup	condensed milk

1. Preheat the oven to 180°C. Lightly butter a 20cm x 30cm shallow tin and line the base and two sides with baking paper.

2. Put the flour and sugar into a food processor and pulse to mix. Drop in the butter a little at a time, then add the vanilla essence and process until the mixture forms coarse crumbs.

3. Weigh the mixture, then set aside one third in a covered bowl in the fridge to chill slightly. This is the topping. Press the remaining crumbs evenly into the prepared tin and chill while you make the filling.

4. Put the butter, golden syrup and sweetened condensed milk in a saucepan and stir over a gentle heat until melted together. Cool the filling to room temperature and spread over the chilled base.

5. Crumble the reserved topping into a bowl, mix with the chopped walnuts and chocolate and sprinkle evenly over the caramel. If the mixture is too firm to crumble then grate it coarsely.

6. Bake for 35 minutes until the topping is an appropriately tan colour. Cool in the tin on a wire rack, cutting into squares or fingers while still warm.

Always read the recipe through before starting to cook.

Baking with Edmonds Mixes

Our Edmonds mixes deliver on our Sure to Rise promise while making baking quick and easy for even novice bakers. The following are some creative ideas for using our classic bread and baking mixes.

Black and Tan Square

Chocolate and caramel are a winning combination. Call dibs on licking the spoon.

BASE
1 packet Edmonds Rich Chocolate
   Cake Mix
60g soft butter or margarine spread

2 eggs
¼ cup water

FILLING
½ cup sweetened condensed milk
25g butter

2 Tbsp golden syrup

1. Preheat the oven to 180°C. Grease and line a 20cm x 30cm shallow tin.
2. Place the cake mix, soft butter or margarine spread, eggs and water into a medium mixing bowl. Using an electric mixer, beat on low speed for 30 seconds to combine. Increase the speed to medium and mix for 2 minutes, scraping down the sides of the bowl occasionally.
3. For the filling, combine all the ingredients in a saucepan and heat until the butter has melted.
4. Spread the cake mixture into the tin. Gently drizzle the filling over. It will sink into the cake mix.
5. Bake for 30–35 minutes or until cooked. When cool, ice using chocolate icing from the cake mix pack if desired and cut into squares.

Cinnamon Pinwheel (Scones)

A quick version of the classic recipe. Try adding a grated apple to the sugar mix for a fruity version.

500g Edmonds Classic Scone Mix
1 cup cold water, approximately

melted butter
milk

SUGAR MIX
3 Tbsp brown sugar

1 tsp ground cinnamon

Caramel Meringue Slice page 81
Coconut Chocolate Brownies page 85, Lemon Bars page 87

Scones page 29

1. Preheat the oven to 220˚C. Lightly grease a baking tray.

2. Place the scone mix and water into a medium mixing bowl. Mix with a wooden spoon to form a soft dough.

3. Roll the dough out into a large rectangle about 5mm thick. Brush the melted butter over the rolled out dough then sprinkle over the combined sugar mix.

4. Roll up the dough towards you to form a long log. Cut the log into 10 equal pieces and arrange these, spiral side up and just touching one another, on the prepared tray. Brush the surface of each scone with a little milk.

5. Bake for 20 minutes or until golden brown. Place on a wire rack to cool.

Cranberry & Lemon Scones

25 HOURS · 12 MAKES

Edmonds Classic Scone Mix allows you to add your own flavours to your scones using whatever you may have to hand — in this case, cranberry and lemon.

500g Edmonds Classic Scone Mix
2 Tbsp icing sugar
grated zest of 1 lemon

1 cup cold water, approximately
1 cup dried cranberries
milk or lightly beaten egg

1. Preheat the oven to 220˚C. Lightly grease a baking tray.

2. Place all the ingredients into a medium mixing bowl. Mix with a wooden spoon to form a soft dough. Roll out onto a floured surface to 2cm thickness and cut into the desired shapes. Place the scones on the prepared tray and rest for 10 minutes before baking.

3. Brush the tops with milk or egg wash for a more golden colour.

4. Bake for 10–12 minutes or until golden brown. Place on a wire rack to cool.

Date Caramel Bars

40 MINS · 16 MAKES

BASE
1 cup chopped dates
60g soft butter or margarine spread
¼ cup milk

1 packet Edmonds Moist Chocolate
Cake Mix
2 eggs, lightly beaten

ICING
1 cup brown sugar
25g butter

2 Tbsp milk
1 cup icing sugar

1. Preheat the oven to 180˚C. Grease a 20cm x 30cm shallow tin.

2. Put the dates, butter or margarine spread and milk in a medium saucepan. Gently heat until the butter has melted, then cool.

3. Add the cake mix and eggs to the cooled dates, beating well to combine. Pour the mixture into the prepared tin.

4. Bake for 20 minutes or until the cake springs back when lightly touched. Cool in the tin on a wire rack.

5. To make the icing, put the brown sugar, butter and milk in a saucepan. Cook over a gentle heat, stirring constantly until the sugar has dissolved.

6. Remove from the heat and sift in the icing sugar, mixing to a smooth paste. If necessary, add more milk to a give a spreading consistency. Spread the icing over the slice.

7. When the icing is almost set, cut into bars with a hot knife. Set aside until cold.

Fruity Citrus Cake

Take a great cake mix and add some extra fruity flavours to it.

1 cup raisins
¼ cup boiling water
1 packet Edmonds Golden Butter
    Cake Mix
2 eggs

¾ cup milk
60g butter, softened
2 tsp finely grated lemon zest
icing sugar

1. Preheat the oven to 170°C. Grease the base of a 20cm cake tin and line with baking paper.

2. Soak raisins in the boiling water for 15–20 minutes. This will stop them sinking to the bottom of the cake.

3. Put the cake mix, eggs, milk and butter into the bowl of an electric mixer. Mix at low speed until the ingredients are combined. Beat for 2 minutes at medium speed, scraping down the sides of the bowl occasionally.

4. Fold in the lemon zest and raisins then pour into the prepared tin.

5. Bake for 50–55 minutes or until the cake springs back when lightly touched. Leave in the tin for 10 minutes before turning out onto a wire rack to cool.

6. When cold, dust with icing sugar.

Golden Lemon Coconut Cake

A fluffy coconut cake with a zing from the creamy lemon icing. A great cake for feeding a crowd.

1 packet Edmonds Golden Butter
    Cake Mix
2 eggs

¾ cup milk
60g butter, softened
1 cup coconut

LEMON CREAM ICING
1 cup icing sugar
1–2 Tbsp lemon juice

75g butter, softened
1 tsp finely grated lemon zest

1. Preheat the oven to 170°C. Grease a 20cm x 30cm shallow tin and line the base with baking paper.

2. Put the cake mix, eggs, milk and butter into the bowl of an electric mixer. Mix at low speed until the ingredients are combined. Beat for 2 minutes at medium speed, scraping down the sides of the bowl occasionally.

3. Fold the coconut through the mixture and pour into the prepared tin.

4. Bake for 20–25 minutes or until the cake springs back when lightly touched. Leave in the tin for 10 minutes before turning out onto a wire rack to cool.

5. To make the icing, beat the icing sugar, lemon juice and butter together until light and creamy.

6. When the cake is cold, ice then sprinkle the lemon zest on top.

Mocha Torte

Makes an impressive-looking celebration cake.

*1 packet Edmonds Moist Chocolate
    Cake Mix*
60g soft butter or margarine spread

2 eggs
¾ cup milk

ICING
50g butter, softened
1¼ cups icing sugar, sifted
2 tsp instant coffee powder
2 tsp hot water

*½ cup chopped walnuts,
    approximately*
8 walnut halves

1. Preheat the oven to 160˚C. Grease and line the bases of two 20cm sandwich tins and line with baking paper.
2. Place the cake mix, soft butter or margarine spread, eggs and milk into a medium mixing bowl.
3. Using an electric mixer, beat on low speed for 30 seconds to combine. Increase the speed to medium and mix for 2 minutes, scraping down the sides of the bowl occasionally.
4. Divide the mixture evenly between the tins.
5. Bake for 20–25 minutes or until the cakes spring back when lightly touched. Leave in the tins for 10 minutes before turning out onto a wire rack to cool.
6. To make the icing, beat the butter, sugar, coffee powder and water together until smooth. Add more water if necessary to form a spreadable icing.
7. When the sponge cakes are cold, sandwich together with one quarter of the icing, then spread the remaining icing over the top and down the sides of the cake.
8. Press the chopped walnuts onto the sides of the cake. Decorate the top with walnut halves.

Pesto, Herb & Cheese Scrolls

You can get the wonderful smell of homemade bread without starting completely from scratch. These savoury scrolls are pretty easy to make – just plan enough time for rising.

*400g Edmonds Soft White
    Bread Mix*
1 cup lukewarm water

5g Edmonds instant dried yeast
5 Tbsp Pesto (page 179)
1½ cups grated cheese

Breadmaker: Add the bread mix, water and yeast to the pan of a breadmaker and initiate dough mode. When the cycle is complete, remove the dough and rest on a floured surface for 10 minutes.
By hand: Place the bread mix in a large bowl and make a well in the centre. Gently pour the lukewarm water into the well and sprinkle the yeast on top. Mix by hand to combine all the ingredients into a dough. Turn the dough onto a floured surface and knead vigorously by hand until smooth and elastic, approximately 10 minutes.

1. Roll the dough into a rectangular shape about 1cm thick and place on a lightly greased baking tray. Cover and stand in a warm place for 10 minutes.
2. Spread the pesto over the dough, leaving 2cm uncovered along one long edge. Sprinkle with 1 cup of the grated cheese and brush the 2cm edge with water. Roll the dough tightly towards the unfilled edge and press to seal. Cut the rolled dough into 12 pieces and place spiral side up on a lined baking tray. Cover and stand in a warm place for 40 minutes.
3. Preheat the oven to 200°C.
4. Sprinkle the dough with the remaining grated cheese and bake for 10–15 minutes. If desired, brush the top of the bread with olive oil while still hot.

Zebra Cupcakes

These marbled cupcakes create a bit of extra fun for celebrations. Alter the colours to suit your theme.

1 packet Edmonds Vanilla Cupcake Mix
60g soft butter or margarine spread
2 eggs

½ cup milk
2 Tbsp cocoa

FROSTING
80g soft butter or margarine spread

2 tsp milk

1. Preheat oven to 180°C. Line a standard 12-hole muffin tin with cupcake cases.
2. Place the cake mix, butter, eggs and milk into a medium mixing bowl. Using an electric mixer, beat on low speed for 30 seconds to combine. Increase speed to medium and beat for 2 minutes, scraping down the sides of the bowl occasionally.
3. Transfer half of the mixture to a separate bowl. Sift the cocoa powder over one half of the mixture and stir to blend well so that there is now one vanilla mixture and one chocolate mixture.
4. Spoon one teaspoon of vanilla mixture into the centre of each cupcake case. Then, spoon one teaspoon of chocolate mixture directly into the centre of the vanilla mixture. Continue spooning mixtures over one another, alternating between chocolate and vanilla, until it is all used up.
5. Bake for 20–25 minutes or until a skewer inserted into the centre of a cupcake comes out clean. Turn cupcakes out onto a wire rack to cool.
6. Make the frosting by placing the frosting mix, butter and milk into a small mixing bowl. Using an electric mixer, beat on low speed for 30 seconds to combine. Increase speed to medium and beat for 3 minutes, scraping down the sides of the bowl occasionally. Spread over cooled cupcakes.

Fillings & Icings

They don't call it 'the icing on the cake' for nothing.
This is where you get to add your own special touches and
fun flourishes to make your cakes and biscuits even more
delicious. These recipes make enough to cover a 20cm cake.

Almond Icing

Homemade almond icing adds real class to any fruit cake.

1 cup icing sugar
225g ground almonds
½ cup caster sugar

1 egg
¼ tsp almond essence or 1 tsp
orange flower water

1. Sift the icing sugar into a bowl and add the other ingredients. Mix together and knead to a smooth paste. Store covered in the fridge.

TO ICE A CAKE
Brush the cake with lightly beaten egg white or sieved apricot jam. Roll out the almond icing to 1cm thickness and cut to fit the cake. Leave to dry for 2–3 days before icing with Royal Icing (page 100).

Butter Filling for Biscuits

A pretty, bright yellow filling for Yoyos or Melting Moments which sets firmly.

2 Tbsp butter, melted
6 Tbsp icing sugar, sifted

1 Tbsp Edmonds custard powder

1. Beat all the ingredients together until smooth.

Buttercream Icing

A rich, soft filling for biscuits or for icing large or small cakes.

2 cups icing sugar
115g butter, softened

½ tsp vanilla essence
1–2 Tbsp milk

1. Sift the icing sugar.
2. Cream the butter with half of the icing sugar, the vanilla and the milk. Beat until smooth and then gradually beat in the remaining icing sugar to give a good spreading consistency.

VARIATIONS
Chocolate Buttercream Icing
Sift 2 tablespoons of cocoa with the icing sugar.
Coffee Buttercream Icing
Beat 1 tablespoon coffee essence or espresso into the buttercream.
Lemon Buttercream Icing
Beat 1 teaspoon finely grated lemon zest into the buttercream.

Caramel Fudge Icing

Brown sugar cooked with milk gives the caramel flavour to this icing – good for sandwiching together plain or chocolate biscuits or for icing cakes.

1 cup brown sugar
25g butter

2 Tbsp milk
1 cup icing sugar

1. Put the brown sugar, butter and milk in a saucepan and cook over a gentle heat, stirring constantly until the sugar has dissolved.
2. Remove from the heat and sift in the icing sugar, mixing to a smooth paste. Add more milk if needed to give a good spreading consistency.

Chocolate Ganache

Rich and delicious, this is a special-occasion filling for a chocolate cake, or for biscuits.

200g dark chocolate
25g butter

½ cup cream

1. Break the chocolate into the top of a double boiler or a heatproof bowl and add the butter and cream. Set over a saucepan of hot, not boiling, water and heat gently, stirring all the time. When the chocolate has melted, remove from the heat and set aside. The ganache will thicken as it cools.
2. You can pour this over a cake as is, or beat hard once it is cold and it will become pale and thick, suitable for spreading and piping.

Cream Cheese Icing

The classic topping for Carrot Cake (page 47), but try it on Citrus Cupcakes (page 67) too.

2 Tbsp butter, softened
¼ cup cream cheese

1 cup icing sugar
½ tsp finely grated lemon zest

1. Beat the butter and cream cheese until creamy. Sift over the icing sugar and add the lemon zest, beating well to combine.

Crème Pâtissière (Pastry Cream)

This traditional French custard filling for éclairs or fruit tarts will lift your baking to another level. It's thoroughly worth the extra effort.

1½ cups milk	**¼ cup Edmonds standard flour**
1 vanilla pod	**2 eggs**
½ cup sugar	**2 egg yolks**

1. Bring the milk to a simmer with the vanilla pod and set aside.
2. Combine the sugar and flour in a saucepan, add the eggs and egg yolks and mix well. Remove the vanilla pod from the milk and pour the milk gently onto the egg mix, stirring.
3. Cook gently, stirring constantly until the mixture just comes to the boil and thickens.
4. Pour into a bowl, cover and cool.

Crumble Topping For Cakes

A baked-on topping which removes the need to ice a plain cake – just dust it with icing sugar before serving. Perfect for when friends drop around unexpectedly.

½ cup brown sugar	**¼ cup fine desiccated coconut**
½ cup Edmonds standard flour	**¼ cup chopped nuts**
100g butter	

1. Combine the sugar and flour in a bowl and rub in the butter with your fingertips until the mixture resembles coarse breadcrumbs. Mix through the coconut and nuts. Sprinkle the topping over cakes before baking. You could also make this in a food processor.

Glacé Icing

The simplest of icings and suitable for many different flavours – it sets to a firm layer and cuts easily. This is a versatile basic icing and one the kids will want to help make so they get to lick the spoon.

2 cups icing sugar	**2 Tbsp hot water**
25g butter, softened	**¼ tsp vanilla essence**

1. Sift the icing sugar into a bowl. Add the butter and enough hot water to bring the icing to a spreadable consistency, then mix in the vanilla.

VARIATIONS
Chocolate Icing
Sift 2 tablespoons cocoa with the icing sugar. Add extra water if necessary.
Coffee Icing
Dissolve 2 teaspoons instant coffee in 1 tablespoon hot water and mix into the icing sugar.
Lemon Icing
Replace the vanilla with 1 teaspoon finely grated lemon zest and replace the water with lemon juice. Add a few drops of yellow food colouring if you wish.

Orange Icing
Replace the vanilla with 2 teaspoons finely grated orange zest and replace the water with orange juice. Add a few drops of yellow and red food colouring if you wish.
Peppermint Icing
Replace the vanilla with ¼ teaspoon peppermint essence and add a drop of green food colouring if you wish.

Mock Cream

Use to replace fresh cream as a filling for sponges and cakes.

100 g butter, softened
1 cup icing sugar
1 Tbsp milk

¼ tsp vanilla essence or
1 tsp finely grated lemon zest

1. Cream butter and sugar until light and fluffy. Add milk and vanilla.
2. Beat until thick and pale like cream.

Royal Icing

Pure white and perfect for icing your Rich Christmas Cake (page 62) or Gingerbread People (page 40). Royal Icing sets very hard and is the best icing for piping decorations. This quantity is sufficient to ice and decorate a 20cm square fruit cake.

4 egg whites
500g icing sugar, sifted

1 Tbsp lemon juice
few drops of glycerine*

1. Beat the egg whites until frothy and liquid.
2. Sift the icing sugar then gradually add to the egg whites, beating all the time. Stir in the lemon juice and glycerine.
3. Keep the bowl of icing covered with a damp cloth until you are ready to use it.

*Glycerine is not essential, but it helps prevent the icing from becoming too brittle and difficult to cut neatly.

Pastry & Savouries

Our tasty savouries and pastries have been perfected over generations and devoured at countless parties, birthdays, weddings, church picnics, school fairs and committee meetings.

How to make perfect pastry:

- 'Cold in the making; brisk in the baking' is the traditional motto for pastry makers. It means keep the butter cold, work quickly and always use a hot oven to cook pastry.
- Chill any water you use and chill the mixing bowl too.
- Use as little water as possible to reduce shrinking when the pastry cooks. Adding a squeeze of lemon juice to the water will help keep pastry tender.
- Use a round-bladed table knife to mix the liquid into the flour, cutting through the mixture until it clumps together.
- You can make short pastry quickly in a food processor, but stop processing when the mixture begins to form clumps. Tip the mixture out onto the bench and knead quickly to bring it together, using the heel of your hand.
- Always chill pastry for at least 10 minutes before rolling it out.
- Roll out pastry on a lightly floured surface and use light strokes of the rolling pin, always working away from you. Keep rotating the pastry on the board.
- Drape the pastry over your rolling pin to lift it onto the baking dish or tin.
- And remember, practice makes perfect. Make pastry often so that it will not be a worrying challenge but a staple of your repertoire – and a guarantee of compliments!

NOTE

If you need to save time you can use the Edmonds range of ready-rolled or block flaky puff, filo and short pastries, available in the freezer section of most supermarkets.

Cheese Pastry

350g MAKES | 20 MINS

A delicious, slightly flaky savoury pastry for pies and quiches.

1½ cups Edmonds standard flour
1 tsp Edmonds baking powder
¼ tsp salt
pinch of cayenne pepper

75g butter
¾ cup grated tasty cheese
3 Tbsp milk, approximately

1. Sift the flour, baking powder, salt and cayenne pepper together.
2. Rub in the butter with your fingertips until the mixture resembles coarse breadcrumbs, then add the grated cheese.
3. Bind to a soft but not sticky dough with the milk and form into a rectangular block. Wrap in greaseproof paper and chill for 10 minutes.
4. Roll the pastry out to 5mm thickness on a lightly floured board and use as required for savoury pies, tarts and quiches.

Try not to stretch pastry when rolling and handling to prevent shrinkage while cooking.

Choux Pastry

Choux pastry is surprisingly easy to make and the crisp pastry shells it produces can be filled with sweet or savoury creams – although Chocolate Éclairs (page 64) and Cream Puffs (page 66) are the perennial favourites.

½ cup Edmonds standard flour
pinch of salt
55g butter

½ cup boiling water
2 eggs

1. Sift the flour and salt onto a sheet of greaseproof paper.
2. Put the butter into a saucepan over a low heat and pour on the boiling water. As soon as the butter has melted, remove the pan from the heat and tip in all the sifted flour in one go.
3. Beat with a wooden spoon until smooth, then return to the heat and keep beating until the mixture forms a ball and leaves the sides of the pan clean. Put the dough into the bowl of an electric mixer or a clean mixing bowl.
4. If you are using an electric mixer, add one of the eggs and beat well on medium speed until the egg is absorbed, then do the same with the second egg. Keep beating until the dough is thick and glossy. If you are using a wooden spoon, beat the two eggs together and add them to the dough 1 tablespoon at a time, beating hard until they are all absorbed and the mixture is thick and glossy. (If you add the eggs too quickly the pastry will become too liquid and difficult to shape.)
5. Use as directed for cream puffs, éclairs or savoury puffs.

Rough Puff Pastry

This is not the true puff pastry (which expands dramatically in the oven) but it is far easier to make and very light and flaky. Once you have mastered the technique, turn to some of the classic puff pastry recipes: Eccles Cakes (page 68), Custard Squares (page 68), Bacon & Egg Pie (page 104), Sausage Rolls (page 107) and many more – the choices are endless.

225g Edmonds standard flour
pinch of salt
170g cold butter*

1 tsp lemon juice
½ cup cold water

1. Sift the flour and salt into a large bowl. Cut the butter into 1cm lumps, dropping it into the flour as you go. Toss the butter through the flour to coat well.
2. Pour in the lemon juice and cold water and mix to a rough dough with a round-bladed table knife, then your fingertips. The lumps of butter will be plainly visible in the pebbly mix. Turn the dough onto a floured board and shape into a roughly rectangular block.
3. With a short side of the rectangle facing you, take a clean, floured rolling pin and begin rolling out the pastry using short, jerky strokes, extending it out into a rectangle about 1cm thick. Try to keep the sides straight and the corners square.
4. Mark the dough across into three equal sections, and fold up the lower third, then fold the top third down over the lower part and push the edges gently with your rolling pin to seal them.
5. Give the dough a quarter turn so that the bottom edge is now on your right and a short side is again facing you. This is one 'turn'.

6. Repeat the rolling, folding and turning three or four more times, using short movements and lifting the rolling pin frequently. After the fourth turn there should no longer be any streaks of butter visible.
7. Wrap in greaseproof paper and chill until quite cold before using.

*Replace 85g of the butter with lard if you wish.

Shortcrust Pastry

Short pastry is typically used for pies, tarts and quiches. It's quick and easy to prepare, then you can call the whole dish your own.

2 cups Edmonds standard flour   **125g butter**
¼ tsp salt   **cold water to mix**

1. Sift the flour and salt together. Rub in the butter with your fingertips until it resembles coarse breadcrumbs, then mix to a stiff dough with a little water.
2. Wrap in greaseproof paper and chill for 10 minutes before using.

VARIATIONS
Wholemeal Pastry
Replace the white flour with Edmonds wholemeal flour and add 1 teaspoon Edmonds baking powder.

Food Processor Pastry
Have the butter and water very cold and dice the butter into small squares. Put the flour and salt into the food processor and drop in the butter a few pieces at a time. Pulse until the mixture resembles coarse breadcrumbs. Add water by the teaspoon and pulse until the mixture begins to clump together. Turn out onto a lightly floured surface, and working quickly, knead lightly using the heel of your hand to push the pastry away from you. Wrap in greaseproof paper and chill for at least 10 minutes.

Sweet Shortcrust Pastry

This recipe will give you perfect crispy pastry shells for sweet pies and tarts.

2 cups Edmonds standard flour   **2 egg yolks**
150g butter   **1–2 Tbsp water**
½ cup caster sugar

1. Sift the flour into a mixing bowl. Cut the butter into small pieces, dropping it into the flour as you go.
2. Rub the butter into the flour with your fingertips until it resembles coarse breadcrumbs.
3. Stir in the sugar, followed by the egg yolks and the water if the mixture seems too dry.

If the weather is warm and the pastry seems difficult to handle, wrap it in greaseproof paper and rest it in the fridge for 15 minutes between rollings. Keep the rolling pin floured and remove any fat or dough that sticks to it.

4. Mix quickly to a stiff dough using a round-bladed table knife. Turn out onto a lightly floured bench and knead lightly until smooth then shape into a rectangular block
5. Wrap in greaseproof paper and chill for 30 minutes before using.

VARIATIONS
Spiced Pastry
Add 4 teaspoons mixed spice to the flour.
Nut Pastry
Add 1 cup chopped walnuts or nuts of your choice, before adding the egg yolks and water.

Bacon & Egg Pie

The best ever picnic pie and a New Zealand favourite. Don't forget to pack a bottle of your homemade Tomato Sauce (page 238) in the picnic basket too.

450g Rough Puff Pastry (page 102) or 2 sheets Edmonds flaky puff pastry, thawed

FILLING
225g lean bacon
6 eggs

salt and pepper
milk or beaten egg

1. Preheat the oven to 200°C. Lightly grease a square 20cm shallow cake tin or pie dish.
2. Roll out half of the rough puff pastry or use 1 sheet of the ready-rolled pastry and line the prepared dish.
3. Snip the bacon rashers into large pieces with kitchen scissors and arrange evenly over the pastry base.
4. Break in the eggs and prick the yolks so that they run slightly. Season with salt and pepper. Brush the edges of the pastry with a little water.
5. Roll out the other piece of pastry or use the second sheet of frozen pastry and lift it carefully onto the filling. Press the edges together to seal.
6. Using a sharp knife, cut away any excess pastry from the edges, arrange it in a stack to keep the layers intact and reroll. Cut out some leaves or other decorative shapes and stick them on the top of the pie with a little water. Make 2–3 slits in the top of the pie. Brush the top with milk or a little beaten egg.
7. Bake for about 30 minutes or until the pie is a beautiful golden brown. Serve warm or cold.

VARIATION
1 small onion, finely chopped
½ cup mixed vegetables

2 Tbsp spicy chutney

Sprinkle the onion and mixed vegetables evenly over the pastry when you scatter over the bacon. Dot the chutney on top and then break in the eggs.

Cheese Straws

40 MINS 30 MAKES

Thin strips of flaky cheese pastry baked to crisp perfection. Serve with dips or spreads.

1 quantity Cheese Pastry (page 101)   **1 egg, beaten**
⅛ tsp dry mustard

1. Preheat the oven to 190°C. Lightly grease a baking tray or line with baking paper.
2. Make the Cheese Pastry as per instructions on page 101, adding the mustard to the sifted ingredients and replacing the milk with the beaten egg.
3. Stir quickly with a round-bladed table knife until the mixture forms a stiff, pliable dough. Wrap in greaseproof paper and chill for 10 minutes.
4. On a lightly floured board, roll out the dough to 5mm thickness and cut into fingers 1cm wide and 5cm long. Place the cheese straws on the prepared tray.
5. Bake for 10 minutes or until pale golden. Place on a wire rack to cool.

Mince Pies

3 HOURS 9 SERVES

You can make one large pie for a meal or a picnic, or 24 small mince pie savouries.

1 tablespoon oil
1 onion, finely chopped
2 cloves garlic, crushed
500g lean beef mince
1½ Tbsp Edmonds standard flour
½ cup beef stock
2 Tbsp tomato purée

salt and pepper
400g Rough Puff or Shortcrust Pastry (pages 102 and 103) or 2 sheets Edmonds savoury short pastry and 2 sheets Edmonds flaky puff pastry
1 egg yolk
1 Tbsp water

1. Put the oil, onion and garlic into a frying pan and cook gently, stirring until the onion is golden – about 15 minutes. Don't rush it or the onion will be crunchy rather than sweet and melting.
2. Add the beef mince. Increase the heat and cook quickly until the meat is browned and crumbly. Stir in the flour and cook for 30 seconds.
3. Gradually add the stock and bring the mixture to the boil, stirring constantly. Add the tomato purée and salt and pepper to taste. Simmer gently for 10 minutes, then set aside to cool.
4. Preheat the oven to 200°C.
5. Cut the pastry in half and on a lightly floured board roll out one half, or use the ready-rolled sheets of short pastry. Line a 22cm pie dish or cut out 18 circles with a 7cm cutter and line patty tins.
6. Wet the edges of the pastry and then spoon in the meat filling.
7. Roll out the remaining pastry to fit the top of a large pie, or cut out circles with a 6cm cutter from the ready-rolled flaky puff pastry for the small pies.
8. Carefully place the pastry over the filling and press the edges together to seal. Finish with any pastry trimmings rolled out and cut into decorative shapes.

9. Combine the egg yolk and water and brush over the tops of the pies. Make two slits in the top of a large pie or one in each of the small pies.

10. Bake for 25 minutes for a large pie and about 15 minutes for the small pies, until the pastry is a dark golden brown.

Quiche Lorraine

1½ HOURS   6 SERVES

A classic of French cooking and a sophisticated and delicious alternative to our traditional bacon and egg pie. Perfect for a special lunch with a crisp green salad.

200g Shortcrust Pastry (page 103) or 1 sheet Edmonds savoury short pastry, thawed

FILLING

3 rashers streaky bacon
½ cup grated gruyère or tasty cheese
3 eggs

275ml cream
salt and pepper

1. Preheat the oven to 180°C.

2. On a lightly floured board, roll out the pastry or use the ready-rolled sheet. Line a 20cm shallow loose bottom tart tin or a quiche dish. Trim away any excess pastry.

3. Put a crumpled sheet of baking paper or tinfoil into the pastry case and fill with dry chickpeas, rice or beans. These stop the pastry from rising as it cooks. They cannot be eaten after this use but if you keep them in a screw-top jar you can use them again for baking blind.

4. Bake for 15 minutes, then remove from the oven and take out the paper and the beans.

5. Return the case to the oven for 5 minutes to dry the pastry, then remove from the oven.

6. While the pastry case is cooking, put the bacon rashers in a dry frying pan and cook until crispy, then chop into small pieces.

7. Scatter the bacon and grated cheese over the cooked pastry case. Whisk together the eggs and cream with some salt and pepper to season and pour carefully into the pastry case.

8. Bake for a further 30–40 minutes or until the filling has risen and is golden brown and set. Serve warm or at room temperature.

Salmon Puffs

30 MINS   20 MAKES

A creamy smoked salmon filling between layers of flaky pastry.

1 sheet Edmonds flaky puff pastry,
 thawed
1 egg yolk
1 Tbsp water
½ cup cream cheese

¼ cup cream, whipped
100g smoked salmon, chopped
1 Tbsp lemon juice
1 Tbsp chopped parsley
pepper

1. Preheat the oven to 200°C. Lightly grease a baking sheet or line with baking paper.

2. Cut out pastry rounds with a 5cm cutter and place on the prepared tray.

3. Mix together the egg yolk and water and brush evenly over the pastry rounds, then prick all over with a fork.

4. Bake for 8–10 minutes or until crisp, puffed and golden. Using a sharp pointed knife, split the pastry rounds through the centre and leave them to cool.
5. Beat together the cream cheese, cream, salmon, lemon juice, parsley and pepper to taste. Spread this mixture onto the bottom rounds and replace the tops.

Sausage Rolls

40 MINS · 20 MAKES

With homemade pastry and good-quality sausages, these are a revelation. Large sausage rolls are good for picnics, but make them tiny to serve as a savoury snack.

500g sausage meat or 500g good-quality sausages of your choice
1 small onion, finely chopped
¼ cup finely chopped parsley
2 Tbsp tomato sauce

450g Rough Puff Pastry (page 102) or 400g block Edmonds flaky puff pastry, thawed
1 egg yolk
1 Tbsp water

1. Preheat the oven to 200°C. Line a baking tray with baking paper.
2. If you are using sausage meat, combine it with the onion, parsley and tomato sauce in a bowl and mix well. If you are using sausages, remove the skins by slitting them down one side and peeling away the skin while you hold them under the cold tap.
3. Roll out the pastry on a lightly floured board to a rectangle measuring 40cm x 30cm, then cut it lengthwise into three strips measuring 40cm x 10cm.
4. With floured hands, lay the skinless sausages end to end down the centre of each strip, or use the seasoned sausage meat, to make three rolls.
5. Brush the edges of each pastry strip with a little water and roll the pastry to enclose the filling. Lift the rolls onto the prepared baking tray.
6. Mix together the egg yolk and water and brush over each roll. Use a sharp knife to make shallow slits across the pastry, marking the eventual size of the sausage rolls. You will cut along these once they are cooked.
7. Bake for 15–20 minutes or until golden.
8. Cool slightly on the baking tray, then slide the rolls onto a cutting board and cut up with a sharp knife. Serve hot or cold.

Savoury Tartlets

40 MINS · 24 MAKES

A bit like mini-quiches, these are a good choice for an afternoon tea savoury.

2 rashers bacon, chopped
1 onion, finely chopped
2 eggs
1 cup milk

salt and pepper
4 sheets Edmonds flaky puff pastry, thawed
1 Tbsp chopped parsley or chives

1. Preheat the oven to 200°C.
2. Gently cook the bacon and onion in a frying pan until the onion is transparent – about 10 minutes. Set aside to cool.
3. Using a fork, beat together the eggs, milk and salt and pepper. You want a well-combined, not frothy mixture.

If you prefer to bake individual sausage rolls, it is a good idea to rinse the knife and wipe it between each cut.

4. Place the pastry on a lightly floured board, and cut out 24 rounds with a 7cm cutter. Line patty tins with the pastry. Spoon a little of the onion mixture into each pastry case, top with the chopped herbs and carefully pour or spoon in some egg mixture.
5. Bake for 15 minutes or until golden and set. Serve hot or warm.

VARIATION
Add 2–3 tablespoons grated tasty cheddar cheese and a dash of cayenne pepper to the egg mixture, or place a small square of feta or brie in each tartlet.

Tomato Tarts

Whip up these simple tarts for a summer lunch in the sun.

1 sheet Edmonds flaky puff pastry,
    thawed
4 Tbsp Pesto (page 179) or
    Red Onion Marmalade (page 180)
1 tomato, sliced
10 yellow cherry tomatoes, halved

40g soft feta
1 Tbsp olive oil
1 Tbsp balsamic vinegar
salt and pepper, to taste
10 leaves fresh basil, approximately

1. Preheat the oven to 190°C. Line a baking tray with baking paper.
2. Half the pastry sheet and lay on the prepared baking tray. Wet the edges of the pastry and fold over to create a 1cm border around each piece of pastry.
3. Spread the pesto or red onion marmalade over the pastry base, keeping inside the pastry border. Top with large tomato slices, then dot with remaining cherry tomato halves and crumble over the feta.
4. Drizzle with olive oil and balsamic vinegar, then season with salt and pepper.
5. Bake for 15–20 minutes or until the pastry is puffed and golden. Scatter the fresh basil leaves over the tarts and serve warm with a green salad.

Vol-Au-Vents

The French words mean 'flying in the breeze' and these light and delicate savouries live up to their name. These crisp, golden puff pastry cases are filled with a little creamy white sauce which can be flavoured in a multitude of ways.

400g block Edmonds flaky puff pastry,
    thawed

FILLING
2 Tbsp butter
1 Tbsp finely chopped onion
2 Tbsp Edmonds standard flour

1 egg yolk
1 Tbsp water

¾ cup full-cream milk, heated
salt and pepper

1. Preheat the oven to 220°C. Dampen a baking tray with a few drops of cold water.
2. On a lightly floured board, roll out the pastry to 1.5cm thickness. Cut rounds with a 5cm cutter and place on the tray.
3. Press halfway through the centre of each pastry round with a 3cm cutter. This will create the lid once the pastry is baked.

Chocolate Éclairs page 64, Custard Squares page 68

Bacon & Egg Pie page 104

4. Mix together the egg yolk and water and carefully brush over the top of each round. Try not to let it run down the sides, as it will stick the layers together and prevent the pastry from rising to its full height.

5. Bake for 15 minutes or until golden and well risen, then place the cases on a wire rack to cool.

6. While the cases are cooling, melt the butter in a saucepan, then add the onion and cook gently for about 10 minutes until it is translucent, but not brown.

7. Stir in the flour and cook for 2 minutes until frothy. Remove from the heat and gradually add in the hot milk, stirring constantly.

8. Return to the heat and cook, stirring, until the mixture thickens and comes to a simmer. Remove from the heat, add flavourings of your choice and season with salt and pepper.

9. Once the pastry cases are cold, use a small, sharp knife to cut around the lid and ease it away from the base. If there is any uncooked pastry in the centre, scrape it away with a teaspoon and discard.

10. Spoon in the filling, with flavourings of your choice, and replace the lid. Warm the vol-au-vents in an oven heated to 180°C for about 5 minutes before serving. Don't reheat in the microwave or the pastry will soften.

FLAVOURINGS

- Grated cheese and chopped ham
- Grated cheese and cooked chopped mushroom
- Smoked fish, finely flaked
- Corned beef, finely chopped, and mustard
- Cooked asparagus and hard-boiled eggs, chopped together
- Cooked prawns, drained and chopped

Soups & Stocks

Well-flavoured stock is a kitchen staple which adds richness and depth to soups and is essential for making Risotto (page 131). You can buy liquid or powdered stock, but it is easy to make your own and you can then control the flavour. The process is simple, but it does take time, since slow simmering is essential to gently extract the flavour of the stock ingredients. If you don't use all the stock immediately, you can freeze it in 1 cup portions for up to 3 months and defrost when you need it.

Beef Stock

6 HOURS | MAKES 1L

1kg uncooked beef bones, fat removed
2L cold water
250g vegetables – e.g. leeks, onions, carrots, celery, roughly chopped
6 black peppercorns

1 bay leaf
sprig of parsley
sprig of thyme

1. Put the bones and water into a large saucepan or stockpot and bring to the boil. Skim off any scum that comes to the surface, then add the vegetables, peppercorns and herbs.
2. Bring to a gentle simmer and cook gently for about 4 hours, partly covered.
3. Strain the stock through a fine mesh sieve, cool and then refrigerate. Once the stock is chilled, remove the fat from the surface.

VARIATION
Rich Meat Stock
Brown the bones well, either in a roasting dish in the oven or in a heavy-based saucepan. Put the bones into the stockpot, drain off the fat, add a little water to the pan and heat for 2–3 minutes, stirring, to dislodge any meat sediment. Then follow the recipe above. You could also add a few soft tomatoes and mushrooms at the start for a richer flavour.

Chicken Stock

4 HOURS | MAKES 2L

2kg chicken bones and wings
2.5L cold water
1 onion, unpeeled, halved
2 carrots, peeled and chopped
2 sticks celery, chopped

2 bay leaves
10 sprigs of parsley
1 sprig of thyme
10 peppercorns
salt

1. Put the chicken bones and wings into a large stockpot with the cold water and bring gently to the boil. Skim off any scum that rises to the surface.

Do not freeze cream soups as they will separate on thawing

2. Add the vegetables, herbs and seasonings and bring back to a simmer.

3. Partly cover the pot and simmer very gently for 2–3 hours. Don't let the stock boil hard or it will be very cloudy.

4. Strain the stock through a fine mesh sieve, cool and then refrigerate. Once the stock is chilled, remove the fat from the surface.

Fish Stock

30 MINS · 1L MAKES

1kg white fish bones and trimmings, including 1 fish head	*1 carrot, sliced*
	1 bay leaf
1L cold water	*1 sprig of thyme*
2 slices of lemon	*3–4 sprigs of parsley*
1 stick celery	*10 peppercorns*
1 onion, unpeeled, chopped	*salt*

1. Wash the fish head then put it into a saucepan with the bones. Add the water and lemon.

2. Bring to a simmer, skim off any scum that rises to the surface and add the other ingredients.

3. Return to a simmer and cook gently for 20 minutes. Strain through a fine mesh sieve, cool and refrigerate.

Vegetable Stock

1.5 HOURS · 2L MAKES

3 onions, unpeeled, quartered	*3–4 sprigs of parsley*
3 leeks, washed and sliced	*4 sprigs of thyme or 1 tsp dried thyme*
3 carrots, sliced	*1 bay leaf*
2 sticks celery, sliced	*10 peppercorns*
3–4 outer leaves of lettuce, chopped	*2L cold water*
3–4 mushrooms	*salt*
2 cloves garlic, unpeeled, slightly crushed	

1. Put all the ingredients into a large stockpot and bring slowly to the boil.

2. Simmer for 45 minutes, partly covered, then strain through a fine mesh sieve. Check and adjust the seasoning. Cool and then refrigerate.

Cream of Asparagus Soup

30 MINS · 4 SERVES

A smooth soup garnished with tender asparagus tips – savoury and satisfying.

500g fresh asparagus	*1 cup milk or a mixture of milk and cream*
1.5L Vegetable or Chicken Stock (page 113, page 112)	*½ tsp salt*
50g butter	*1 tsp sugar*
4 Tbsp Edmonds standard flour	*pinch of nutmeg*

1. Break off the tough ends of the asparagus and cut the spears into small pieces, keeping the tips separate.
2. Cook the tips until tender in a little boiling, salted water. Drain and set aside.
3. Bring the stock to the boil then add the rest of the chopped asparagus and cook until tender. Purée using a wand blender or food processor.
4. Melt the butter in a large saucepan and then add the flour and cook, stirring, until frothy.
5. Remove from the heat and add the puréed asparagus, stirring, followed by the milk, salt, sugar and nutmeg. Return to the heat and bring to a simmer. Check and adjust the seasoning. Serve with the reserved asparagus tips as a garnish.

Cream of Tomato Soup

30 MINS 6 SERVES

Brings out the sweet flavour of tomatoes at the end of summer.

450g tomatoes, peeled, or 400g can
  chopped tomatoes in juice
1 onion, finely chopped
1 carrot, finely chopped
450ml Chicken Stock (300ml if using
  canned tomatoes) (page 112)

1 tsp sugar
salt and pepper
150ml milk
130ml cream
extra cream
chopped chives

1. Put the tomatoes, onion, carrot, chicken stock, sugar and seasoning in a large saucepan and bring gently to the boil. Reduce the heat to low and simmer gently until the vegetables are tender, about 15 minutes.
2. Purée the soup using a wand blender or food processor and then add the milk and cream. Heat gently but do not boil.
3. Serve with a swirl of cream on top and a few chopped chives.

Cream of Mushroom Soup

25 MINS 6 SERVES

A robustly flavoured soup for autumn. Use flat, dark, meaty mushrooms if you can.

25g butter
500g mushrooms, sliced
1 clove garlic, crushed
2 cups milk
1 cup Chicken Stock (page 112)
½ tsp salt

pepper
50g butter
2 Tbsp Edmonds standard flour
1 Tbsp lemon juice
2 rashers streaky bacon
1 Tbsp chopped parsley

1. Melt the first measure of butter in a large saucepan and add the sliced mushrooms and the crushed garlic. Cook gently, stirring, for 10 minutes.
2. Add the milk, stock and seasonings, bring to the boil and simmer for 5 minutes. Then purée the soup with a wand blender or in a food processor.
3. Knead the second measure of butter with the flour until it forms a paste and add this in small lumps to the soup, stirring all the time.

Finely chop the vegetables for cream soups using a food processor if you wish.

4. When the soup has simmered for a few minutes and thickened a little add the lemon juice and taste for seasoning.
5. Grill the bacon until crisp, then cool a little and crumble. Serve the soup garnished with the bacon crumbs and parsley.

French Onion Soup

1½ HOURS SERVES 4

Bubbling hot cheese and tender bread with flavoursome onion soup. This is a French classic and a simple winter favourite.

50g butter
6 onions, chopped
1 Tbsp Edmonds standard flour
4 cups Beef Stock (page 112)

salt and pepper
1 bay leaf
4 slices crusty baguette
½ cup grated tasty cheese or gruyère

1. Heat the butter until foamy in a large, heavy-based saucepan and add the onions. Lower the heat and cook very gently, stirring, until the onions are golden brown and very tender, about 20 minutes.
2. Stir in the flour and cook for 2–3 minutes, then remove from the heat.
3. Bring the beef stock to the boil in another saucepan and pour it onto the onions, stirring. Add the seasoning and the bay leaf, return to the stove and simmer, uncovered, for 30 minutes. Remove the bay leaf.
4. Preheat the oven to 200°C.
5. Place the slices of bread in the base of four ovenproof soup dishes and pour on the hot soup to cover. Sprinkle the top of each dish thickly with the grated cheese and cook in the oven for 10 minutes or until the top is golden and bubbling.

Leek & Potato Soup

1 HOUR SERVES 4

A calming and comforting creamy soup, perfect for chilly winter nights.

4 large leeks
60g butter
2 potatoes, peeled and diced
1 onion, finely chopped
salt and pepper
850ml Chicken or Vegetable Stock
  (page 112, page 113)

1 cup milk
½ cup cream
extra cream to garnish
chopped chives to garnish

1. Trim away the coarse green leaves and roots of the leeks and cut them in half lengthwise. Slice thinly and wash well in cold water to remove any dirt. Lift them out of the water and drain in a colander.
2. Melt the butter gently in a large, heavy-based saucepan and add the leeks, potatoes and onion, stirring to coat in the butter. Season with salt and pepper, cover the pan and cook over a very low heat for 10 minutes.
3. Add the stock, milk and cream and bring back to a gentle simmer, then replace the lid and cook very gently for another 20 minutes. Don't have the heat too high or the milk may boil over.

4. Purée the soup with a wand blender or in a food processor. Return to the stovetop, reheat gently and check and adjust the seasoning. Serve with a swirl of cream and a sprinkling of chopped chives on top.

Minestrone

OVERNIGHT   SERVES 8

A thick and hearty Italian vegetable soup which includes both dried beans and fresh vegetables. Served with crusty bread, it is a meal in itself.

½ cup haricot or red kidney beans
¼ cup oil
2 Tbsp butter
2 onions, finely chopped
2 carrots, chopped
2 sticks celery, sliced
2 courgettes, sliced
1 potato, peeled and diced

1 cup shredded cabbage
100g chopped green beans
2 x 400g cans tomatoes in juice,
   chopped
5 cups Beef Stock (page 112)
salt and pepper
grated parmesan cheese

1. Cover the beans with cold water and soak overnight, then drain.
2. Heat the oil and butter in a large saucepan, add the onions and cook gently for 10 minutes, until golden.
3. Add the carrots, celery, courgettes, potato, cabbage and green beans and cook for 8 minutes, stirring frequently.
4. Add the undrained tomatoes, stock, soaked, drained haricot beans and salt and pepper to taste.
5. Bring to the boil then reduce the heat, partly cover and simmer gently for 1½–2 hours or until the soup is thick. Serve with plenty of parmesan cheese.

Old-Fashioned Vegetable Soup

HOURS 4   SERVES 8

Winter vegetables slow-cooked in beef stock with lentils and pearl barley to give it body. This is a winner every time.

1kg beef bones, fat removed
3L water
½ cup red lentils
½ cup pearl barley

½ cup split peas
3 cups chopped vegetables –
   e.g. carrots, potatoes, parsnips
salt and pepper

1. Put the bones, water, lentils, barley and split peas into a large saucepan. Bring to the boil and simmer for 2–3 hours or until the meat is falling off the bones.
2. Remove the bones, fat and gristle from the soup and add the chopped vegetables. Cook for 30–45 minutes until the vegetables are cooked. Season with salt and pepper to taste.

Pea & Ham Soup

2 HOURS   6 SERVES

Ham gives the sweet, slightly grainy peas a salty tang in this classic soup.

500g bacon or ham bones
2 cups green split peas
1 onion, finely chopped
2 carrots, peeled and diced
3L cold water

2 cloves garlic, peeled
1 sprig of thyme
black pepper
1 bay leaf
Croûtons (page 119)

1. Put all the ingredients except the Croûtons into a large saucepan. Bring slowly to the boil then partly cover and simmer for about 1½ hours or until the peas are tender.
2. Remove the bay leaf, sprig of thyme and the bacon bones. Cut any meat off the bones and dice it.
3. Purée the soup with a wand blender or in a food processor and adjust the seasoning. If it is too thick, add a little water. Return the soup to the pan and the meat to the soup.
4. Reheat and serve with Croûtons.

Pumpkin Soup

40 MINS   6 SERVES

One of New Zealand's most popular go-to comfort meals – a traditional, creamy pumpkin soup.

1 Tbsp oil
1 onion, chopped
750g pumpkin, peeled and chopped
1 large potato, peeled and chopped

4 cups Chicken Stock (page 112)
salt and pepper
pinch of nutmeg

1. Put the oil and onion in a large saucepan and cook gently until the onion is translucent, about 10 minutes.
2. Add the pumpkin, potato and stock and bring slowly to the boil. Partly cover and cook gently until the vegetables are soft, about 20 minutes.
3. Remove 1 cup of the stock and set aside. Purée the soup in a blender, adding the reserved stock if you need it to thin the soup.
4. Season with salt, pepper and nutmeg to taste.

VARIATIONS
Cook a ham hock with the vegetables or add ½ teaspoon ground cumin to the onion as it cooks.

Seafood Chowder

40 MINS — 6 SERVES

You can use pretty much any kind of fresh fish in this, from delicate snapper to oily kahawai. You could also add shellfish, such as mussels or pipis.

4 cups Chicken Stock (page 112)
few sprigs of parsley
1 bay leaf
6 black peppercorns
2 Tbsp butter
2 leeks, thinly sliced

3 carrots, thinly sliced
1 potato, peeled and sliced
2 sticks celery, thinly sliced
500g white fish fillets, cut into
   large chunks
salt and white pepper

1. Place the stock, parsley, bay leaf and peppercorns in a saucepan and bring to the boil. Partly cover with a lid, then simmer for 10 minutes.
2. While the stock is simmering, melt the butter in another saucepan and add the leeks, carrots, potato and celery. Gently cook without colouring until the vegetables are glossy and just tender, about 20 minutes.
3. Place the fish on top of the vegetables and pour in the stock through a sieve. Reheat until the fish is opaque (about 5 minutes) and season with salt and pepper to taste.

Spicy Lentil Soup

1½ HOURS — 6 SERVES

Lentils, spices and bacon bones make this a particularly satisfying soup.

2 tsp butter
2 tsp oil
1 clove garlic, crushed
1 carrot, finely chopped
1 onion, finely chopped
1 stick celery, finely chopped
1 tsp curry powder

1 cup brown lentils
500g bacon bones
400g can tomatoes in juice, chopped
4 cups Beef Stock (page 112)
salt and pepper
2 Tbsp chopped parsley

1. Heat the butter and oil in a large saucepan and add the garlic, carrot, onion and celery. Cook gently for about 10 minutes until the onion is translucent.
2. Add the curry powder and cook, stirring constantly, for 30 seconds.
3. Add the lentils, bacon bones, tomatoes and juice, stock and bring gently to the boil. Partly cover and simmer for 45 minutes or until the lentils are cooked.
4. Remove and discard the bacon bones and season the soup with salt and pepper to taste. Serve garnished with chopped parsley.

Croûtons to serve with soup

Sprinkle onto any soup to add a crunch.

2–3 slices bread of your choice

1. Preheat the oven to 190°C.
2. Cut bread slices into small dice and place on a shallow baking tray.
3. Bake for 10 minutes or until evenly browned on all sides, shaking the tray occasionally during cooking. Or fry the diced bread in a little oil and butter and drain on paper towels.

Eggs

Surely one of the most versatile ingredients in the kitchen, eggs are easy, good value, and always on hand.

Boiled Eggs

Put room-temperature eggs into a saucepan of cold water and place over a medium heat. When the water comes to a simmer, turn off the heat and put the lid on the saucepan. Leave in the pan until cooked the way you like them – see times below.

Soft-boiled	3–4 minutes
Firm white, soft yolk	4–7 minutes
Hard-boiled	8 minutes

As soon as hard-boiled eggs are cooked, put them under cold running water for a few minutes. This prevents a grey ring forming on the outside of the yolk. Have eggs at room temperature before cooking to discourage cracking.

Frittata

30 MINS | 6 SERVES

An Italian dish of eggs and vegetables – perfect for a quick lunch or light meal. Started on the top of the stove and finished under the grill.

50g butter
2 onions, chopped
3 cups grated vegetables – e.g.
courgettes, carrots, potatoes

salt and pepper
4 eggs
4 Tbsp cream or milk
¼ cup grated parmesan cheese

1. Preheat the oven to 180°C.
2. Melt the butter in a large heavy-based ovenproof frying pan, add the onions and cook gently until translucent, about 10 minutes.
3. Add the grated vegetables, season well with salt and pepper, and cook, stirring, for 10 minutes or until just tender.
4. Preheat the grill. Beat together the eggs and cream or milk and pour over the vegetable mixture.
5. Cook gently until the egg begins to cook at the edges, then sprinkle over the parmesan and grill for 8–10 minutes until the egg is set. Serve cut into wedges.

Impossible Quiche

1 HOUR — 6 SERVES

If you add a little flour to a savoury mixture of eggs, vegetables, cheese and milk you can create a savoury picnic or lunch dish which slices easily without the need for a pastry crust.

1 large onion, finely chopped
¼ tsp salt
25g butter
3 eggs
1 cup milk
½ cup Edmonds self raising flour*

2 cloves garlic mashed with ½ tsp salt
2 potatoes, peeled, cubed and cooked
1 cup grated tasty cheese
2 cups finely chopped greens and herbs**
2–3 Tbsp grated parmesan

1. Preheat the oven to 220°C and butter a 20cm shallow ovenproof serving dish.
2. Put the onion, salt and butter into a small, heavy-based frying pan, cover and set over a gentle heat. After 10 minutes, remove the lid and raise the heat a little. Stir regularly for another 10 minutes until the onion is soft and golden, but not browned. Set aside to cool.
3. In a large mixing bowl, beat together the eggs and milk with the flour and the crushed garlic. Once the flour is incorporated, add the onion, potatoes, tasty cheese and greens. Mix gently with a spatula until everything is well combined, and spread out evenly in the prepared dish.
4. Sprinkle over the grated parmesan and bake for about 30 minutes. Serve warm or at room temperature.

*Substitute chickpea flour and ½ tsp baking powder if you want a gluten-free result.

**Use what you have. Leafy greens like spinach, silverbeet, sorrel, parsley, chives and tarragon go in raw, but you'll need to pre-cook other green vegetables like broccoli or asparagus.

Omelette

5 MINS — 1 SERVES

Simple, fast, golden and delicious – a perfect, quick meal at any time.

2 eggs
1 Tbsp milk
salt and pepper

2 tsp butter
chopped herbs to garnish

1. Lightly beat the eggs and milk and season with salt and pepper to taste.
2. Heat an omelette pan, add the butter and when the butter is foaming, but not brown, pour in the egg mixture.
3. Cook over a moderate heat, lifting the mixture at the edges as it sets and tipping the pan to allow the uncooked egg to run underneath.
4. Cook until the egg is set and golden. Add any filling you wish, then tip the pan and use a spatula to help the omelette fold in half, enclosing the filling. Turn onto a hot plate and serve with a sprinkling of herbs.

Poached Eggs

By cooking them in shallow water in a frying pan you can achieve perfect poached eggs, every time.

1. Pour hot water into a frying pan, add 1 tablespoon of vinegar and bring to a simmer.
2. Break each egg into a saucer and slip them carefully into the pan.
3. Cover the pan and turn off the heat. Leave for 3 minutes, after which the whites will be set and the yolks covered with a light coating of white.
4. Remove with a slotted spoon, drain on paper towels and serve on hot buttered toast.

NOTE
Do not try to poach more than 4 eggs at a time as the water will not stay at the right temperature.

Scotch Eggs

Hard-boiled eggs wrapped in spiced sausage meat, then crumbed and deep fried – these are perfect for a picnic with homemade tomato sauce.

vegetable oil for deep frying
400g sausage meat or skinned sausages
¼ cup finely chopped onion
1 Tbsp tomato sauce
salt and pepper
1 tsp finely grated lemon zest
4 hard-boiled eggs (page 120)
1 egg, beaten
1 cup fine, crisp breadcrumbs

1. Heat the vegetable oil in a saucepan or deep-fryer.
2. Put the sausage meat or skinned sausages, onion, tomato sauce, salt and pepper and lemon zest in a bowl and mix well to combine.
3. Shell the eggs and divide the sausage meat mixture evenly into four. With wet hands, mould the sausage meat mixture around each egg.
4. Roll in the beaten egg, then in the breadcrumbs.
5. Deep-fry in hot oil for 8 minutes or until golden. Drain on paper towels.
6. Cut in half lengthwise and serve hot or cold.

NOTE
You can reduce the amount of oil you need for deep frying by using a heavy wok rather than a saucepan.

Scrambled Eggs

The trick with scrambled eggs is not to overcook them but keep them creamy and soft.

2 eggs
1 Tbsp milk or cream
salt and pepper
1 Tbsp butter
chopped herbs to garnish

1. Lightly beat the eggs with the milk or cream and the salt and pepper.
2. Melt the butter in a small heavy-based frying pan, pour in the egg mixture and cook

---

gently, lifting the egg as it sets on the base of the pan and turning it over with a spoon or spatula. Keep cooking until the eggs are set and are a creamy consistency, and always stir gently. Stop just before you think the eggs are ready as they will continue to cook for a minute after you remove them from the pan.

3. Add the chopped herbs and serve on hot, buttered toast.

VARIATIONS
Add finely sliced mushrooms to the uncooked egg mixture.
Fold in cooked, chopped bacon after the eggs are cooked.
Fold in chopped smoked salmon after the eggs are cooked.

Stuffed Eggs

20 MINS · 16 MAKES

Once essential on shared supper tables at community events, these tasty eggs remain a popular snack.

8 hard-boiled eggs (page 120)
1 tsp curry powder
2–3 Tbsp Mayonnaise (page 178)
or Edmonds whole egg mayonnaise

salt
chopped chives
lettuce leaves

1. Shell the eggs and cut them in half lengthwise. Carefully remove the yolks.
2. Using a fork, mash the yolks with the curry powder, mayonnaise and salt to taste until they are smooth.
3. Spoon or pipe the egg yolk mixture back into the halved egg whites, sprinkle with chopped chives and serve on small lettuce leaves.

Using the Whites and Yolks of Eggs

Here are some suggestions for using up leftover egg yolks or whites. Remember that egg whites can be frozen very successfully and used as fresh when defrosted, but yolks cannot.

Egg Yolks
Crème Brûlée (page 188)
Crème Caramel (page 189)
Cheese Straws (page 105)
Crème Pâtissière (page 99)
Mayonnaise (page 178)
Sweet Shortcrust Pastry (page 103)

Egg Whites
Friands (page 70)
Meringues (page 72)
Pavlova (page 191)
Royal Icing (page 100)

Have eggs at room temperature to prevent cracking on immersion in hot water.

Pasta & Rice

New Zealanders eat a lot more pasta and rice than they once did, and the selection available has grown enormously. These recipes use mainly basic pasta and standard rice varieties but feel free to substitute more exotic variations.

How to cook perfect pasta:

- For every 250g of pasta use 2 litres of water and 2 teaspoons of salt.
- Bring the water to a very fast, rolling boil in a large saucepan. Add the pasta, stir well, and return to the boil. Cook with the lid off until 'al dente' or firm to the bite but with no white centre. Drain well and serve.
- Cook dried pasta for the time indicated on the packet – usually 8–12 minutes.
- Fresh pasta cooks in a much shorter time, usually 2–3 minutes, but stuffed pasta like ravioli takes up to 9 minutes.

How to cook perfect rice:

- Many types of rice are available in New Zealand. Long grain rice, white or brown, is used mostly for savoury dishes and short grain rice for sweet dishes. Italian risotto, however, is always made with short grain rice, as is Japanese sushi.
- It is best to wash all rice before cooking. Swirl the rice in a bowl with 2–3 changes of cold water then drain well. You can also soak long grain rice, especially Indian basmati rice, for 30 minutes before cooking, to keep the grains white and separate.
- Rice trebles in volume when it is cooked, so 1 cup of dry rice will make 3 cups of cooked rice.

Almond Pilaf

Fluffy rice studded with raisins and toasted almonds; this is a wonderful accompaniment to any curry. Try it with the Curried Chicken on page 155.

½ cup sliced almonds
25g butter
1 onion, chopped
1 clove garlic, crushed

2 Tbsp raisins
1½ cups Chicken Stock (page 112)
salt and pepper
1 cup long grain rice

1. Preheat the oven to 180°C.
2. Place the sliced almonds in a shallow baking tray and toast for about 5 minutes until golden. Watch them closely as they burn easily. Set aside to cool.
3. Melt the butter in a saucepan, add the onion and garlic and cook until the onion is soft and translucent, about 10 minutes.
4. Stir in the raisins, stock and salt and pepper to taste. Cover and bring to the boil.
5. Add the rice, give the mixture a good stir, put on the lid, then reduce the heat to very low. Cook for 20 minutes without lifting the lid.

6. After 20 minutes, give the rice a gentle stir, preferably with a wooden fork or chopsticks, and then stir through most of the almonds.
7. Spoon the rice into a serving dish and garnish with the remaining almonds.

Basic Homemade Egg Pasta

You can make your own pasta very quickly in the food processor using just flour and eggs – well worth a try and the results are sure to please.

2½ cups Edmonds standard flour   3 eggs

1. Put the flour in the food processor and, with the motor running, drop in the eggs, one at a time. Keep pulsing until the mixture forms clumps.
2. Turn out onto a floured board and knead for about 5 minutes, until the dough is smooth and springy.
3. Divide the dough into quarters, roll them into flattish balls and set aside to rest, covered in a bowl, for 10 minutes.
4. Now flour the board and, working with one piece of dough at a time, roll the pasta out to 2mm thickness. Keep the rolling pin and the board dusted with flour.
5. When you have a large sheet of pasta rolled out, lay it on a clean tea towel to dry it a little while you roll out the next sheet.
6. Once the four sheets are all rolled out, take the first one, lay it on the board and loosely roll up into an 8cm wide roll. Cut across the roll with a sharp knife to make noodles, between 3mm wide (fettuccine) and 15mm wide (pappardelle). For lasagne, cut 10cm wide strips. Or you can roll out and cut the pasta using a pasta machine and by following the maker's instructions.
7. Form the noodles into loose 'nests' and leave covered with a tea towel until you are ready to cook.
8. Drop the pasta into a large saucepan of salted, boiling water and cook for 2–3 minutes until al dente or slightly firm to the bite.
9. Toss with the sauce of your choice and serve hot.

NOTE
If you allow the pasta to dry completely it will keep for 2–3 weeks in a cool cupboard but will take a little longer to cook. To make a larger quantity of pasta, use the formula of 1 egg to 1 cup of flour.

Basic Recipe for Long Grain Brown Rice

This method ensures tender, nutty-tasting, well-cooked rice.

1 cup long grain rice   1½ cups water

1. Wash the rice and put it in a saucepan with the water and soak for 30 minutes.
2. Bring to the boil with the lid on, stir once, then lower the heat and cook for 25 minutes without lifting the lid.
3. Turn off the heat, leave for 15 minutes, then fluff up the rice with a wooden fork or chopsticks and serve.

Basic Recipe for White Rice

30 MINS · 2 SERVES

This is called the absorption method and it works for any quantity of rice.

1 cup rice
1 cup water

pinch of salt

1. Wash the rice and put it in a saucepan which has a close-fitting lid. Add the water and the salt.
2. With the lid off the pan, bring the water to a fast boil.
3. Stir once, put on the lid and reduce the heat to very low. A simmer mat is useful over a gas flame.
4. Leave the rice for 20 minutes and do not lift the lid!
5. Remove from the heat, then lift the lid and stir the rice gently with a wooden fork or a pair of chopsticks (this prevents the grains from breaking). Replace the lid and leave for 5 minutes, then serve.

Coconut Chilli Rice

30 MINS · 4 SERVES

1 cup long grain rice
375ml can coconut cream

1 chilli, seeded and chopped, or
1 tsp prepared chopped chilli

1. Put the rice into a medium saucepan with the coconut cream and chilli.
2. Cover and bring to the boil, then reduce the heat to a minimum and cook, covered, for 20 minutes.
3. Stir the rice gently with a wooden fork or chopsticks and serve.

Fried Rice

20 MINS · 4 SERVES

Quickly made and packed with flavour, this is a meal in itself.

3 Tbsp oil
2 eggs, beaten
1 onion, finely chopped
1 clove garlic, finely chopped
2 tsp grated fresh ginger
2 rashers bacon, finely chopped

1 stick celery, diced
1 tsp white sugar
2 cups long grain rice, cooked
1 Tbsp soy sauce
6 spring onions, finely chopped

1. Heat 1 tablespoon of the oil in a wok, pour in the eggs and once set and bubbling around the edges, turn the egg over. Remove from the wok with a spatula and drain on paper towels.
2. Wipe out the wok and heat the remaining oil. Add the onion, garlic, ginger, bacon and celery and cook for 1 minute.
3. Add the sugar, stir well, then add the rice, soy sauce and spring onions. Stir until the rice is heated through. Lastly fold in the cooked egg to serve.

Scotch Eggs page 122
Impossible Quiche page 121

Vegetarian Lasagne page 132, Macaroni Cheese page 130

Lasagne with Meat Sauce

2 HOURS   6 SERVES

In this Bolognese meat sauce, called a ragù, the beef is cooked very slowly in milk before the tomatoes are added, creating a meltingly tender result. You can use this classic sauce with other pasta if you wish.

MEAT SAUCE

2 Tbsp oil	salt
1 Tbsp butter	1 cup white wine
1 onion, chopped	½ cup milk
2 Tbsp chopped carrot	pinch of nutmeg
2 Tbsp chopped celery	400g can tomatoes in juice, chopped
350g lean beef mince	

CHEESE SAUCE

50g butter	¾ cup grated cheese
3 Tbsp Edmonds standard flour	½ tsp salt
1½ cups milk, heated	pepper

PASTA
250g wide lasagne, cooked

TOPPING
2 Tbsp grated parmesan cheese

1. Put the oil, butter and onion in a large deep saucepan and cook over a gentle heat, stirring occasionally, until the onion is translucent and golden, about 10 minutes. Then add the carrot and celery and cook for 2 minutes.

2. Add the minced meat and stir until all trace of redness has gone, then add the salt and the wine. Increase the heat and cook for 5 minutes until the wine has almost evaporated.

3. Now add the milk and nutmeg, reduce the heat and simmer for 5 minutes. Lastly add the tomatoes and their juice and stir well.

4. When the sauce just begins to simmer, reduce the heat and cook very gently, barely bubbling, for 1 hour with the lid off, stirring occasionally. Set aside to cool.

5. Make the cheese sauce when the meat sauce is almost cooked. Melt the butter in a saucepan, add the flour and cook until frothy.

6. Remove from the heat and gradually add the hot milk, stirring constantly, then return to the stove and cook, stirring, until the mixture boils and thickens. Remove from the heat and stir in the cheese.

7. Season with the salt and pepper to taste. Set aside until cool, covered.

8. Preheat the oven to 180°C.

9. Place half of the lasagne in a greased ovenproof dish. Spread with half the meat mixture and half the cheese sauce, then repeat the layers, finishing with the cheese sauce. Sprinkle with the parmesan.

10. Cook for 20 minutes or until golden and heated through.

Lemon Rice

30 MINS · SERVES 4

Serve with fish or chicken curries.

1 cup long grain rice
1 cup water
25g butter

1 Tbsp finely grated lemon zest
2 Tbsp lemon juice
salt and pepper

1. Put all the ingredients into a medium saucepan which has a close-fitting lid and bring quickly to the boil, uncovered.
2. Put on the lid and reduce the heat to minimum. A simmer mat is useful on a gas flame.
3. Cook for 20 minutes without lifting the lid, then stir the rice, preferably with a wooden fork or chopsticks.
4. Rest for 5 minutes with the lid on and then serve.

Macaroni Cheese

1 HOUR · SERVES 6

This Sunday evening special needs no description – other than the promise that plates will be emptied very quickly.

2 Tbsp butter
1 onion, finely chopped
2 Tbsp Edmonds standard flour
½ tsp dry mustard
2 cups milk, heated

salt and pepper
2 cups grated tasty cheese
2 cups macaroni elbows, cooked
2 Tbsp dry breadcrumbs

1. Preheat the oven to 190°C.
2. Melt the butter in a saucepan, add the onion and cook gently for about 10 minutes or until the onion is translucent.
3. Stir in the flour and cook, stirring, until frothy. Then add the mustard.
4. Remove from the heat and add the hot milk gradually, stirring.
5. Return to the heat and cook, still stirring, until the sauce boils and thickens. Remove from the heat, season with salt and pepper and add half the grated cheese, and the macaroni.
6. Combine well and put into an ovenproof dish.
7. Mix the breadcrumbs into the remaining grated cheese and sprinkle over the top.
8. Cook for 20 minutes or until golden and heated through.

VARIATION
Add chopped, cooked bacon or ham to the sauce if you wish.

Simple Risotto

If you use Italian risotto rice, which has very round, plump grains, you will find it easy to make a perfect, creamy risotto. A well-flavoured stock is also helpful. This is a simple recipe using tomato as the flavouring. When you have mastered the technique, try it with other vegetables like mushrooms, red capsicum, courgettes or asparagus.

1 onion, finely chopped
2 cloves garlic, finely chopped
2 Tbsp olive oil
30g butter
750ml stock or water
250g risotto rice

250g fresh or canned tomatoes, chopped
salt and pepper
3 Tbsp grated parmesan cheese
1 Tbsp butter

1. Put the onion, garlic, oil and butter into a heavy-based, wide saucepan. Cook over a gentle heat, stirring occasionally, until the onion is soft and golden, about 10 minutes.
2. While the onion is cooking, put the stock in another saucepan and bring to a very gentle simmer.
3. Add the rice to the onion and give it a good stir so that each grain is coated with oil. Then add the tomatoes and a ladleful of the hot stock.
4. For the next 20 minutes you need to be fully committed to stirring the risotto, to make sure that the rice cooks evenly. Add another ladleful of stock whenever the rice dries out and keep the heat under the pan at medium to high – but not so high that the stock boils away as soon as you add it or the rice will be chalky inside.
5. Once all the stock is added and absorbed the rice will be creamily bound together. Taste and season with salt and pepper.
6. Add the grated parmesan and the butter, and stir just to melt them into the rice. Tip onto a warmed dish and serve immediately.

Spaghetti and Meatballs

An American dish which you are unlikely to find in Italy, but a New Zealand family favourite and easy to make since the meatballs are baked rather than fried.

TOMATO SAUCE
4 Tbsp olive oil
1 onion, chopped
400g can tomatoes in juice

salt and pepper
¼ tsp sugar

MEATBALLS
450g lean beef mince
1 onion, very finely chopped
½ cup soft breadcrumbs
1 egg

1 clove garlic, crushed
pinch of dried marjoram
salt and pepper
3 Tbsp grated parmesan cheese

500g spaghetti, cooked

1. Place the olive oil and onion in a saucepan and cook gently until the onion is translucent, about 10 minutes.
2. Add the tomatoes and their juice, salt and pepper to taste, and sugar. Cook gently,

just simmering, with the lid off, for about 20 minutes. Set aside.

3. Preheat the oven to 200°C. Grease a baking tray.

4. Combine all the meatball ingredients in a large bowl, and mix thoroughly together using your hands.

5. Measure out tablespoonfuls of mixture and shape it into balls. Place the meatballs on the prepared tray.

6. Bake for 8–10 minutes or until cooked through.

7. Add the hot meatballs to the reheated sauce and serve with the cooked spaghetti.

Tuna Sauce for Pasta

Very tasty and made in a jiffy from pantry basics. This is a good one for anyone about to go flatting to have in their cooking repertoire.

2 Tbsp butter
1 small onion, finely chopped
2 x 185g cans tuna, flaked
250g sour cream

1 red capsicum, finely chopped
salt and pepper
250g pasta, cooked

1. Melt the butter in a saucepan, add the onion and cook gently until translucent, about 10 minutes.

2. Add the tuna and the sour cream and heat together but do not let the sauce boil. Stir in the chopped red capsicum and season with salt and pepper. Toss through hot pasta.

Vegetarian Lasagne with Spinach and Walnuts

Every bit as good as meat lasagne, with the same cheese sauce. Walnuts add their rich flavour and texture to the spinach and ricotta layer. Light and delicious.

CHEESE SAUCE
Cheese Sauce (page 184)

SPINACH LAYER
130g baby spinach
225g ricotta cheese
50g chopped walnuts

200g grated tasty or mozzarella cheese
salt and pepper
100g blue vein cheese (optional)

PASTA
250g lasagne sheets, ready to use

TOPPING
100g grated tasty cheese or mozzarella

1. Preheat the oven to 180°C. Grease a 23cm ovenproof square dish well.

2. Make the cheese sauce first and set aside to cool.

3. Put the spinach leaves in a bowl of cold water, then lift them out and put them into a large saucepan.

4. Cook with the lid on over a medium heat until the spinach collapses and becomes tender, about 2–3 minutes.

5. Drain well in a colander or sieve and squeeze out as much of the water as you can with your hands.

6. Chop the spinach very finely and combine with the ricotta, walnuts, grated cheese and salt and pepper. Add about 2 tablespoons of the cheese sauce and mix well. Add the crumbled blue vein cheese if you wish.

7. Spread a layer of lasagne in the base of the dish and follow with a layer of spinach and then one of cheese sauce.

8. Repeat the layers until the dish is full, finishing with cheese sauce, and the extra cheese topping.

9. Cook the lasagne for about 1 hour until golden on top and bubbling. Allow to rest for about 10 minutes before serving with green salad.

VARIATION

Add more flavour and colour with a layer of roasted and peeled red capsicum in the middle of the lasagne.

Seafood

New Zealanders are lucky to have access to a wide variety of fresh seafood. Long may this continue to be the case! Whether you catch it yourself or pick it up on the way home, fish and shellfish are always a nutritious and delicious meal option.

How to choose whole fish:

Look for fish that has:
- no smell of ammonia or strong odour
- translucent, firm flesh
- intact scales
- bright red gills
- bulging, bright eyes, and
- no blood in the body cavity.

How to cook whole fish or fillets:

Poaching

Weigh the fish and allow 10–15 minutes cooking time per 500g. Wrap the fish in tinfoil or place on a steaming rack and put in a saucepan with enough water to just cover it. Put the lid on and simmer very gently until the fish is tender. The surface of the water should barely shake. Drain and serve with the sauce of your choice. For fillets allow 4–6 minutes cooking time.

Steaming

Place the fish in a lightly greased steamer and cook until done. Or place the fish fillets in a deep plate that will fit in your steamer. Sprinkle with a little grated ginger and garlic, some soy sauce, a drizzle of sesame oil, some chopped coriander and spring onions and sliced chilli if you wish.

Grilling

Heat the grill and oil the grilling rack. Remove the head, fins and tail from whole fish and cut 2–3 slashes in the flesh of thick fish to allow the heat to penetrate. Brush with melted butter or oil. While the fish is cooking, brush it again with more melted butter or oil. Grill a whole fish for 10 minutes per 500g and fillets for 4–5 minutes.

Baking

Preheat the oven to 180°C. Remove the fins from whole fish, weigh the fish and allow 20 minutes' cooking time per 500g. Put 2 slices of lemon into the cavity and place the fish in a greased baking dish or roasting pan. Brush with melted butter or oil and bake until cooked.

Frying

Wipe the fish fillets and cut into serving-sized pieces if you wish. Dust with seasoned flour and fry quickly in oil and butter over medium heat. Or dip in egg and coat in breadcrumbs before frying in oil and butter.

To test for doneness

Fish is cooked when the flesh flakes easily, when the flesh separates from the bones, or when a creamy white juice comes from the flesh.

Basic Battered Fish

Thin, crisp, golden batter, just veiling the perfectly cooked fish. Make sure the batter is well rested and the oil is hot.

¾ cup Edmonds standard flour	½ cup milk
pinch of salt	oil for deep-frying
1 egg	6 fish fillets
1 Tbsp oil	extra flour

1. Sift the flour and salt into a mixing bowl. Make a well in the centre and break in the egg and pour in the oil.
2. Mix with a fork, gradually incorporating the flour and adding the milk a little at a time.
3. Whisk until smooth and then rest for 15 minutes before using.
4. Heat the oil in a large saucepan or heavy wok.
5. Dry the fillets, dip them in flour and then in the batter.
6. Deep-fry the fillets in the hot oil until golden and crisp. Lift out and drain on paper towels.

VARIATIONS

Beer Batter

½ cup Edmonds standard flour	½–⅔ cup beer, approximately
½ tsp salt	

Sift the flour and salt into a bowl. Add the beer slowly until the mixture reaches a blendable consistency and mix to a smooth batter. Makes about 1 cup.

Crisp Batter

¼ cup Edmonds Fielder's cornflour	¼ tsp salt
½ cup Edmonds standard flour	½ cup milk
1 tsp Edmonds baking powder	

Sift the cornflour, flour, baking powder and salt into a bowl and add the milk gradually, mixing until smooth. Makes about 1 cup.

Use a heavy-based wok as it takes less oil to achieve the required depth for deep frying.

Fish Cakes

1 HOUR · 4 SERVES

A delicious English specialty, fish cakes must be well seasoned and have a high proportion of fish to potato. Use white fish or salmon.

500g potatoes, peeled
30g butter
500g white fish fillets
1 small onion, finely chopped
2 Tbsp chopped tarragon or parsley
salt and pepper

½ cup Edmonds standard flour
1 egg
1 Tbsp water
1–1½ cups dried breadcrumbs
oil for shallow frying
lemon wedges

1. Boil the potatoes in salted water until tender. Drain and mash with the butter.
2. Poach the fish in lightly salted water or steam it. Cool slightly.
3. Flake the fish and mix it gently into the potato with the onion, herbs and salt and pepper. Taste and adjust the seasoning then form the mixture into 8 flat cakes. Combine flour with salt and pepper. Lightly coat the fishcakes with the seasoned flour.
4. Beat the egg with the water and dip the fish cakes first in the egg mixture, then in the breadcrumbs.
5. Heat a little oil in a heavy-based frying pan and fry the fish cakes over a moderate heat for 2–3 minutes on each side or until golden.
6. Drain on paper towels and serve with lemon wedges.

Fish Cooked En Papillote

30 MINS · 4 SERVES

A traditional French method of cooking fish in paper parcels. Tender, flavoursome and very easy.

4 large white fish or salmon fillets
salt and pepper
3 Tbsp chopped parsley
2 cloves garlic, very finely chopped

1 Tbsp finely grated lemon zest
1 Tbsp lemon juice
3 Tbsp butter, softened

1. Preheat the oven to 200°C.
2. Lay each fish fillet in the centre of a piece of baking paper large enough to enclose it. Sprinkle with salt and pepper.
3. Combine the parsley, garlic and lemon zest in a small bowl, then divide the mixture evenly over the fillets. Sprinkle with the lemon juice and add a few small dabs of butter.
4. Bring the paper up to enclose the fish and secure by folding the edges together several times. Carefully lift the fish parcels onto baking trays using a spatula.
5. Bake for about 15 minutes. Transfer the parcels onto heated plates and serve immediately.

Fish Pie Supreme

1 HOUR · 6 SERVES

This recipe has always been high up in the Edmonds Cookery Book Top 20. It's a great way to use up leftover smoked kahawai and a classic Kiwi winter warmer.

TOPPING
25g butter
1 Tbsp milk
3 cups cooked mashed potatoes, hot

¾ tsp salt
pepper

FILLING
1 Tbsp butter
1 Tbsp Edmonds standard flour
1 cup milk, heated

500g smoked fish, flaked
1 Tbsp chopped parsley
2 hard-boiled eggs, chopped

1. Preheat the oven to 190°C. Grease a 20cm pie dish.
2. Add the butter and milk to the hot mashed potatoes and beat with a fork to combine. Season with the salt and pepper to taste.
3. Spread half of the potatoes evenly over the base of the pie dish.
4. Melt the butter in a saucepan, stir in the flour and cook until frothy.
5. Remove from the heat and gradually add the hot milk, stirring.
6. Return to the heat and cook, still stirring, until the sauce boils and thickens.
7. Remove from the heat and gently stir through the fish, parsley and eggs. Pour this mixture into the lined pie dish and cover with the remaining mashed potato.
8. Cook for 20 minutes or until golden brown on top.

VARIATION
If you have small pie dishes, make individual pies for a change.

Fried Oysters and Mussels

Tender shellfish in a breadcrumb coating.

oil for shallow frying
1½ dozen oysters or mussels, shelled
¼ cup Edmonds standard flour
½ tsp salt

black pepper
1 egg
¾ cup soft breadcrumbs
lemon wedges

1. Heat the oil in a large frying pan or heavy wok.
2. Drain the oysters and remove the beards from the mussels.
3. Combine the flour, salt and pepper in one dish. Beat the egg and place in a second dish, and place the breadcrumbs in a third dish.
4. Coat each oyster or mussel with seasoned flour, then dip in the egg and coat with the breadcrumbs.
5. Fry the shellfish in the hot oil in batches and cook until golden. Drain on paper towels and serve with lemon wedges.

Dipping Sauce for Fried Oysters or Mussels

4 Tbsp sweet chilli sauce
1 Tbsp lime or lemon juice or cider

vinegar
1 Tbsp cold water

Mix everything together and serve in a small bowl.

Kedgeree

20 MINS · SERVES 4

An Anglo-Indian dish originally served at breakfast time. There are many versions of this recipe, but the principal ingredients nowadays are fish and rice. A good way to use up some leftover rice, but if it is very dry, steam it for a few minutes before using.

50g butter
1 onion, finely chopped
1 clove garlic, crushed
1 tsp grated fresh ginger
1 tsp curry powder
1 cup long grain rice, cooked

250g smoked fish, flaked
1 Tbsp lemon juice
salt and pepper
2 hard-boiled eggs, quartered
2 Tbsp toasted flaked almonds
1 Tbsp chopped parsley

1. Melt the butter in a saucepan, add the onion and cook gently until the onion is translucent, about 10 minutes.
2. Add the garlic, ginger and curry powder and stir for a minute. Then add the rice and stir until it is coloured and warmed through.
3. Gently fold in the flaked fish, add the lemon juice and salt and pepper to taste. Cook gently until the fish is heated through.
4. Transfer to a serving dish and garnish with the boiled eggs, almonds and parsley.

Marinated Raw Fish

2½ HOURS · SERVES 6

This is a popular dish throughout the Pacific Islands and a great choice for a light summer meal. The lemon juice 'cooks' the fish and turns the flesh white, then coconut milk adds flavour and moisture.

500g firm white fish fillets – e.g.
    snapper, tarakihi or gurnard
1 tsp salt
¼ cup lemon juice

1 onion, finely chopped
½ cup coconut milk
2 tomatoes, diced
½ cup cucumber, chopped

1. Cut the fish into bite-sized pieces, sprinkle with salt then lemon juice, and cover.
2. Chill for 2 hours or until the fish whitens, stirring occasionally, then drain and stir in the onion and coconut milk.
3. Put in a serving dish and sprinkle over the tomatoes and cucumber. Serve chilled.

Mussel or Whitebait Fritters

1½ HOURS · SERVES 4

If you are lucky enough to have whitebait, you can use this recipe for whitebait fritters, although purists would leave out the flour and add another egg. With freshly opened mussels, this is perfection.

12 fresh mussels or 125g whitebait
1 egg
1 Tbsp Edmonds standard flour
¼ tsp Edmonds baking soda

salt and pepper
2 Tbsp chopped parsley or coriander
oil for shallow frying
lemon wedges

1. Open the mussels by pouring hot water over them in a bowl, or steaming them slightly in an open pan with a little water. Remove from the shells and clean, then chop finely or whiz in a food processor, leaving the mixture a little chunky. If you are using whitebait, drain it well.

2. With a fork, whisk together the egg, flour, baking soda, salt and pepper to taste and the herbs. Add the chopped mussels or whitebait and chill the mixture for 1 hour if you have the time.

3. Heat the oil gently in a heavy-based frying pan and fry large tablespoons of the mixture until golden brown on both sides.

4. Drain on paper towels and serve with lemon wedges.

Pan-Fried Fish with Lemon and Capers

A very simple, fast and delicious way to cook fillets of white fish.

800g white fish fillets	*juice of 1 large lemon*
3 Tbsp Edmonds standard flour	*2 Tbsp capers*
4 Tbsp olive oil	*1 Tbsp chopped parsley*
2 Tbsp butter	

1. Preheat the oven to 200°C.

2. Dust the fish fillets with the flour. Heat the olive oil in a frying pan and add the fish. Pan-fry the fillets over a medium heat on both sides until golden brown. Transfer to an ovenproof platter and put in the oven until the fish is just cooked. This will take about 5 minutes. Check that the fish flakes easily when you insert a knife.

3. Pour the oil out of the frying pan, add the butter and when the butter is bubbling but not brown, add the lemon juice, capers and parsley. Cook over a gentle heat for a few seconds just until the mixture thickens a little.

4. Spoon over the cooked fish and serve immediately.

Seafood Cocktail

A 1960s classic that dropped off the radar for a while but has made a comeback, thanks to its delicious flavours and a certain retro charm.

2 cups mixed seafood – e.g. shrimps,	*2 tsp lemon juice*
crab, prawns, oysters, crayfish	*white pepper*
1 cup cream	*1 cup shredded iceberg lettuce*
¼ cup tomato sauce	*paprika or chopped parsley*

1. Combine the seafood and set aside while preparing the sauce.

2. Put the cream in a bowl and beat until thickened slightly, then beat in the tomato sauce, lemon juice and pepper.

3. Place a small amount of shredded lettuce into individual serving dishes and top with the seafood mixture. Spoon the cream over the seafood and sprinkle with paprika or chopped parsley.

VARIATION
Replace the cream with unsweetened yoghurt mixed with a pinch of sugar.

Squid Rings

Crumbed and cooked very quickly to keep them soft.

oil for deep-frying
500g squid rings
2 cloves garlic, crushed
1 egg

1 Tbsp Edmonds Fielder's cornflour
1 Tbsp milk
1 cup toasted breadcrumbs,
    approximately

1. Heat the oil in a large frying pan or heavy wok.
2. Put the squid and garlic in a bowl, mix together and leave for 15 minutes.
3. Beat the egg, cornflour and milk together and dip the squid rings into the mixture, then into the breadcrumbs.
4. Deep-fry in hot oil for 2 minutes or until golden. Do not overcook as this will toughen the squid. Serve with a dipping sauce.

Steamed Mussels

Quickly steamed just until they open, mussels can be eaten immediately, added to fish soups or made into fritters.

20–30 fresh mussels in the shell
1 cup water or white wine

chopped parsley to garnish (optional)

1. Scrub the mussels well, removing and discarding the beards, and place them in a large, wide saucepan or frying pan.
2. Add the water or white wine and place over a medium heat. Watch the mussels closely and as the shells open, remove the mussels with tongs to a hot dish. Discard any that do not open.
3. If you used wine to open the mussels, add 2 tablespoons of butter to the pan and bring to a quick simmer. Strain the liquid over the mussels and sprinkle with chopped parsley.

You can drain fried food on stale bread slices instead of absorbent paper.

Meat

New Zealanders don't eat quite as much red meat as they used to, back when a meal wasn't really a meal unless there was a sizeable chunk of lamb or beef involved. However, we do enjoy more choice of cuts and a higher quality overall.

How to choose roast meat:

- The best joints of meat for roasting are the larger ones. If the meat weighs less than 1.5kg kilograms you should pot roast it (page 142) to keep it moist and prevent it drying out.
- Make sure the meat is at room temperature, not straight from the refrigerator, and tie it into a compact shape with string if necessary so that it will cook evenly.
- Weigh the meat and place it fatty side up on an oiled rack in a roasting dish. If you intend to roast vegetables alongside the meat, and don't want to use a rack, place it on a layer of chopped onions, celery and herbs like rosemary or parsley. These will flavour the meat and stop it sticking to the pan.
- If the meat has no fat layer, spread it with soft butter or brush it with oil and season with salt and pepper.
- Preheat the oven to 220°C and place the meat in the centre. After 20 minutes, reduce the heat to 180°C and continue to roast, basting with the pan juices every 20 minutes. Put any vegetables you wish to roast – potatoes, kumara, pumpkin, parsnips, cut to similar sizes – around the meat at this point and turn them over in the pan juices.
- When the meat is cooked to your liking, remove the vegetables to a warm serving dish. Lift out the meat onto another warm dish, cover with tinfoil and leave to rest in a warm place for 15–20 minutes before carving. If the vegetables need more cooking, return them to the oven while the meat rests. The resting time ensures that the meat will be tender and gives you time to make the gravy and cook any green vegetables.
- Always warm the dinner plates when you are serving a roast meal.

Times for roasting meat

Weigh the joint of meat and allow the number of minutes given below per 500g, then add the extra minutes to give the total roasting time.

MEAT		MINUTES PER 500G	EXTRA TIME
Beef	rare	15	15 minutes
	medium	20	20 minutes
	well done	25	25 minutes
Lamb	medium rare	20	20 minutes
	well done	30	30 minutes
Pork	with skin	30	30 minutes
	without skin	35	35 minutes

How to roast pork with crackling:

1. Have the butcher score the skin well. Place the meat in the kitchen sink and pour a kettleful of boiling water over it, then drain and dry the meat and rub salt into the skin.
2. Preheat the oven to 220˚C. Put the meat on a rack in a roasting dish with 1 cup of water in it and cook for about 20 minutes, until the skin starts to bubble and crisp.
3. Reduce the heat to 180˚C for the rest of the cooking time. Keep the dish topped up with hot water, but don't baste the pork or cover the roasting dish, or the crackling will lose its crackle.

Basic Gravy From Roasted Meat

30 MINS   4 SERVES

1 Tbsp fat from roasting dish
1½ Tbsp Edmonds standard flour
1½ cups water, stock or
   vegetable water

salt and pepper
1 tsp soy sauce (optional)

1. After you have removed the joint of meat and roasted vegetables, pour off most of the fat from the roasting dish, leaving about 1 tablespoon and any seasoning vegetables that were under the meat.
2. Sprinkle on the flour and cook over a medium heat, stirring until foamy.
3. Remove from the heat and gradually add the liquid, stirring well with a whisk or wooden spoon.
4. Simmer until the gravy comes to the boil, then season with salt and pepper to taste, adding a little soy sauce if the gravy seems too pale.
5. Strain out the seasoning vegetables and pour the gravy into a warmed jug or gravy boat.

Beef Pot Roast

3 HOURS   6 SERVES

Tender slices of well-cooked beef served with its own juices.

1 Tbsp oil
1 Tbsp butter
1–1.5kg piece of beef topside, trimmed
   of fat
2 carrots, chopped
2 onions, chopped
2 sticks celery, chopped

1 bay leaf
2–3 sprigs of parsley and thyme
1½ cups beef stock, or beef stock
   and red wine
salt and pepper
1 tsp wholegrain mustard (optional)

1. Heat the oil and butter in a large heavy-based saucepan, put in the meat and brown it on all sides.
2. Remove the meat and add the chopped vegetables, cover the pan and cook gently for 5 minutes.
3. Return the beef to the pan on top of the vegetables. Tie the herbs into a small bundle with kitchen string and return to the pan, then pour on the liquid. Season with salt and pepper.

4. Bring to a simmer, cover and cook over a gentle heat for 2 hours or until the meat is very tender.

5. Remove the meat from the pan, cover and keep warm. Add the wholegrain mustard to the pan if you wish, increase the heat and boil the liquid until it thickens slightly and becomes syrupy. Strain out the vegetable solids and serve alongside the meat in a warmed jug, or slice the meat onto a warm platter and pour the meat juices over it.

VARIATION
You could also cook the roast in an ovenproof casserole dish for 2 hours in the oven at 160˚C.

Chilli Con Carne

1½ HOURS · SERVES 8

A Texan dish of beans and minced beef which was originally made very hot indeed. Adjust the amount of chilli powder to suit your taste.

2 Tbsp oil
1 onion, finely chopped
1 clove garlic, finely chopped
750g lean beef mince
425g can chopped tomatoes in juice
2 x 425g cans kidney beans, drained

1 bay leaf
2 tsp–2 Tbsp chilli powder (to taste)
salt
¼ tsp brown sugar
tortillas or corn chips

1. Put the oil, onion and garlic into a large saucepan and cook very gently, stirring occasionally, until the onions are golden and tender, about 10 minutes.

2. Add the minced beef and brown very lightly, then add all the other ingredients.

3. Bring to a slow simmer, cover with a close-fitting lid and cook very gently for about 1 hour or until the beef is tender.

4. Discard the bay leaf and serve with tortillas or corn chips.

Corned Beef

3 HOURS · SERVES 10

A very economical dish, excellent served hot with boiled potatoes or cold in a sandwich with pickle or chutney. 'Corned' is an old English word for salted meat.

1.5–2kg corned silverside
1 onion, peeled, halved and stuck with 6 cloves
1 Tbsp malt vinegar
10 black peppercorns
1 bay leaf

2–3 sprigs each of parsley and thyme
2 Tbsp brown sugar or golden syrup
Mustard Sauce (page 179), to serve

1. Put all the ingredients into a large saucepan and cover with cold water.

2. Bring to a simmer and cook, covered, for 30 minutes per 500g of meat or until the meat is tender when tested with a fine skewer.

3. Let the meat sit in its liquid for 20 minutes before slicing thickly to serve. If you want to serve the meat cold, let it cool in the liquid then remove and slice thinly. Reserve 1 cup of the liquid if you intend to make Mustard Sauce.

4. Serve hot with Mustard Sauce or bake for another hour with the spicy glaze below.

VARIATION
Corned Beef with a Spicy Glaze

12 whole cloves	*⅓ cup tomato sauce*
1 Tbsp mustard	*3 Tbsp vinegar*
⅓ cup brown sugar	*3 Tbsp water*

1. Preheat the oven to 180°C.
2. Stud the cooked corned beef with the cloves and place in an ovenproof dish.
3. Combine all the remaining glaze ingredients and pour the mixture over the corned beef.
4. Cook for 1 hour, basting every 15 minutes with the glaze. Serve hot.

Curried Sausages

Unknown in India but an old-fashioned New Zealand favourite in the British tradition of adding a curry-flavoured sauce to a variety of foods. Serve with rice or on toast.

8 sausages	*1 tsp hot curry powder*
1 Tbsp oil	*1 Tbsp Edmonds standard flour*
1 onion, chopped	*¾ cup chicken or vegetable stock*
1 clove garlic, crushed	*1 Tbsp relish or chutney*

1. Put the sausages into a saucepan of cold water and bring to the boil. Simmer for 5 minutes or until they are cooked, then drain. Remove the skins when they are cool enough to handle, then slice into chunks.
2. Put the oil, onion and garlic into a large saucepan and cook very gently, stirring occasionally, until the onion is golden and tender, about 10 minutes.
3. Stir in the curry powder and cook for 30 seconds, then add the flour and cook for another 30 seconds.
4. Add the stock gradually, stirring constantly, until the mixture boils. Simmer for 5 minutes, then add the sausages and relish and cook gently until the sausages are hot.

Hearty Beef Casserole

Very simply flavoured, this family casserole has plenty of gravy, so serve it with lots of fluffy mashed potato.

1kg chuck or blade steak, trimmed of excess fat	*2 carrots, sliced*
	salt and pepper
2 Tbsp oil	*1 bay leaf*
1 onion, chopped	*1 sprig thyme*
¼ cup Edmonds standard flour	*1 sprig parsley*
3 cups beef stock (page 112)	

1. Preheat the oven to 160°C.
2. Cut the meat into 2.5cm cubes. Put the oil and chopped onion into a heavy-based frying pan and cook gently for 10–15 minutes until the onion is translucent, but not browned. Use a slotted spoon to remove the onion and place it in a casserole dish.
3. Coat the meat in flour and, working in small batches, quickly brown it in the frying pan. Add the browned meat to the casserole.
4. Pour the beef stock slowly into the frying pan and bring to the boil, stirring to

Mussel Fritters page 138, Fish Pie Supreme page 136

Meat Loaf page 148, Any Fruit Chutney page 232

incorporate any meat residue. Add the carrots and season with salt and pepper to taste.

5. Make a bouquet garni by tying together the bay leaf, thyme and parsley with kitchen string. Add this to the meat in the casserole dish and then pour over the hot stock.

6. Cover the casserole and cook for 1½ hours or until the meat is tender. Remove the bouquet garni before serving.

VARIATIONS

Beef and Mushroom Casserole
Replace half the beef stock with red wine. Add ¼ cup tomato purée and 1 cup sliced mushrooms.

Beef and Mustard Casserole
At end of the cooking time, stir in 1 tablespoon wholegrain mustard.

Beef and Capsicum Casserole
Add 1 chopped red or green capsicum when cooking the onions.

Irish Stew

2½ HOURS   8 SERVES

Heavy on the potato and with tender, flavoursome lamb, this is a simple and delicious winter dish.

2kg potatoes
1kg lamb shoulder chops, trimmed of excess fat
500g onions, thickly sliced
salt and black pepper

2 cups water
2 bay leaves
several sprigs each of parsley and thyme

1. Slice three of the potatoes and halve the rest.

2. Put the sliced potatoes in a deep, heavy-based saucepan and then add the meat, the halved potatoes, onions, salt and pepper and the water. Tie the herbs in a bundle with kitchen string and put in the pan.

3. Bring to a gentle simmer, then cover with a close-fitting lid and cook gently for 2 hours. The stew will be thick and creamy. Remove the herb bundle before serving.

Lamb Curry

3 HOURS   4 SERVES

A delicious creamy sauce coating tender cubes of lamb, this curry is quick to put together and can also be made with pork or beef. Serve with Raita (page 180).

500g boned lamb shoulder, cut into cubes, or pork pieces or chuck steak
1 onion, finely chopped
2.5cm piece of fresh ginger, finely chopped
200g canned tomatoes in juice
3 Tbsp chopped coriander
1 fresh green chilli, sliced
¼ tsp turmeric

1 tsp ground cumin
4 Tbsp natural unsweetened yoghurt
1 Tbsp tomato purée
salt
3 Tbsp butter or oil
4 cloves garlic, finely chopped
½ cup hot water
rice
extra chopped coriander

Brown meat in batches. Browning too much meat at once causes the meat to stew in its own juices making it tough.

1. Combine all the ingredients except the butter, garlic, water, rice and extra coriander in a bowl and mix well.

2. Heat the butter gently in a heavy-based saucepan with the chopped garlic. When the garlic becomes slightly golden and aromatic, after about 30 seconds, add all the other ingredients.

3. Bring to a simmer, cover and cook very gently for 1½ hours, or 2 hours for beef. Serve with rice and sprinkled with more chopped coriander.

Liver & Bacon

30 MINS   4 SERVES

Richly favoured liver and salty bacon are perfect partners.

500g lamb's liver (lamb's fry), skin removed
1½ Tbsp Edmonds standard flour
salt and pepper

1 Tbsp butter
8 rashers bacon, rind removed
¼ cup hot water
lemon wedges and chopped parsley

1. Slice the liver into 1cm thick slices then coat in flour seasoned with salt and pepper.

2. Heat the butter in a frying pan and cook the liver for 2–3 minutes on each side over a high heat, then place in a warmed serving dish.

3. Fry the rashers of bacon in the same pan until crisp and place on the liver. Season with salt and pepper.

4. Pour the hot water into the pan and bring to the boil, stirring up all the juices from the meats, then pour this gravy over the liver and bacon. Squeeze over a little lemon juice and sprinkle with parsley.

Meat Loaf

1½ HOURS   10 SERVES

A classic picnic dish, delicious hot or cold.

MEAT LOAF
500g lean beef mince
500g sausage meat, or peeled sausages
1 onion, finely chopped
2 cloves garlic, crushed
1 egg

1 cup grated carrot
½ cup chopped parsley
2 tsp prepared mustard
2 tsp mixed herbs
1 tsp salt
pepper

TOPPING
2 Tbsp rolled oats
1 Tbsp brown sugar

2 Tbsp tomato sauce
¼ cup chopped parsley

1. Preheat the oven to 190°C.

2. Combine the meat loaf ingredients and mix well. Combine all the topping ingredients.

3. Press the meat loaf mixture into a 22cm loaf tin, spread with the prepared topping and cover with tinfoil.

4. Cook for 30 minutes, then remove the foil and cook for a further 30 minutes or until the juices run clear when tested with a skewer. Serve hot or cold.

Pork Chops Baked with Apple & Rosemary

1½ HOURS   4 SERVES

Soaking pork chops in a salt water brine for just half an hour before cooking them adds flavour and tenderises the meat. Brining is a good idea with today's very lean pork, which can be dry when cooked.

BRINE
4 Tbsp salt   *4 cups cold water*

PORK
4 large pork chops   *3 Tbsp olive oil*
3 apples, peeled and sliced   *salt and pepper*
2 tsp chopped rosemary

1. Dissolve the salt in the water, pour over the pork chops in a shallow ovenproof dish so that they are covered, and chill for 30 minutes to 2 hours.
2. Preheat the oven to 190°C.
3. Drain the pork chops and pat them dry with paper towels. Using a sharp knife or kitchen scissors make small cuts into the fat along the edge of the chops. This will keep them flat as they cook.
4. Combine the sliced apples, rosemary and 1 tablespoon of the oil and scatter over the base of an ovenproof dish that will fit the pork chops in a single layer.
5. Season the chops with salt and pepper. Place the remaining oil in a heavy-based frying pan and sear the pork chops until they are golden brown on both sides then lie them on top of the apples. Cover with tinfoil.
6. Bake for 25 minutes, then remove the cover and cook for another 10 minutes or until the chops are very tender.

Shepherd's Pie or Cottage Pie

1½ HOURS   6 SERVES

Shepherd's Pie is made with lamb and Cottage Pie with beef. Both were originally ways of using up leftover roast meat by chopping it finely, mixing with stock or gravy and reheating with a good layer of mashed potato on the top. You can also make either pie from minced raw meat.

FILLING
1 Tbsp oil   *1 Tbsp tomato purée*
1 onion, chopped   *¾ cup beef stock*
500g lean lamb or beef mince   *1 Tbsp chutney or relish*
2 Tbsp Edmonds standard flour

TOPPING
3 potatoes, chopped   *salt and black pepper*
50g butter   *½ cup grated tasty cheese*
1 Tbsp finely chopped onion

1. Put the oil and onion in a large saucepan and cook very gently, stirring occasionally, until the onion is translucent and tender, about 10 minutes.
2. Add the mince and cook until just browned, stirring constantly. Add the flour and cook for 1 minute, stirring, then add the tomato purée, stock and chutney or relish.
3. Bring to a simmer and cook gently for 15–20 minutes.

4. Cook the potatoes in boiling, salted water until tender, then drain and return to the pan. Heat gently to remove excess moisture, shaking the pan.

5. Preheat the oven to 190°C.

6. Mash the potato with the butter, onion, salt and pepper and half of the grated cheese. Beat until smooth and creamy.

7. Put the mince into a pie dish and top with the mashed potato. Sprinkle with the remaining grated cheese.

8. Bake for 20 minutes or until the top is crisp and golden.

Steak & Kidney Pie

4 HOURS   6 SERVES

Golden flaky pastry over tender savoury meat – slow cooked to melting perfection.

1kg beef chuck or blade steak
2–3 lamb kidneys
1 Tbsp Edmonds standard flour
1 tsp salt
1 tsp black pepper
½ tsp mixed dried herbs
½ cup water

200g Rough Puff Pastry (page 102) or
* 2 sheets Edmonds flaky puff pastry,*
* thawed*
1 egg yolk
1 Tbsp water
salt

1. Make the steak and kidney filling first. Cut the meat into 2.5cm cubes, core the kidneys and chop them into small pieces.

2. Toss the meats with the flour, salt and pepper and mixed herbs, put them into a deep casserole and pour over the water.

3. Cover tightly and cook, just at a simmer, for about 2 hours – or cook in the oven at 160°C for 2½ hours. Cool.

4. Preheat the oven to 200°C.

5. Put the steak and kidney filling into a deep pie dish. On a lightly floured board, roll out the pastry to 3cm larger than the pie dish or join the ready-rolled sheets.

6. Cut a 3cm wide strip off the edge, wet the edge of the pie dish with water and place the pastry strip all round. Cover the filling with the rest of the pastry, pressing the edges firmly together.

7. Pierce holes in the centre of the pastry top and decorate with pastry trimmings rolled out and cut into decorative shapes. Chill for 20 minutes. Beat the egg yolk, water and salt together and brush over the pastry.

8. Bake for 20 minutes, and then reduce the heat to 180°C and bake for another 30 minutes. Cover the pastry with tinfoil to prevent overbrowning.

VARIATION
Steak and Kidney Pie with Mushrooms
Add 120g sliced or quartered mushrooms to the steak and kidney mixture before cooking.

Wiener Schnitzel

1 HOUR   6 SERVES

Crunchy on the outside and tender inside, this is a favourite dish in Germany and Austria. Traditionally made with veal, but also with beef or pork.

1 egg	*6 x 100g pieces of beef*
1 Tbsp water	* or pork schnitzel*
½ cup Edmonds standard flour	*2 Tbsp oil*
1 cup fine, dry breadcrumbs	*50g butter*
	lemon wedges

1. Beat the egg and water together and pour them on a shallow plate. Put the flour on another plate and the breadcrumbs on a third.

2. Dip the pieces of schnitzel first into the flour, then the egg, then the breadcrumbs, and set aside on a plate. Cover and chill for 20 minutes. The chilling helps the coating to set and stops it falling off when you fry the schnitzel.

3. Heat the oil and butter in a frying pan, add the schnitzel in two or three batches and cook until golden on both sides, turning once. Add a little more oil for each batch. Serve with lemon wedges.

Yorkshire Pudding

1½ HOURS   4 SERVES

A basic batter, baked in the oven to puffy, golden perfection. Designed to accompany a good roast of beef.

1 cup Edmonds standard flour	*300ml milk, approximately*
pinch of salt	*2 Tbsp beef dripping or butter*
1 egg	

1. Sift the flour and salt together and make a well in the centre. Break in the egg and add enough milk to mix to a smooth batter.

2. Beat well, cover and let stand for at least 30 minutes and up to 4 hours.

3. Preheat the oven to 200°C.

4. Put the beef dripping or butter in a pan or pie dish and heat in the oven until smoking hot.

5. Pour in the batter and bake for 30–40 minutes until browned and puffy and crisp at the edges. Cut into squares to serve with roast beef.

Chicken

Only a generation ago, chicken was a luxurious treat for most Kiwi families. Today this versatile white meat is something many enjoy every other day.

How to roast a chicken:

- Make sure the chicken is at room temperature by taking it from the refrigerator 30 minutes before you start cooking.
- Preheat the oven to 200°C.
- Season the chicken's cavity with salt and pepper and, if you wish, a few sprigs of thyme, a crushed garlic clove and half an unpeeled lemon.
- If you have made a stuffing, fill the cavity loosely and close the opening with a short bamboo skewer.
- Weigh the chicken after it is stuffed to work out the cooking time.
- Roasting time for chicken is 25 minutes per 500g, plus 20 minutes.
- Rub the skin generously with olive oil or softened butter and season with salt and pepper.
- Put the chicken in a roasting dish, not much larger than the bird, breast side down. Pour in 1 cup of hot water or stock and roast for 35 minutes.
- Take the roasting dish out of the oven, carefully turn the chicken onto its back, squeeze the juice of the other lemon half over the breast and roast for the remaining time.
- Test by piercing the thickest part of the thigh with a fine skewer. If clear juice runs out the chicken is cooked.
- Leave the cooked chicken in a warm place to rest for 5–10 minutes before serving it.
- Always warm the dinner plates for a roast meal.

Basic Sage and Onion Stuffing

An old-fashioned stuffing, but a good one. Try to use fresh sage leaves since dried sage has a musty flavour.

3 cups soft breadcrumbs
1 onion, finely chopped
1 tsp chopped fresh sage leaves

2 Tbsp melted butter
1 egg
salt and pepper

1. Combine all the ingredients in a bowl and mix well. Stuff the chicken loosely and bake any extra stuffing in a small, oiled ovenproof dish.

VARIATIONS

Sausage Stuffing
Add 200g sausage meat or skinned sausages to half a quantity of sage and onion stuffing.

Orange and Rosemary Stuffing
Add 2 tablespoons finely grated orange zest and replace the sage with 2 teaspoon's finely chopped rosemary.

Apricot Stuffing
Replace the sage with ½ cup chopped dried apricots which have been soaked in ¼ cup orange juice for 2 hours.

Chicken and Orange Casserole

1 HOUR · 4 SERVES

A spicy casserole with a tangy orange sauce which can be made on the stove-top or oven baked.

50g butter
8 chicken pieces
1 onion, finely chopped
1 cup sliced celery
½ cup orange juice
1 Tbsp finely grated orange zest

¼ tsp cinnamon
¼ tsp ground ginger
½ cup chicken stock (Page 112)
1 Tbsp Edmonds Fielder's cornflour
1 Tbsp white vinegar

1. Preheat the oven to 180°C if using.

2. Melt the butter in a large frying pan or heatproof casserole dish. Add the chicken and quickly brown on all sides. Remove from the pan and set aside.

3. Add the onion and celery to the pan and cook gently, stirring occasionally, until the onion is translucent and tender, about 10 minutes.

4. Add the orange juice and zest, spices and stock and bring to a simmer, then return the chicken pieces to the pan.

5. Cover and bake in the oven for about 40 minutes or for 30 minutes on the stove-top. Test that the chicken is cooked by piercing the thickest part of the meat; if the juices run clear it is done.

6. Mix the cornflour and vinegar to a smooth paste, add to the casserole and stir until the juices thicken. Taste for seasoning and serve with rice or potatoes and green vegetables.

Chicken Cashew Nut Stir-fry

40 MINS · 4 SERVES

Using chicken thighs is best to keep the meat moist and juicy.

300g skinless, boneless chicken thighs
2 tsp Edmonds Fielder's cornflour
1 egg white
¼ tsp salt
2 Tbsp hoisin sauce
1 Tbsp soy sauce
2 tsp sesame oil
1 tsp chilli sauce

3 Tbsp vegetable oil
½ cup cashew nuts
1 clove garlic, finely chopped
1 tsp finely chopped fresh ginger
1 red capsicum, seeded and finely sliced
100g button mushrooms, sliced
2 spring onions, sliced

1. Slice the chicken thighs into thin strips. Combine the cornflour, egg white and salt, mix with the chicken and chill for 20 minutes.
2. Combine the hoisin sauce, soy sauce, sesame oil and chilli sauce and set aside.
3. Heat a wok or large frying pan with 1 tablespoon of the oil and stir-fry the cashew nuts until lightly browned. Drain on paper towels.
4. Add the remaining oil to the wok and quickly stir-fry the garlic and ginger for about 30 seconds, then put in the chicken strips and toss for 1 minute.
5. Add the capsicum and mushrooms and stir-fry until the chicken is white and cooked, about 1–2 minutes.
6. Pour over the combined sauces and cook for another 2 minutes, making sure everything is coated with the sauce.
7. Add the cashew nuts and spring onions, stir once and place on a heated serving dish. Serve at once with steamed jasmine or short grain rice, crunchy lettuce and a tomato and cucumber salad.

Chicken Enchiladas

A famous Mexican dish of chicken-filled tortillas quickly baked with hot tomato sauce and cheese. Tender homemade tortillas and a creamy sauce make this dish a real treat.

TOMATO SAUCE

450g tomatoes	*2 Tbsp vegetable oil*
1 clove garlic	*½ tsp salt*
2–3 jalapeño or serrano chillies (canned), or ½ tsp chilli powder	*½ cup sour cream, at room temperature*

ENCHILADAS

2 Tbsp oil	*1 onion, very finely chopped*
8 fresh Flour Tortillas (page 15)	*¾ cup grated tasty cheese*
1½ cups shredded, cooked chicken	*1 Tbsp chopped parsley or coriander*

1. Halve the tomatoes and cook them on an oiled griddle or in a heavy-based frying pan, turning once, until the skin is slightly charred and the flesh is soft.
2. In a blender or food processor, purée the tomatoes, garlic and chillies until smooth, then fry the mixture in the oil for about 5 minutes until it has thickened slightly.
3. Add the salt, and then stir in the sour cream and heat very gently. Don't allow the sauce to boil or it will curdle.
4. Preheat the oven to 180°C.
5. Heat the oil in a frying pan and fry each tortilla quickly for about 15 seconds, turning once, without letting them become crisp. They should be just slightly heated.
6. Dip each tortilla in the warm tomato sauce, letting the excess drip off, and then transfer to a plate and spread with 2 tablespoons of the shredded chicken and sprinkle with chopped onion. Roll up loosely and place side by side in an ovenproof dish. (This is a slightly messy operation, but do persevere – it is worth it.)
7. Pour the remaining tomato sauce over the tortillas and sprinkle with the grated cheese and any remaining onion.
8. Bake for just 10 minutes to heat through and melt the cheese, sprinkle with chopped parsley or coriander and serve immediately.

Do not use the same cutting board for raw chicken and vegetables.

NOTE
Make extra batches of the tomato sauce while tomatoes are cheap and plentiful and freeze. Just don't add the sour cream until after you have defrosted the sauce.

Coronation Chicken Canapés

1 HOUR   24 MAKES

Coronation Chicken was served at the luncheon after the coronation of Queen Elizabeth II in June 1953 and it has remained popular ever since. Tender pieces of chicken are combined with a mild curry-flavoured mayonnaise and, in this variation, served in crisp bread cases as canapés.

24 slices white sandwich bread
150g butter, melted
250g chicken breast or boneless thighs
50g Mayonnaise (page 178) or
    Edmonds whole egg mayonnaise

2 Tbsp mango or other fruit chutney
1 tsp curry powder
2 Tbsp lemon juice
salt and pepper
chopped parsley

1. Preheat the oven to 200°C. Cut out 24 rounds, one from each piece of bread with a 7cm cutter. Brush the rounds with the melted butter and place them, butter side down, in patty tins.
2. Bake for 8 minutes or until crisp and golden, and set aside to cool.
3. Poach the chicken over a gentle heat in just enough water to cover it for about 10 minutes or until cooked. Cool and chop into small pieces.
4. Gently mix together all the remaining ingredients except the parsley and adjust seasoning.
5. Put spoonfuls of the coronation chicken into the bread cases, sprinkle with chopped parsley and serve immediately.

Curried Chicken

40 MINS   4 SERVES

This is a quickly made, mildly spiced curry, relatively sweet because of the apple. If you would like more heat add ¼–½ teaspoon chilli powder with the curry powder.

1 Tbsp oil
1 onion, finely chopped
6 boneless chicken thighs,
    600g approximately
2 cloves garlic, crushed
1 tsp grated fresh ginger
1 Tbsp curry powder

1 tsp Edmonds Fielder's cornflour
1 cup chicken stock
1 apple, peeled and cut into small
    cubes (optional)
1 Tbsp lemon juice
2 Tbsp toasted, shredded coconut

1. Place the oil in a large frying pan with the onion. Cook gently until the onion is translucent, about 10 minutes.
2. Cut the chicken into bite-sized chunks while the onion is cooking.
3. Add the crushed garlic and grated ginger and stir for 10 seconds, then add the curry powder and cook, stirring, for 30 seconds.
4. Add the chicken chunks, and stir for 2–3 minutes until lightly browned on all sides.

Coronation chicken also makes an excellent sandwich filling and the bread cases can be used with other savoury fillings.

5. Mix the cornflour with a little of the stock until smooth, then add the rest of the stock and pour this mixture into the pan. Cook, stirring, until the mixture thickens a little. Simmer gently for 5 minutes, and then add the apples if using and simmer for 10 minutes more, stirring occasionally. Mix through the lemon juice and adjust seasoning.

6. Sprinkle with toasted coconut and serve with White Rice (page 126) or Almond Pilaf (page 124) and some fruit chutney on the side.

Family Chicken Pie

Serve with a green salad for the perfect family meal.

8 boneless chicken thighs
2 Tbsp oil
3 rashers bacon, chopped
100g mushrooms
1 onion, chopped
1 clove garlic, crushed
2 Tbsp Edmonds standard flour
1 cup chicken stock
¼ tsp mixed herbs

½ cup milk
½ tsp salt
white pepper
1 cup sweet corn kernels
200g Rough Puff Pastry (page 102) or
    2 sheets Edmonds flaky puff pastry,
    thawed
1 egg yolk
1 Tbsp water

1. Skin the chicken thighs and cut the meat into 2.5cm pieces.

2. Place the oil in a large saucepan with the bacon, mushrooms, onion and garlic and cook gently, stirring, until the onion is translucent and tender, about 10 minutes.

3. Stir in the flour and cook until frothy, then gradually add the stock and bring to the boil.

4. Add the chicken pieces, herbs, milk, salt and pepper to taste, then cook gently for 20 minutes, stirring occasionally. Remove from the heat and allow to cool.

5. Add the sweet corn kernels – drained if from a can, thawed if frozen – and pour the mixture into a 20cm pie dish and brush the edge of the dish with water.

6. Preheat the oven to 200°C.

7. On a lightly floured board, roll out the pastry to a circle large enough to fit the top of the pie dish or join the ready-rolled sheets. Carefully place the pastry over the filling and press to the edges of the dish to firmly seal. Trim away any excess and reroll, then cut out some decorative shapes and place them on the pie, holding them in place with a little water.

8. Brush the pastry top with the egg yolk beaten with the water and make a few slits in the top of the pie to allow the steam to escape.

9. Bake for 10 minutes, then reduce the heat to 180°C and bake for a further 20 minutes until the pastry is golden and well risen.

Toast coconut by stirring it in a dry frying pan over a gentle heat until it turns
a pink-gold colour and smells toasted.

Lemon Fried Chicken Drumsticks

5 HOURS | 4 SERVES

Tender, golden and flavoursome, these drumsticks are economical and always popular. The chicken is marinated in lemon juice, then quickly fried and finished off in the oven to ensure that it cooks completely and the outside does not burn. Great for a crowd or a picnic.

8 chicken drumsticks, skin on
¼ cup lemon juice
1½ tsp salt
3 cloves garlic, crushed

½ tsp ground black pepper
½ cup Edmonds standard flour
1 cup vegetable oil for frying

1. Arrange the chicken drumsticks in a single layer in a shallow dish. Mix together the lemon juice, 1 teaspoon of the salt, the garlic and half the pepper and pour over the chicken.

2. Cover the dish and refrigerate for 4 hours or overnight. Turn the pieces over in the juice a couple of times.

3. When you are ready to cook, preheat the oven to 180°C.

4. Drain the chicken legs and discard the lemon juice. Place the flour and the remaining salt and pepper in a large plastic bag and shake the drained chicken in the bag a few pieces at a time, then remove and set aside.

5. Heat the oil in a wok or heavy-based frying pan and brown the chicken pieces, a few at a time, turning once. When the pieces are golden brown, remove from the pan and transfer to a shallow ovenproof dish.

6. Bake in the oven for about 30 minutes or until cooked. Test by inserting a fine skewer into the thickest part of a drumstick; if clear juice runs out the chicken is ready. Drain on paper towels and serve hot or cold.

Marinated Chicken Nibbles

1¾ HOURS | 6 SERVES

Sticky, spicy, delicious and both quick and easy to make.

3 cloves garlic, crushed
3 Tbsp soy sauce
2 Tbsp liquid honey
pepper

1 Tbsp tomato sauce
1 Tbsp grated fresh ginger
500g chicken nibbles or wings
2 tsp sesame seeds

1. Combine the garlic, soy sauce, honey, pepper, tomato sauce and ginger and pour over the chicken in a shallow dish and cover. Alternatively, put the marinade and chicken into a large snaplock bag, seal and shake the bag so that the chicken is coated with the marinade. Chill for 1 hour.

2. Preheat the oven to 200°C. Line a shallow ovenproof tray with baking paper.

3. Lie the chicken pieces on the prepared tray and sprinkle with the sesame seeds.

4. Bake for 30–35 minutes or until crisp and golden and serve hot or at room temperature.

Press garlic cloves with the flat of the knife to remove skin.

Vegetables

'Meat and two veg' used to be the rule, but New Zealanders now enjoy more vegetables and have a much wider variety to choose from. When you can, select seasonal vegetables as they will most likely be fresher, locally grown, and less expensive than out-of-season produce.

How to store vegetables:

Store most fresh vegetables and herbs in the refrigerator crisper. Always keep tomatoes at room temperature and keep potatoes, kumara, onions, garlic and pumpkins in a cool, dark, dry place.

How to cook vegetables:

Steaming

A quick and efficient way of cooking many vegetables. Put the prepared vegetables in a steaming basket or a perforated steamer set over rapidly boiling water and cover with a lid. You could use a metal sieve or colander instead of a custom-made steamer. Steam the vegetables until they are just tender.

Boiling

Put the prepared vegetables into a small amount of boiling water in a saucepan. Root vegetables like potatoes and kumara require more cooking water than green vegetables. Cover and bring the water quickly back to boiling point. Cook the vegetables over a moderate heat until they are tender, then drain. You can use the cooking water, which is a light vegetable stock, for sauces, soups, risotto or gravy.

Roasting winter vegetables

Preheat the oven to 200°C. Peel the vegetables if you wish – potatoes, kumara, pumpkin, parsnips, and onions – and cut them into wedges or chunks of a similar size. If you are roasting garlic, peel the cloves if you wish and leave them whole. Put 2–3 tablespoons of oil in a roasting pan and heat on top of the stove then add the vegetables and turn them over in the hot oil, and season with salt and pepper and some chopped herbs. Roast for 45 minutes to 1 hour, turning the vegetables at least once. Keep warm until ready to serve.

Stir-frying

Onions, carrots, mushrooms, capsicums and all green vegetables are suitable for stir-frying. Cut them into fine sticks, rounds or small florets so they will cook quickly. Heat a small amount of oil in a frying pan or wok and add the vegetables that need longer cooking first, for example broccoli, carrot, cauliflower or onion. Cook quickly, tossing the vegetables so that they are constantly on the move. When the first vegetables are almost cooked, add the remaining ones – mushrooms, cabbage, lettuce, spinach, spring onions – which need a shorter cooking time. Cook all the vegetables until they are tender but still crisp.

Microwaving

Cut the vegetables to a similar size and place in a shallow microwave dish with a small amount of water. Cover. Stir once during the cooking time and then leave the vegetables to stand for about one-third of the total cooking time, still covered. Add salt and other seasonings after cooking.

Baked Potatoes

1 HOUR   4 SERVES

Old, floury potatoes are best for baking – Agria is a good variety.

4 large potatoes of about the same size

TOPPINGS

butter or sour cream
crisply cooked bacon, crumbled

grated cheese
chopped chives

1. Preheat the oven to 200°C.
2. Scrub the potatoes and dry them well then pierce the skin in several places with a fine skewer.
3. Put the potatoes directly onto the rack in the centre of the oven and cook for about 1 hour.
4. Test the potatoes with a skewer to check if the centre is completely soft.
5. Remove from the oven with care – they will be extremely hot – cut a cross in the top of each potato with a sharp knife and push in at the sides so that the top opens out. Serve with butter or other toppings of your choice.

Cauliflower Cheese

40 MINS   6 SERVES

Cauliflower in cheese sauce is always a winner – you could extend it with some macaroni as well if you wish.

1 cauliflower, divided into large florets
25g butter
2 Tbsp Edmonds standard flour
2 cups milk, heated

¾ cup grated tasty cheese
salt and white pepper
½ tsp mustard (optional)

1. Preheat the oven to 190°C.
2. Steam the cauliflower or cook it in boiling salted water until tender, then drain well.
3. While the cauliflower is cooking, melt the butter in a saucepan, stir in the flour and cook until frothy.
4. Remove from the heat and gradually add the milk, stirring.
5. Return to the heat and cook gently, stirring, until the sauce boils and thickens.
6. Remove from the heat and add ½ cup of the cheese, salt and pepper to taste, and the mustard.
7. Put the drained cauliflower into an ovenproof serving dish, pour over the sauce and sprinkle with the remaining cheese.
8. Cook for 20 minutes or until golden.

Curried Cabbage

30 MINS · SERVES 6

A warming winter dish to accompany casseroles and roasts.

½ cabbage, shredded
1 Tbsp oil or butter
1 small onion, finely chopped

2 bacon rashers, chopped
1 tsp curry powder
salt and pepper

1. Add the cabbage to a saucepan of boiling water and lightly boil for 5–6 minutes. Just enough to cook the cabbage but still leave a bit of crunch. Drain.
2. Add the oil to a frypan and cook the onion until it is soft. Add the bacon and cook for another 2 minutes.
3. Sprinkle over the curry powder, add the cooked cabbage and stir until combined and heated through. Season to taste with salt and pepper to serve.

Gratin Dauphinois

2 HOURS · SERVES 4

A famous French dish of sliced potatoes cooked with cream – simple and superb.
Use waxy potatoes which hold together when cooked, like Nadine or Jersey Benne.

50g butter
500g waxy potatoes
1 clove garlic, crushed

300ml cream
salt and pepper

1. Preheat the oven to 170°C. Grease a shallow ovenproof dish with the butter.
2. Peel the potatoes and slice them as thinly as you can, about 5mm.
3. Place the garlic and cream in a saucepan and heat until almost boiling.
4. In the ovenproof dish, layer the potatoes in overlapping rounds, seasoning each layer with salt and pepper, and pour over the cream
5. Bake for 1½ hours, then increase the heat to 200°C for another 10 minutes to create a golden crust.

Hash Brown Potatoes

1 HOUR · SERVES 6

Use leftover boiled potatoes for this classic American breakfast dish – especially great with a fried egg on top.

1kg floury potatoes, halved
salt and pepper
2 rashers bacon

50g butter
2 Tbsp olive oil
1 onion, finely chopped

1. Cook the potatoes in boiling salted water until tender, drain well and cut into 1cm cubes. Season with salt and pepper.
2. Put the bacon in a large frying pan and cook until crisp and brown. Remove from the pan and drain on paper towels.
3. Add the butter, oil and chopped onion to the pan with the bacon fat and cook gently until the onion softens, about 5 minutes.

4. Spread the potatoes evenly over the onion, press down with a spatula and cook over a low heat for at least 20 minutes, shaking the pan occasionally. The underside should be a deep golden brown.

5. Loosen the potatoes with a spatula, then cover the pan with a large plate, turn the pan over so that the potatoes drop onto the plate, and slide them back into the pan.

6. Cook the other side, pressing down with a spatula until golden and crisp. Serve with cooked bacon.

Mashed Potatoes

For a really creamy mash choose floury potatoes like Agria, cook them whole to prevent them becoming waterlogged and use hot milk to keep them fluffy and light.

6 potatoes, peeled
50g butter

½ cup hot milk
salt and pepper

1. Put the potatoes in a saucepan of cold, salted water and bring to the boil. Cover and cook for about 25 minutes until the potatoes are tender when pierced with a sharp knife.

2. Drain well, return to the saucepan and heat gently, shaking the pan until the potatoes are dry.

3. Mash with a potato masher, then beat until smooth with a wooden spoon or a whisk.

4. Add the butter and hot milk and beat until fluffy, seasoning with salt and pepper to taste.

Mixed Vegetable Fritters

Make these with one or two different vegetables for a bright combination of colours and tastes.

2 eggs
¼ cup milk
½ cup Edmonds self raising flour
1 tsp curry powder
½ tsp salt
ground black pepper
¼ cup chopped parsley

2 cups grated raw vegetables –
  e.g pumpkin, carrots, kumara,
  courgette, beetroot
1 onion, grated
2 Tbsp oil
Yoghurt Dressing (page 184)

1. Beat the eggs and the milk together, then add the flour, curry powder, salt and pepper, and whisk until smooth. Stir in the parsley and set aside for 10 minutes.

2. Add the grated vegetables and onion to the batter and combine thoroughly.

3. Heat the oil in a heavy-based frying pan and drop in large tablespoonfuls of the mixture.

4. Cook until golden underneath then turn over with a spatula and cook the other side. Drain on paper towels and serve hot, or keep warm in the oven at 160°C for up to 20 minutes. Serve with the Yoghurt Dressing.

Mock Whitebait Patties

30 MINS · 2 SERVES

These have been a favourite in the Edmonds Cookery Book for many decades. They taste nothing like whitebait, of course, but you could add a pinch of poppy seeds to the batter to mimic those tiny black eyes...

2½ Tbsp Edmonds standard flour
2 Tbsp milk
3 Tbsp grated cheese
salt and pepper

1 egg, beaten
1 potato, peeled and grated
1 tsp Edmonds baking powder
3 Tbsp oil

1. Add the flour, milk, cheese and seasonings to the beaten egg and set aside for 10 minutes.
2. Add the grated potato to the batter with the baking powder just before you cook the patties.
3. Heat the oil in a heavy-based frying pan and drop in tablespoonfuls of the mixture.
4. Cook for 5 minutes on each side until golden, drain on paper towels and serve hot, or keep warm in the oven at 160°C for up to 20 minutes.

Mushrooms on Toast

15 MINS · 1 SERVES

A quick lunch or breakfast dish of meaty mushrooms in a creamy sauce.

30g butter
200g large, flat mushrooms,
  thickly sliced
1 Tbsp Edmonds standard flour
salt and pepper
¼ cup milk

¼ cup cream
1 tsp lemon juice
2 slices buttered toast
finely chopped parsley

1. Melt the butter gently in a frying pan and add the mushrooms. Cook, stirring, until the mushrooms are dark brown and tender, then sprinkle over the flour and mix well.
2. Season with salt and pepper then add the milk and cream and bring to the boil, stirring.
3. Mix through the lemon juice and spoon the mushrooms onto the buttered toast. Sprinkle with parsley and serve.

Orange and Ginger Carrots

20 MINS · 6 SERVES

Cooking carrots this way accentuates their sweetness and beauty.

4–6 carrots, cut into sticks
1 tsp ground ginger
½ cup orange juice
2 Tbsp water

½ tsp salt
2 Tbsp brown sugar
2 Tbsp butter

1. Put all the ingredients into a saucepan. Bring to the boil, stirring until the sugar has dissolved.

Almond Pilaf page 124
Lemon Fried Chicken
Drumsticks page 157
Curried Chicken page 155

Sweet & Sour Red Cabbage page 166
Hearty Beef Casserole 144
Orange & Ginger Carrots page 162

2. Reduce the heat and simmer, uncovered, until the carrots are just tender and the liquid has reduced to a glaze. This should take 8–10 minutes.

NOTE
TO MICROWAVE
Put the carrots, ginger and orange juice in a microwave-proof dish with the water. Cook on high power (100%) for 5–7 minutes or until just tender. Add the salt, brown sugar and butter and cook for 1 minute.

Potato Bake

1½ HOURS · SERVES 4

In this famous Swedish dish, called Jansson's Temptation, shredded potatoes and onions are baked with anchovies and cream and topped with crispy breadcrumbs. The anchovies melt into the potatoes giving a subtle, salty tang.

30g butter
2 onions, thinly sliced
8 potatoes, peeled
12 anchovy fillets

300ml cream
30g butter
1 Tbsp dried breadcrumbs

1. Preheat the oven to 220°C. Grease an ovenproof dish with butter.
2. Heat the first measure of butter in a frying pan and cook the onion gently for 5 minutes.
3. Cut the potatoes into fine matchsticks, or grate them coarsely.
4. Cover the base of the dish with a third of the potatoes, top with half the onions and half the anchovies. Repeat the layers and finish with the last of the potatoes.
5. Pour half the cream over the dish, dot with pieces of butter and sprinkle with the breadcrumbs.
6. Bake for 45 minutes, then pour the remaining cream around the edges of the potatoes and return to the oven for another 5 minutes.

Pumpkin, Spinach & Feta Bake

1½ HOURS · SERVES 4

Roasted buttercup pumpkin baked with feta cheese and spinach makes a flavoursome vegetarian dinner.

1kg buttercup or butternut pumpkin,
   peeled and seeded
1 tsp fennel seeds (optional)
4 cloves garlic, chopped
2 small dried red chillies, finely
   chopped
3 Tbsp olive oil
100g spinach or silver beet

300g feta cheese
¼ cup sour cream or natural
   unsweetened yoghurt
¼ cup grated parmesan
1 egg, beaten
1 spring onion, finely chopped
extra parmesan
fresh basil leaves, torn

1. Preheat the oven to 200°C. Line a shallow baking tray with baking paper.
2. Cut the pumpkin into 1cm slices and toss in the baking tray with the fennel seeds if using, garlic, chilli and olive oil. Cover the tray with tinfoil and roast for 30 minutes or until tender.

3. Wash the spinach or silver beet, steam for 2–3 minutes until wilted, then drain and roughly chop.

4. Mash the feta roughly and mix in the sour cream or yoghurt, parmesan and egg. Add the steamed spinach and spring onion.

5. Put the roasted pumpkin into an oiled ovenproof dish, or divide between individual dishes and top with the feta and spinach mixture. Sprinkle with extra parmesan cheese and torn basil.

6. Bake for 20–25 minutes or until golden.

VARIATION

Line the dish with 3 sheets Edmonds filo pastry, lightly brushed with melted butter, then layer in the pumpkin and the cheese mixture, and top with 3 more sheets of pastry, crumpled at the edges to seal. Brush with water and bake as above. A delicious vegetable pie.

Ratatouille

Here is a simple method of cooking this famous medley of summer vegetables. You can eat it warm or cold with meat or an omelette, or with crusty bread for lunch – imagine yourself in the South of France.

1 onion, sliced
1 aubergine, unpeeled, cubed
2 red capsicums, seeded
*   and cut into strips*
3 courgettes, cut into rounds

4 tomatoes, sliced
¼ cup olive oil
salt and pepper
6 cloves garlic, peeled

1. Layer the vegetables in a deep, heavy-based saucepan in the order given, sprinkling a little olive oil and salt and pepper over each layer and tucking the garlic cloves between the layers.

2. Cook over a gentle heat with the lid on for about 1 hour. Remove the lid and allow any excess liquid to evaporate.

NOTE

You can adjust the quantities of vegetables. Courgettes are not essential, but ratatouille must include tomatoes.

Sweet & Sour Red Cabbage

Meltingly tender, slow-cooked cabbage – perfect with sausages, meat loaf or corned beef.

½ red cabbage, shredded
3 Tbsp butter
1 onion, finely chopped
1 apple, cored and thinly sliced

2 Tbsp brown sugar or honey
2 Tbsp vinegar
pinch of caraway seeds (optional)
salt and pepper

1. Soak the red cabbage in cold water for 15 minutes.

2. While the cabbage is soaking, melt the butter in a large, heavy-based saucepan and gently fry the onion until soft and golden, about 10–15 minutes.

3. Lift the cabbage out of the water with your hands, leaving it moist, and add to the pan with the remaining ingredients. Stir to combine then bring gently to a simmer.

4. Cover and cook very gently for about 1½ hours until the cabbage has absorbed most of the liquid and is very tender. Check to see that it is not sticking during this time and add a little hot water if necessary. Taste and season with salt and pepper.

Sweet Corn Fritters

20 MINS   6 SERVES

Always popular for a weekend brunch.

¾ cup Edmonds standard flour
1 tsp Edmonds baking powder
½ tsp salt
pepper
1 egg

440g can cream-style sweet corn
2 Tbsp oil
tomato or chilli sauce
  and sour cream

1. Sift the flour, baking powder, salt and pepper into a bowl and add the egg, mixing to combine.

2. Stir in the sweet corn and set aside for 10 minutes.

3. Heat the oil in a heavy-based frying pan and drop in large tablespoonfuls of the mixture.

4. Cook until golden underneath then turn over with a spatula and cook the other side. Drain on paper towels and serve hot with tomato or chilli sauce and a dollop of sour cream.

Salads

Salads have become more adventurous recently with all sorts
of exotic combinations of vegetables, fruits, nuts and pulses.
But a salad doesn't have to be over-complicated to taste delicious.
These are all tried and trusted New Zealand stand-bys.

Coleslaw

1 HOUR | SERVES 8

*An American cabbage salad which goes well with sausages, and barbecued
or cold meats.*

4 cups finely shredded cabbage
1 green capsicum, finely sliced
½ cup diced celery
1 Tbsp finely chopped onion

¼–½ cup French Dressing (page 175),
   Mayonnaise (page 178),
   Yoghurt Dressing (page 184) or
   Blue Cheese Dressing (page 174)

1. Crisp the shredded cabbage by putting it in iced water for 30 minutes, then drain.
2. Mix together the cabbage, capsicum, celery and onion and then mix through the
dressing of your choice. Chill before serving for a wilted coleslaw, or dress just before
serving for crisp.

VARIATIONS
Add any of the following to the coleslaw with the dressing:

1 cup grated carrot
1 cup grated cheese
½ cup chopped walnuts or peanuts
½ cup raisins, sultanas, chopped dates
   or chopped dried apricots

1 orange, peeled and diced
½–1 cup pineapple pieces
1 apple, finely diced
2 Tbsp chopped parsley
1 tsp caraway seeds

Kumara Salad

1 HOUR | SERVES 4

*Unpeeled kumara roasted to bring out their sweetness then drizzled with a lightly
curried mayonnaise.*

2–3 large kumara, washed
1 Tbsp olive oil
salt and pepper
¼ cup Mayonnaise (page 178) or
   Edmonds whole egg mayonnaise
¼ cup sour cream or natural
   unsweetened yoghurt

½ tsp curry powder
1 tsp lemon juice
3 spring onions, finely sliced or
   1 red onion, thinly sliced
1 Tbsp toasted chopped walnuts
   or almonds

1. Preheat the oven to 200°C.
2. Cut the unpeeled kumara into large chunks, toss in the oil and season with
salt and pepper.

3. Roast in a shallow baking tray for 30 minutes or until tender. Cool.
4. Mix together the mayonnaise, sour cream or yoghurt, curry powder and lemon juice and season with salt and pepper to taste.
5. Arrange the kumara in a shallow serving dish, drizzle over the dressing and finish with the spring onions and toasted nuts.

NOTE
Vary the type of kumara used to create more colour in the dish.

Pasta Salad with Tuna and Olives

A good picnic or summer evening dish.

250g penne or other short pasta
1 red onion, finely sliced
1 red capsicum, seeded and diced
3 sticks celery, finely sliced

200g can tuna in oil, drained
10 black or green olives, pitted
10 cherry tomatoes, halved

DRESSING
1 clove garlic crushed with ¼ tsp salt
1 tsp mustard
1 Tbsp lemon juice
* or white wine vinegar*

salt and pepper
3 Tbsp olive oil
1 tsp chopped parsley or tarragon

1. Cook the pasta in plenty of boiling, salted water until just tender or al dente and drain well.
2. Make the dressing by combining all the ingredients in a small glass jar and shaking well to combine.
3. Place the pasta in a large bowl, add the dressing and set aside to cool – but not in the fridge.
4. Add the red onion, caspsicum, celery and tuna and toss again. Garnish with the olives and halved cherry tomatoes and serve at room temperature.

Potato Salad

Open to many variations and always popular, but make sure the potatoes are not too cold and hard. They should be soft enough to absorb some of the dressing.

2–3 potatoes
½–1 cup Mayonnaise (page 178),
* French Dressing (page 175) or*
* Yoghurt Dressing (page 184) or*
* Edmonds whole egg mayonnaise*

2–3 spring onions, sliced
2 hard-boiled eggs, chopped
1–2 tsp finely chopped mint

1. Cook the whole potatoes in plenty of boiling water for about 25 minutes or until tender. Drain and cool a little.
2. Peel away the skin from the warm potatoes, cut them into medium-sized chunks and combine with the dressing of your choice while they are still slightly warm.

3. Gently mix through the spring onions, eggs and mint, or variations of your choice, and serve immediately or at room temperature.

VARIATIONS
Add any of the following to your taste:

1 green or red capsicum, sliced
1 Tbsp chopped chives or parsley
2–3 rashers bacon, cooked, sliced
*   and crumbled*

¼ cup toasted sunflower
*   or sesame seeds*
¼ cup sliced gherkins
4 radishes, sliced

NOTE
If you want to use leftover boiled potatoes, it is best to reheat them just a little before adding the dressing so that some of it is absorbed.

Rice Salad with Ham & Peas

1 HOUR   8 SERVES

Rice salads can include a wide variety of ingredients. This is a good combination, but alter to suit your taste.

2 cups long grain rice, washed
*   and drained*
2 cups water
250g diced ham or chicken
*   or cooked prawns*
1 cup cooked peas or sliced green beans

½ cup chopped parsley
5 spring onions, finely sliced
3 radishes, diced
salt and pepper
3 Tbsp toasted flaked almonds

DRESSING
2 tsp Dijon mustard
½ cup olive oil

3 Tbsp wine vinegar
1 clove garlic crushed with ¼ tsp salt

1. Put the rice into a large saucepan with a close-fitting lid. Add the water and bring to a rolling boil, then stir, put on the lid and cook over the lowest possible heat for 20 minutes – without lifting the lid!
2. While the rice is cooking, whisk together the dressing ingredients.
3. After 20 minutes, remove the lid and fluff up the rice, preferably with a wooden fork or chopsticks, then replace the lid and leave for another 10 minutes.
4. Tip the rice into a bowl and mix with the dressing, then add the ham, chicken or prawns, the peas or beans, parsley, spring onions, radishes and season with salt and pepper.
5. Transfer to a serving dish and sprinkle with the toasted almonds.

Roasted Vegetable Salad

1 HOUR · 6 SERVES

A summer dish of roasted vegetables, made particularly delicious with the addition of some crumbled feta cheese.

½ butternut pumpkin, peeled, seeded
   and cut into thin slices
1 kumara, halved and thinly sliced
1 aubergine, cut into cubes
2 courgettes, diced
1 red capsicum, seeded
   and thinly sliced
1 yellow capsicum, seeded
   and thinly sliced

1 red onion, cut into wedges
   and layers separated
6 cloves garlic, peeled
3 Tbsp olive oil
salt and pepper
¼ tsp chilli flakes (optional)
200g feta cheese (optional)

DRESSING
¼ cup olive oil
1 Tbsp tomato purée

½ tsp paprika (optional)
2 Tbsp lemon or lime juice

1. Preheat the oven to 220°C. Line a shallow roasting dish with baking paper.
2. Toss all the vegetables with the olive oil and plenty of salt and pepper and the chilli flakes if you wish. Spread evenly in the roasting dish.
3. Cook for 30–40 minutes, turning the vegetables after 20 minutes. They should all be tender and browned at the edges.
4. Make the dressing by shaking the ingredients together in a glass jar, then transfer the cooked vegetables to a large serving dish and toss with the dressing. Top with crumbled feta cheese if you wish.

Waldorf Salad

20 MINS · 6 SERVES

Invented at New York's Waldorf Hotel in the 1890s, this dish was originally a combination of apples, celery and mayonnaise. Green grapes and walnuts were added by the 1920s and it has remained popular ever since as a crisp and refreshing salad.

3 crisp tart apples, peeled
   and cut into long strips
juice of ½ a lemon
1 cup cold water
6 sticks celery, cut into fine strips
   4cm long

½ cup walnut pieces
¼ cup Mayonnaise (page 178) mixed
   with ¼ cup natural unsweetened
   yoghurt or whipped cream
½ cup seedless grapes, halved

1. Drop the apple strips into a bowl with the lemon juice and cold water.
2. If the celery is not crisp, soak it in chilled water for 10 minutes, then drain well.
3. Combine the drained apples, the celery and the walnuts with the mayonnaise dressing and place in a serving dish. Scatter with the green grapes. Chill slightly before serving.

NOTE
Add 1 teaspoon finely grated orange zest to the mayonnaise for an extra burst of flavour.

Dressings, Sauces & Marinades

Whether it is an accompaniment or an integral part of the meal, a well-made sauce, dressing or marinade can elevate the most humble dish to a whole new level. They are often surprisingly easy to prepare once you have the knack.

Aioli

CUPS

A garlic-scented mayonnaise from the South of France, wonderful with hot or cold boiled potatoes, hard-boiled eggs, chickpeas or even barbecued meat. This is a quick blender version.

2 eggs, at room temperature
2 cloves garlic crushed with ½ tsp salt
ground black pepper

½ cup olive oil
½ cup vegetable oil
1 tsp lemon juice

1. Put the eggs into a food processor or blender with the crushed garlic, and pepper and pulse to combine.
2. Combine the oils in a small jug which pours easily and, with the motor running, very slowly trickle the oil onto the eggs. The mayonnaise will thicken and become creamy.
3. Once all the oil is added, stir in the lemon juice and taste for seasoning. For a more mellow garlic flavour, try roasting or steaming the garlic cloves in their skins until they are soft, then squeeze out the purée and use in the dressing as above.

Apple Sauce

CUPS

Serve cold with roast pork, or a grilled pork chop – or hot with ice cream or a sponge pudding.

3–4 cooking apples, peeled
  and chopped
1 Tbsp lemon juice
50g butter

1 strip of lemon zest
1–2 Tbsp sugar
1 Tbsp brandy (optional)

1. Sprinkle the apples with the lemon juice. Melt the butter in a heavy-based saucepan over a low heat. Add the apples and lemon zest and lay a piece of baking paper on top of the fruit to keep in the steam. Put the lid on the pan and cook gently until the apples are soft, about 10 minutes.
2. Drain off any liquid and remove the lemon zest, then purée in a blender, return to the pan and add sugar to taste. Simmer for about 5 minutes until thickened then add the brandy if you wish.

Barbecue Marinade

½ CUP

This mixture can be used as a marinade and basting sauce for barbecued meats.

¼ cup tomato sauce
1 tsp sugar
1 Tbsp soy sauce

¼ cup chilli sauce
2 cloves garlic, crushed

1. Combine all the ingredients in a bowl. About 20 minutes before cooking, pour over the meat to be barbecued.
2. Cook as usual, basting with the marinade in the last few minutes.
Watch carefully as the sugars in the sauce can burn or make the meat stick.

Béarnaise Sauce

1 CUP

A rich, buttery sauce traditionally served with grilled sirloin or fillet steak. A special occasion treat.

2 Tbsp chopped tarragon
2 Tbsp tarragon vinegar
150ml dry white wine
1 Tbsp finely chopped spring onion,
    white part only

1 tsp ground black pepper
3 egg yolks
1 Tbsp cold water
pinch of salt
175g butter, cut into small cubes

1. Put the tarragon, vinegar, white wine, spring onion and black pepper in a small saucepan and boil hard until it has reduced to 2 tablespoons of liquid. This is called making a 'reduction' and it contributes a fresh, sharp flavour to the sauce. Set aside.
2. Whisk together the yolks, cold water and salt in the top of a double boiler or heatproof bowl over a saucepan of simmering water. Don't let the water boil hard.
3. Strain in the reduction and then whisk constantly as you add the butter a cube at a time. Wait until each cube has been absorbed before adding the next.
4. Once all the butter has been added and the sauce is thick and fluffy, taste for seasoning and serve.

Berry Sauce for Ice Cream

1 CUP

15 MINS

A very quickly made sauce, best with dark, tart berries like blackberries, blueberries or blackcurrants.

2 cups berries, fresh or frozen
2 Tbsp caster sugar
4 Tbsp water

½ tsp Edmonds Fielder's cornflour
1 Tbsp water

1. Put the berries, sugar and first measure of water into a small saucepan and heat gently just until the juices start to run – about 2 minutes for fresh berries, 3 minutes for frozen. Keep the berries whole.
2. Pour the mixture into a sieve and put the berries in a serving bowl. Return the juice to the saucepan.

3. Combine the cornflour with the second measure of water and add to the juice in the pan. Bring the mixture to the boil, stirring, and simmer for 1 minute until it thickens slightly.
4. Pour the sauce over the berries and serve the sauce with Ice Cream (page 190) or Cheesecake (page 186) or other cool desserts.

Blue Cheese Dressing

Rich and creamy and with the strong flavour of blue cheese, this is a simple dressing for green salads or grilled steak – or try it as a dip with raw vegetables.

75g blue vein cheese
1 Tbsp white wine vinegar
¼ cup olive oil

¼ cup sour cream or natural
  unsweetened yoghurt
pepper

1. Mash the cheese with the vinegar, then stir in the oil and sour cream or yoghurt.
2. Taste and season with pepper.

Cashew Cream

A delicious alternative to mayonnaise, this cream is very good with cold chicken and with shredded vegetable salads.

50g cashew nuts
½ clove garlic crushed with ¼ tsp salt
½ cup water
3 Tbsp lemon juice

½ cup vegetable oil
salt
white pepper
pinch of chilli powder

1. Put the cashew nuts, crushed garlic, water and lemon juice into a blender and purée until smooth.
2. With the motor running, add the oil gradually through the hole in the lid. Season to taste with salt, pepper and a pinch of chilli.

Caramel Fudge Sauce

A hot sauce for ice cream or Moist Date Pudding (page 205).

125g butter
¾ cup brown sugar
1½ Tbsp Edmonds Fielder's cornflour

1 cup water
1 Tbsp golden syrup
½ cup cream

1. Heat the butter and sugar in a saucepan, stirring constantly until the sugar dissolves. Boil for 3 minutes, stirring occasionally, and then remove from the heat.
2. Combine the cornflour, water and golden syrup in a bowl and mix until smooth, then add to the saucepan and bring the mixture back to the boil, stirring constantly. Boil for 2 minutes.
3. Remove from the heat and mix in the cream.

Custard Sauce

1 CUP · 15 MINS

A richer custard with an added egg.

1 Tbsp Edmonds custard powder
1 cup milk
½ tsp vanilla essence

1 egg, beaten
1 tsp sugar

1. Mix the custard powder and 2 tablespoons of the milk to a smooth paste in a saucepan.
2. Add the remaining milk, vanilla, beaten egg and sugar and cook, stirring constantly until the custard thickens. Do not bring to the boil.

Cooked Salad Dressing

1 CUP

This dressing keeps well in the fridge and can be thinned with milk or yoghurt.

1 Tbsp flour
1 tsp dry mustard
½ tsp salt
1 Tbsp sugar
1 egg

25g butter, melted
¼ cup white or malt vinegar
¾ cup milk
pinch of cayenne pepper

1. Put the flour, mustard, salt and sugar in the top of a double boiler or a heatproof bowl which will fit over a saucepan.
2. Add the egg, melted butter and then the vinegar and mix well.
3. Add the milk gradually and when well blended, place over simmering water. Cook until thick, stirring constantly. Season with cayenne. Keep in a jar in the refrigerator.

French Dressing (Vinaigrette)

½ CUP

The classic oil and vinegar dressing which is best made in small quantities and used immediately.

⅓ cup olive oil
1 Tbsp white wine vinegar
  or lemon juice
¼ tsp dry mustard powder or
  ½ tsp prepared mustard

1 small clove garlic, crushed
salt and pepper
1 Tbsp chopped parsley, chives or basil

1. Put all the ingredients into a screw-top jar and shake well.

VARIATIONS
Mustard Vinaigrette
Add 2 teaspoons wholegrain mustard.

Green Peppercorn Sauce

Little bursts of flavour come from the plump green peppercorns in this creamy sauce. Serve with steaks, poached chicken or fish.

50g butter
2 Tbsp lemon juice
2 Tbsp green peppercorns, rinsed
4 egg yolks

¼ cup cream
2 Tbsp sour cream
1 tsp prepared mustard
salt and pepper

1. Melt the butter in a saucepan and add the lemon juice.
2. Stir in the peppercorns, egg yolks, cream, sour cream and mustard and cook over a gentle heat until the sauce thickens. Do not allow it to boil.
3. Season with salt and pepper to taste.

Hollandaise Sauce

Like a hot mayonnaise made with butter, this sauce adds richness to asparagus, salmon, steamed potatoes or broccoli. And it softly enfolds poached eggs in a classic Eggs Benedict.

1 Tbsp lemon juice
1 Tbsp cold water
salt and white pepper

3 egg yolks
175g unsalted butter, cut into small cubes

1. Whisk together the lemon juice, cold water, salt, pepper and egg yolks in the top of a double boiler or in a heatproof bowl over a saucepan of simmering water. Don't let the water boil hard.
2. Add the butter a cube at a time, whisking constantly. Wait until each cube has been absorbed before adding the next.
3. When all the butter has been added, remove from the heat and whisk for 2 minutes, then return to the heat and whisk for another 2 minutes.
4. Keep the sauce warm over gently simmering water until needed or you could put it in a Thermos flask. It will not separate as it cools.

Honey Soy Marinade

An excellent marinade for oven-baked chicken wings. Goes well with pork too.

¼ cup dry sherry
1 Tbsp soy sauce
1 Tbsp grated fresh ginger

2 cloves garlic, crushed
1 Tbsp honey
½ tsp chilli powder (optional)

1. Combine all the ingredients in a bowl and mix well. Place the meat in the marinade, stirring to coat.
2. Cover and leave to marinate for at least 1 hour.

Hot Chocolate Sauce

A rich, dark chocolate sauce which you can serve warm with ice cream, or allow it to cool and spread it over a cake.

170g dark chocolate
300ml water

100g sugar
pinch of cinnamon

1. Chop the chocolate and put it in a saucepan with the water. Set over a gentle heat and stir until the chocolate is melted and smooth.
2. Add the sugar and cinnamon and stir over the heat until the sugar dissolves, then bring to the boil and simmer gently for 10–15 minutes or until the sauce has a rich and syrupy consistency.

Hummus

You can use this as a dip, spread on pita bread or as an accompaniment to salad.

1 cup chick peas
½ tsp salt
1 spring onion, finely chopped
3 Tbsp tahini (sesame seed paste)
2 cloves garlic, crushed

2 Tbsp lemon juice
1 Tbsp parsley, finely chopped
2 Tbsp olive oil
extra oil

1. Put the chick peas into a bowl. Cover with boiling water. Stand for 1 hour. Drain. Cook in boiling, salted water for 1 hour or until tender. Drain and allow to cool.
2. Put chick peas into a food processor or blender. Add onion, tahini, garlic, lemon juice, salt, parsley and oil. Process until smooth. More oil may be required to blend to a smooth paste. Chill until ready to serve.

Kiwifruit Marinade

A tenderising marinade for steaks or lamb chops.

2 kiwifruit, finely chopped
1 Tbsp honey

2 tsp grated fresh ginger
coarsely crushed peppercorns

1. Combine all the ingredients in a bowl and mix well. Place the meat in the marinade, stirring to coat.
2. Cover and leave to marinate for at least 1 hour.

Mayonnaise

1¼
CUPS

The classic smooth, golden mayonnaise.

2 egg yolks, at room temperature
½ tsp Dijon mustard
½ tsp salt

1 Tbsp white wine vinegar
  or lemon juice
300ml olive oil and vegetable oil, mixed
  salt and pepper

1. Put the egg yolks into a bowl with the mustard, salt and 1 teaspoon of the vinegar or lemon juice. Using a whisk or an electric beater on slow speed, whisk the mixture until fluffy.
2. Add the oil half a teaspoon at a time, making sure that each amount of oil is incorporated before adding the next.
3. Continue whisking and adding the oil until about 2 tablespoons have been incorporated and the mixture has begun to thicken.
4. Now add the remaining oil in a very thin stream, whisking constantly.
5. Once all the oil has been incorporated the mayonnaise should be very thick and floppy. Whisk in the remaining lemon juice or vinegar and season with salt and pepper to taste.

Mint Sauce

½
CUP

Serve with roast lamb for the complete Kiwi roast experience.

2 Tbsp sugar
2 Tbsp boiling water
2 Tbsp finely chopped green mint

4 Tbsp vinegar
pinch of salt

1. Put the sugar and boiling water into a small saucepan and boil for 1 minute.
2. Put the mint into a small bowl and pour over the hot water and the vinegar. Allow to stand for 15 minutes, add salt to taste, then pour into a small jug and stir well before serving.

Mushroom Sauce

1½
CUPS

Try this delicious sauce with roast chicken or use twice the quantity of sliced mushrooms to make a chunky mushroom sauce for pasta.

100g button mushrooms, chopped
1½ cups chicken stock, made with
  a cube
1 Tbsp lemon juice

25g butter
1 Tbsp Edmonds standard flour
4 Tbsp cream
salt and pepper

1. Put the mushrooms, chicken stock and lemon juice in a pan and bring to the boil. Simmer for about 20 minutes until the liquid has reduced by half. Purée in a blender or food processor or leave as is for a more textured sauce.
2. Melt the butter in a small saucepan, sprinkle on the flour and cook for 1 minute, stirring constantly.
3. Remove from the heat and gradually add the mushrooms.

4. Return to the heat, bring to a gentle simmer and cook for about 5 minutes, stirring, then mix in the cream and season with salt and pepper.

Mustard Sauce

A perennially popular sauce for corned beef.

1 egg
2 Tbsp sugar
1 Tbsp Edmonds standard flour
2 tsp dry mustard powder

1 cup water or corned beef
    cooking liquid
¼ cup malt vinegar
salt and pepper

1. Beat the egg and sugar together and put into a saucepan.
2. Whisk in the flour and mustard, then gradually add the water and vinegar.
3. Cook over a low heat until the sauce thickens, then season with salt and pepper to taste, adding more sugar if you wish.

Peanut Sauce for Satay

Satay is an Indonesian word for small pieces of meat – chicken, pork or beef – grilled on skewers and usually served with a spicy peanut sauce. Here is a tasty, simplified version of the sauce. Also try it as a dip with raw vegetables or with cold chicken.

2 Tbsp oil
1 clove garlic, crushed
1 onion, chopped
¼–½ tsp chilli powder
½ cup crunchy peanut butter

1 Tbsp soy sauce
1 Tbsp lemon juice
1 Tbsp brown sugar
¾ cup coconut cream
salt

1. Put the oil, garlic, onion and chilli powder in a saucepan and place over a moderate heat. Cook gently until the onion is translucent, about 10 minutes.
2. Stir in the peanut butter, soy sauce, lemon juice and sugar, then add the coconut cream. Season with salt to taste.

Pesto

The versatile and beautiful basil sauce for pasta, from Genoa in northern Italy. Try it with tomato salads, in a chicken sandwich or dolloped into Minestrone (page 116).

100g basil leaves
100ml olive oil
25g pine nuts

2 cloves garlic, lightly crushed
½ tsp salt
50g parmesan cheese, grated

1. Put the basil, olive oil, pine nuts, garlic and salt in a blender or food processor and process at medium speed until a green paste forms. Add the grated cheese and process again briefly.

NOTE
If you have basil in the garden, make a big batch without the parmesan cheese, freeze it in small containers and add parmesan once the sauce has defrosted.

VARIATION
Pesto Linguine
Cook 350g linguine in lots of boiling, salted water with 2 potatoes cut into thin sticks and 50g thin green beans – they will all cook at the same time. Drain well and toss with pesto (made without the pine nuts) and serve.

Raita (Cucumber Yoghurt Sauce)

The cooling accompaniment to any curry.

1 cucumber, seeded and chopped
1 tsp salt
1 tsp cumin seeds

2 spring onions, chopped
1 cup natural unsweetened yoghurt
1 Tbsp lemon juice

1. Put the cucumber in a bowl, sprinkle with salt and set aside for 15 minutes. Rinse under cold water and drain.
2. Put the cumin seeds into a small frying pan and heat gently until aromatic.
3. Combine the cucumber, cumin seeds, spring onions, yoghurt and lemon juice in a small bowl.

Red Onion Marmalade

Caramelised onions cooked gently with wine, vinegar and a little sugar make a very tasty accompaniment to any cold meat or cheese. They keep very well in the fridge.

3 red onions, thinly sliced
1 Tbsp olive oil
¼ tsp salt
1 bay leaf

4 Tbsp brown sugar
4 Tbsp balsamic vinegar
½ cup dry red wine

1. Put the onions in a large, heavy-based frying pan with the olive oil, salt and bay leaf.
2. Cover the pan and cook gently for 15 minutes until the onions begin to soften then remove the lid and cook for another 15 minutes until they are dark and sticky and very well cooked. Stir occasionally to make sure the onions do not stick or burn.
3. Add the brown sugar, balsamic vinegar and red wine and bring to a simmer then cook, uncovered, stirring often for about 15 minutes until most of the liquid has evaporated. The onions should be shiny and dark red. Store in a jar in the refrigerator.

Quick Blender Mayonnaise

Made quickly with a whole egg, this is lighter and paler than true mayonnaise.

1 egg, at room temperature
1 Tbsp white wine vinegar
   or lemon juice
½ tsp Dijon mustard

salt
2 Tbsp cold water
300ml olive oil
pepper

1. Put the egg into the blender with the vinegar or lemon juice, mustard and a pinch of salt.

Pesto, Herb & Cheese Scrolls page 95

Kumara Salad page 168

2. Add the cold water, cover and blend at high speed for about 5 seconds.
3. With the motor running, add the oil slowly through the hole in the blender lid.
Season to taste with salt and pepper.

Tahini Cream

¾ CUP

A Middle Eastern dip to serve with pita breads or raw vegetables. Tahini is made from crushed sesame seeds.

1 clove garlic crushed with ½ tsp salt
150ml tahini
2–3 Tbsp lemon juice

1 Tbsp water
1 Tbsp chopped parsley
½ tsp ground cumin seeds

1. Put the crushed garlic into a small mixing bowl and add the tahini. Stir in
1 tablespoon of the lemon juice and taste. Add more lemon juice if you need to
and use the water to thin the dressing.
2. Put into a bowl and sprinkle with chopped parsley and some ground cumin seeds.

Tartare Sauce

1 CUP

Serve with simply pan-fried fish – or fish and chips.

1 Tbsp chopped parsley
1 Tbsp finely chopped capers
1 Tbsp chopped gherkins

1 Tbsp finely chopped chives
1 cup Mayonnaise (page 178) or
   Edmonds whole egg mayonnaise

1. Combine all the ingredients. Use immediately or store in the refrigerator until needed.

Uncooked (Condensed Milk) Salad Dressing

2 CUPS

A New Zealand tradition, this sweet salad dressing keeps in a jar in the fridge and can be thinned with milk or yoghurt. Use it on lettuce or potato salads.

1 egg
395g can sweetened condensed milk
1 tsp mustard powder

½ tsp salt
⅓ cup milk
¼ cup vinegar

1. Put the egg in a mixing bowl and beat well, then add the other ingredients in order,
beating constantly.
2. Set aside for 15 minutes to thicken. Store in a jar in the refrigerator.

VARIATION

Horseradish Sauce
Add 2 tablespoons grated horseradish to 1 cup salad dressing. A wonderful
accompaniment to roast beef.

White Sauce

The basic sauce which is a base for many flavour variations. This is a great one for those who are just starting out. Get the hang of this and you have a huge range of sauces you can make just by adding a few other ingredients.

2 Tbsp butter
2 Tbsp Edmonds standard flour

1 cup milk, heated
salt and pepper

1. Melt the butter in a small saucepan over a medium heat. Stir in the flour and cook for about 1 minute until frothy.
2. Remove from the heat and gradually add the milk, stirring constantly. Return to the heat and cook, stirring, until the sauce boils and thickens.
3. Cook for another 2 minutes, then season with salt and pepper to taste.

VARIATIONS
Béchamel Sauce
The French version of white sauce made with flavoured milk. Heat the milk with a bay leaf, a few peppercorns and a blade of mace and let it steep for about 10 minutes. Strain the milk and use it to make the white sauce as above.
Caper Sauce
Add 1 teaspoon prepared mustard, 1 tablespoon drained capers and 1 tablespoon lemon juice once the sauce is cooked.
Cheese Sauce
Stir in ½ cup grated tasty cheese once the sauce is cooked.
Curry Sauce
Add 1–2 teaspoons curry powder with the flour.
Gluten Free White Sauce
Replace the Edmonds standard flour with an equal quantity of Edmonds gluten free plain flour.
Parsley Sauce
Add 2–4 tablespoons chopped parsley once the sauce is cooked.

Yoghurt Dressing

A lighter alternative when mayonnaise seems too rich.

1 cup natural unsweetened yoghurt
salt and pepper

1 Tbsp lemon juice
¼ tsp dry mustard

1. Stir all the ingredients together until combined and chill before using.

Cold Desserts

Desserts are a welcome treat, especially so since they're something we no longer have with every other meal. These cold desserts are perfect for special summer meals – but they'll be popular whatever time of the year you serve them.

Blancmange

4½ HOURS   4 SERVES

Blancmange may be an old-fashioned dessert, but it is certainly worth a revival. A cool and refreshing custard of sweetened milk which sets in a mould and turns out very easily. Particularly wonderful with poached plums or other summer fruit.

3 Tbsp Edmonds Fielder's cornflour   **600ml milk**
2 Tbsp sugar   **few drops of vanilla essence**

1. Mix the cornflour and sugar to a smooth cream with a little of the cold milk.
2. Heat the remainder of the milk in a saucepan and pour it onto the cornflour mixture, stirring. Return the mixture to the pan and cook until the milk thickens, then cook for 5 minutes longer, stirring all the time.
3. Remove from the heat, add the vanilla and pour into a wet mould or basin. Cool then chill for about 4 hours in the refrigerator until set.
4. Unmould onto a serving dish and serve with fruit and cream.

VARIATION
Coconut Blancmange
Replace 300ml of the milk with canned coconut cream, and add a pinch of salt.

Brandy Snaps

1 HOUR   16 MAKES

The perfect crunchy vehicle for whipped cream. They keep well in an airtight tin, but fill them just before serving to keep them snappy.

3 Tbsp golden syrup   **½ cup Edmonds standard flour**
75g soft brown sugar   **1 tsp ground ginger**
75g butter   **150ml cream, whipped and flavoured**
½ tsp finely grated lemon zest   **with a little brandy**

1. Preheat the oven to 180°C. Grease several baking trays very lightly.
2. Put the golden syrup, brown sugar and butter into a saucepan and heat gently, stirring, until melted together, but not boiling. Pour into a mixing bowl and cool for 5 minutes.
3. Add the lemon zest, sift in the flour and ginger, then mix well.
4. Drop the mixture in small teaspoonfuls onto the trays, allowing 4 to a tray. They will spread so keep them well apart.

Preheat your measuring spoon in hot water to easily measure golden syrup.

5. Bake one tray at a time for 8–10 minutes until the brandy snaps have spread out and are golden brown.
6. Leave them on the tray for a minute or two to set, then lift them one at a time with a spatula and roll around the handle of a wooden spoon, or a conical cream horn mould. Leave on a rack to cool, join side down.
7. Fill with whipped cream just before serving.

NOTE
Don't grease the cream horns but grease the wooden spoon handle if using.

Cheesecake (Baked)

OVERNIGHT HOURS SERVES

A very rich, delicious dessert to be served in small slices. Malt biscuits, gingernuts or plain wine biscuits are good for the crumb base.

BASE
1 cup plain biscuit crumbs *50g butter, melted*

FILLING
500g cream cheese, softened *finely grated lemon zest*
250g sour cream *¼ cup lemon juice*
1 cup caster sugar *3 eggs, lightly beaten*
2 Tbsp Edmonds standard flour

1. Preheat the oven to 150°C.
2. Crush the biscuits finely in a food processor or with a rolling pin. Mix together the biscuit crumbs and butter and press evenly over the base of a 20cm springform tin. Chill while you prepare the filling.
3. Place the cream cheese, sour cream, sugar, flour, lemon zest and juice in a food processor and blend until smooth.
4. With the motor running on slow speed, gradually add the beaten eggs, processing until well blended. Pour the filling onto the biscuit base.
5. Bake for 1 hour 50 minutes or until firm. Cool in the tin, then cover and refrigerate for at least 6 hours, or overnight before serving.

Cheesecake (Unbaked)

OVERNIGHT HOURS SERVES

Fold some fresh berries or pitted cherries through the filling to vary the flavour.

BASE
250g packet digestive or ginger *1 Tbsp lemon juice*
* biscuits* *75g butter, melted*
1 tsp finely grated lemon zest

FILLING
2 tsp gelatine *½ cup caster sugar*
2 Tbsp water *2 Tbsp lemon juice*
250g cream cheese *1 tsp finely grated lemon zest*
250g sour cream *1 tsp vanilla essence*

1. Crush the biscuits finely in a food processor or with a rolling pin and mix with the lemon zest, juice and butter.
2. Press the crumb mixture over the base and sides of a 20cm springform tin. Chill while you make the filling.
3. Sprinkle the gelatine over the cool water and leave to swell for 10 minutes.
4. Beat the cream cheese until soft, add the sour cream and beat again. Then stir in the sugar, lemon juice and zest and the vanilla. Beat well until the sugar has dissolved.
5. Put the bowl with the swelled gelatine over simmering water and allow it to melt, and then mix quickly into the cheese filling.
6. Pour the filling onto the crumb crust and leave it to set in the fridge for at least 4 hours or overnight.

Chocolate Log

2½ HOURS   8 SERVES

The traditional French Christmas cake and a very good choice for a celebratory dessert.

3 eggs
½ cup caster sugar
½ tsp vanilla essence
25g butter, melted
1 Tbsp hot water
¼ cup Edmonds standard flour

1 tsp Edmonds baking powder
2 Tbsp cocoa
jam and whipped cream
icing sugar and extra cocoa (optional)
Chocolate Buttercream Icing (page 98)

1. Preheat the oven to 200°C. Lightly butter a 20cm x 30cm sponge roll tin and line the base and two sides with baking paper.
2. Beat the eggs, sugar and vanilla until pale yellow and very thick and fluffy, about 10 minutes.
3. Fold through the melted butter and hot water, and then sift on the flour, baking powder and cocoa. Fold gently through until the mixture is smooth and has no streaks. Pour the mixture into the prepared tin.
4. Bake for 10–12 minutes or until the cake springs back when lightly touched. While the cake is baking put a piece of baking paper on the bench and dust with icing sugar.
5. Turn the cake onto the baking paper and spread it thinly with jam, then roll it up from a short side, using the baking paper to help it along.
6. Leave the roll wrapped in the paper until cold, then unroll it and fill with whipped cream.
7. Reroll and either dust with icing sugar or cocoa, or spread it with Chocolate Buttercream Icing. Use a fork to make bark patterns in the icing and dust again with icing sugar to represent snow on the log. Chill for at least 1 hour before serving.

Chocolate Mousse

3 HOURS   4 SERVES

The formula for a smooth, rich chocolate mousse is 1 egg and 25g dark chocolate per person. Serve in tiny glasses or espresso coffee cups.

100g dark chocolate
2 Tbsp water or espresso coffee
4 eggs, separated

1 Tbsp rum or orange liqueur
whipped cream and grated chocolate

1. Chop the chocolate and place in a heatproof bowl with the water or coffee. Set the bowl over a saucepan of hot water. Leave for 5 minutes then stir gently until the mixture is smooth and well combined.

2. Beat the egg yolks until fluffy and then gradually stir in the warm chocolate, followed by the rum or liqueur.

3. Whisk the egg whites until stiff and fold half into the chocolate mixture. When incorporated, add the remaining egg white and continue to fold gently together until combined and there are no white streaks.

4. Spoon into 4 small dishes or 1 large one and leave in a cool place for several hours or overnight. The mousse will become firm as the chocolate sets, but may be a little too hard if set in the refrigerator.

5. Serve decorated with whipped cream and grated chocolate.

Crème Brûlée

The name means 'burnt cream' and this chilled rich custard has a glassy layer of caramelised sugar on the top which will crack into delicious shards when you hit it with your spoon.

2 cups cream
1 vanilla pod
½ cup caster sugar

5 egg yolks
1 tsp Edmonds Fielder's cornflour

CARAMEL
100g sugar

1. Heat the cream almost to boiling point with the vanilla pod, then set aside.

2. Beat together the caster sugar and the egg yolks for about 3 minutes until pale yellow and fluffy, and then beat in the cornflour.

3. Remove the vanilla pod and stir the hot cream into the egg mixture, then pour everything into the top of a double boiler or a heatproof bowl set over a pan of simmering water.

4. Stir constantly until the custard thickens, but do not let it come to the boil. Remove from the heat and strain into a jug, then pour into 4 individual heatproof ramekins or custard cups. Cool then chill for at least 4 hours.

5. Make the caramel topping about an hour before you intend to serve the custards. Put the sugar into a heavy-based saucepan over a very low heat and let it melt gently. Don't stir the sugar, just shake the pan occasionally.

6. When all the sugar has melted and turned a pale caramel colour, pour it carefully over the surface of the chilled custards. After a few minutes the caramel will harden to a golden layer on the custard.

NOTE
Don't try to scrape all the unused caramel from the pan, just fill it with hot water and bring back to the boil to melt the caramel and clean the pan.

Crème Caramel

OVERNIGHT HOUR SERVES

In this dessert the caramelised sugar is baked under the custard and creates a melting golden top layer when you turn them out. This is an excellent choice for a dinner party since it must be made in advance – make individual servings or one large custard.

¾ cup sugar
½ cup water
4 eggs or 6 egg yolks
2 Tbsp sugar

1 cup full-cream milk
1 cup cream
½ tsp vanilla essence

1. Preheat the oven to 160°C. Have ready an ovenproof dish in which the dish or ramekins for the custard will fit neatly.
2. Combine the first measure of sugar and water in a heavy-based saucepan and heat gently, stirring constantly until the sugar dissolves.
3. Bring to the boil, stop stirring and watch closely, shaking the pan occasionally. When the sugar has become a rich, dark – but not burnt – caramel, carefully pour a little into each ramekin. Tilt the ramekins around to spread the caramel over the base and put them into the ovenproof dish.
4. Beat together the whole eggs or egg yolks with the second measure of sugar, milk and cream until well combined but not frothy. Add the vanilla and strain into a jug.
5. Pour the custard into the caramel-lined ramekins and pour enough hot water into the dish to come halfway up the sides of the ramekins. Slide the whole assembly carefully into the oven.
6. Bake for 30–40 minutes or until the custard is just set, but still wobbly in the centre. Lift the custards out, cool on a rack, then chill overnight.
7. To serve, loosen the edges with a round-bladed table knife and invert them onto individual plates – each custard will be surrounded with a pool of thin, golden caramel.

Cream Chantilly

MAKES

Sweetened whipped cream which holds its shape very well if used as a topping.

½ cup cream
¼ tsp vanilla essence

1 Tbsp icing sugar

1. Combine the cream, vanilla and icing sugar and whip the cream as usual.

Flummery

HOURS SERVES

Simply made and always pretty – all you need to do is choose the flavour of the jelly crystals. Make individual servings or one impressive dessert.

2 packets jelly crystals
1½ cups boiling water

375ml can evaporated milk, chilled until very cold

1. Dissolve the jelly crystals in the boiling water and leave to cool – about 30 minutes. Pour ½ cup of the jelly into your dish.

2. Put the chilled evaporated milk into a chilled bowl and beat with an electric beater until foamy, about 2 minutes. Add the remaining cooled jelly and beat again for 3 more minutes until very thick.

3. Spoon the mixture on top of the plain jelly and leave to set in the fridge – about 1 hour.

VARIATION
Yoghurt Flummery
Omit the evaporated milk. Chill the jelly until the consistency of raw egg white, then beat until thick and foamy. Stir in 300g yoghurt, plain or flavoured. Pour into a serving dish and chill until set.

Fruit Sorbet

Light and refreshing and filled with fresh fruit flavour.

500g summer fruit – e.g. grapes, boysenberries, plums or strawberries
½ cup sugar

1 cup water
¼ cup lemon juice
2 egg whites

1. Purée the fruit then strain to remove the skins and seeds.

2. Combine the sugar and water in a saucepan and heat gently, stirring until the sugar dissolves. Cool slightly then combine with the fruit purée and the lemon juice.

3. Pour into a shallow container, cover and freeze until the mixture starts to freeze on top and at the sides.

4. Transfer the sorbet to a bowl, add the egg whites and beat until fluffy and well combined.

5. Return to the container and freeze again until set, about 4 hours. Serve in chilled glasses.

Ice Cream

This recipe involves combining three beaten mixtures, so make sure you have three mixing bowls. It makes a rich and creamy vanilla ice cream which you can flavour in many ways.

4 eggs, separated
½ cup caster sugar

1 tsp vanilla essence
300ml cream

1. Beat the egg whites until stiff peaks form and gradually add half of the sugar, 1 tablespoon at a time. Beat until each spoonful dissolves before adding the next.

2. In a separate bowl, beat the egg yolks and the remaining sugar until thick and pale. Add the vanilla.

3. Fold the egg yolks into the egg white mixture.

4. Whip the cream until thick then fold into the egg mixture with any other flavourings.

5. Pour the ice cream into a shallow container, cover and freeze for 2 hours or until firm.

VARIATIONS
Add any of the following after the cream:

1 cup chocolate chips
1 cup chopped nuts

1 cup puréed berry fruit – e.g.
* strawberries or raspberries*

Lemon Tart

1½ HOURS   6 SERVES

Crisp sweet pastry and a creamy lemon filling. A nice light summer dessert.

300g Sweet Shortcrust Pastry (page 103) or 400g block Edmonds sweet short
** pastry, thawed**

FILLING
4 eggs	*¾ cup caster sugar*
⅓ cup lemon juice	*1 cup cream*
1 Tbsp finely grated lemon zest	*icing sugar*

1. Preheat the oven to 190°C.
2. On a lightly floured board roll out the pastry and lift it into a 23cm shallow tart tin. Trim the edges and chill for 10 minutes.
3. Put a crumpled sheet of greaseproof paper or tinfoil into the pastry case and fill with dry chickpeas, rice or beans. This process is called 'baking blind' and the beans stop the pastry from rising as it cooks. The beans cannot be eaten after this use but if you keep them in a screw-top jar you can use them again for baking blind.
4. Bake the pastry case for 15 minutes, then remove it from the oven and take out the paper and the beans. Return the case to the oven for 5 minutes to dry the pastry, then cool on a wire rack.
5. Make the filling by beating the eggs, lemon juice, zest and sugar until combined. Lightly beat in the cream and pour the mixture into the baked pastry crust.
6. Bake for 5 minutes then reduce the temperature to 150°C and cook for a further 20–25 minutes or until the tart is set.
7. Dust with icing sugar and serve warm or cold.

Pavlova

OVERNIGHT   1 HOUR   10 SERVES

The recipe for a lofty meringue cake evolved slowly in both Australia and New Zealand, but the name arrived in 1935 when Bert Sachse, chef at the Esplanade Hotel in Perth, named his cake in honour of Russian ballerina Anna Pavlova. Sachse later acknowledged that the recipe he used was from a 1929 cookery book, The New Zealand Dairy Exporter.

6 egg whites	*1½ tsp vanilla essence*
pinch of salt	*1½ tsp Edmonds Fielder's cornflour*
2 cups caster sugar	*whipped cream and fresh fruit*
1½ tsp vinegar	

1. Preheat oven to 150°C. Line a baking tray with baking paper and draw a 20cm circle on it. Turn over the baking paper so that the pencil line doesn't transfer to your pavlova.
2. Using an electric mixer, beat the egg whites with the salt until stiff, then add the

sugar very gradually while still beating. Keep beating for 5 minutes to dissolve the sugar.

3. Slow the beater speed and add the vinegar, vanilla and cornflour.

4. Pile the meringue in the centre of the circle and use a spatula to spread it out to the edge of the circle, keeping it as round and even as possible. Make a slight dip in the top.

5. Bake for 45 minutes, then leave to cool in the oven overnight.

6. Using two spatulas, lift it carefully onto a serving plate and fill the central depression with whipped cream and fresh fruit.

Pecan Tart

An American classic; luscious and sweet with a delightful nutty crunch.

200g Sweet Shortcrust Pastry (page 103) or 1 sheet Edmonds sweet short pastry, thawed

FILLING
100g butter, softened
½ cup brown sugar
3 eggs

3 Tbsp liquid honey
200g pecan nuts

1. Preheat the oven to 190°C.

2. On a lightly floured board, roll out the pastry or use the pre-rolled sheets, and lift it into a 20cm shallow tart tin. Trim the edges and chill for 10 minutes.

3. Put a crumpled sheet of greaseproof paper or tinfoil into the pastry case and fill with dry chickpeas, rice or beans. This process is called 'baking blind' and the beans stop the pastry from rising as it cooks. The beans cannot be eaten after this use but if you keep them in a screw-top jar you can use them again for baking blind.

4. Bake the pastry case for 15 minutes, then remove from the oven and take out the paper and the beans. Return the case to the oven for 5 minutes to dry the pastry then cool on a wire rack.

5. Reduce the oven temperature to 180°C.

6. Cream the butter and sugar until light and fluffy. Add the eggs one at a time, beating well after each addition. Stir in the honey and pecans.

7. Pour the filling onto the cooked pastry base. Return to the oven and bake for a further 30 minutes or until filling is set.

Sherry Trifle

The layered confection we now call a trifle took several centuries to evolve and remains a Christmas must-have in many households. A gloriously silly and utterly delicious dessert, trifle deserves the best fruit and the best sherry or liqueur you have.

200g Three Minute Sponge (page 59)
¼ cup raspberry or apricot jam

¼ cup sherry or fruit liqueur
2 cups fresh berries or poached fruit

CUSTARD
4 Tbsp Edmonds custard powder
3 Tbsp sugar

2 cups full-cream milk

TO DECORATE
300ml cream, whipped

1 Tbsp toasted slivered almonds

1. Cut the sponge in half horizontally and fill with jam, then cut into large cubes and put in a pretty glass bowl.

2. Spoon sherry or liqueur over the sponge, then arrange the fruit and any syrup over the top. Set aside while you make the custard.

3. Mix the custard powder, sugar and ¼ cup of the milk to a smooth paste. Add the remaining milk and cook over a low heat, stirring constantly until mixture boils and thickens.

4. Remove from the heat, cover and leave until cool, then pour the custard over the fruit. Chill for 1 hour then cover with whipped cream and toasted almonds, or other decorations.

VARIATION

If you have egg yolks to use up, make the custard in the Crème Brûlée recipe (page 188) and use it in your trifle.

Spanish Cream

2 HOURS   6 SERVES

A silky custard set with gelatine which separates into two layers – one fluffy, one smooth. Spanish cream is an old-fashioned dessert, both refreshing and pretty subtly flavoured with vanilla and lemon.

2 Tbsp water
1½ tsp gelatine
1 cup full-cream milk
½ cup cream

2 strips of lemon zest
2 eggs, separated
2 Tbsp caster sugar
1 tsp vanilla essence

1. Put the water into a small bowl, sprinkle on the gelatine and leave for 5 minutes to swell.

2. Put the milk, cream and lemon zest into a saucepan and heat gently until tiny bubbles appear around the edge. Remove from the heat.

3. Whisk the egg yolks with the caster sugar until pale and fluffy. This will take about 2 minutes with a whisk or hand beater. Pour some of the hot milk onto the egg yolks, still whisking hard, then pour it all back into the saucepan.

4. Add the soaked gelatine, set the saucepan over a low heat and cook for 3–4 minutes until the mixture thickens very slightly. Don't let it come to the boil.

5. Strain the custard into a bowl, discarding the lemon zest, and put the bowl into the sink filled with about 5cm of cold water. Stir every few minutes until the custard is warm, not hot. Stir in the vanilla.

6. Beat the egg whites until stiff and very gently fold them through the warm custard using a metal spoon.

7. Pour the Spanish Cream into 4–6 individual glasses or 1 pretty glass bowl. Put in the fridge to set for about 1 hour.

VARIATION

Snowflake Cream

Add ½ cup fine desiccated coconut to the custard with the egg whites and pour on the top of some soft berries or other summer fruit.

Summer Fruit Salads

2 HOURS   6 SERVES

The best plan is to have three or four varieties of the best, ripest fruit you can find and avoid canned fruit if possible. Cut the fruit into bite-sized pieces, and add a very small amount of syrup – fruit salads should not be swimming in sweet syrup. Stone fruits like peaches, plums, apricots, nectarines and mango can go in raw but are delicious if you cook them briefly with a little sugar and water, then leave to cool.

SYRUP
2 slices fresh ginger
a few sprigs of fresh mint

3 Tbsp sugar
6 Tbsp water

1. Put the ginger and mint into a cup.
2. Bring the sugar and water to a simmer, stirring until the sugar dissolves.
3. Pour the syrup into the cup and leave to cool. Strain out the mint and ginger and pour the syrup over the fruit.

A few possible fruit salads:
- Strawberries sliced and mixed with a little icing sugar and a squeeze of lemon juice
- Strawberries, raspberries and blueberries with orange juice
- Melon with fresh pineapple and a few raspberries
- Apricots and a few sliced red plums
- Sliced peaches and strawberries
- Sliced oranges and chopped dates with a syrup made from orange juice and a little orange flower water
- Watermelon and blackberries or blueberries.

Hot Puddings

Is there anything more perfect on a cold winter night than a hot pudding? These desserts lift any meal and make it into more of a family occasion.

Apple Pie

HOUR SERVES

"Good apples pies are a considerable part of our domestic happiness." Jane Austen in a letter to her sister Cassandra, in the autumn of 1815. We couldn't have put it better ourselves.

200g Sweet Shortcrust Pastry (page 103) or 2 sheets Edmonds sweet short pastry, thawed
milk or water

FILLING
4–6 Granny Smith apples, peeled and cored
½ cup sugar
25g butter, melted

2 Tbsp Edmonds standard flour
¼ tsp ground cloves
extra 2 tsp sugar

1. Preheat the oven to 200°C.
2. Prepare the filling first. Slice the apples thinly, then combine with the sugar, butter, flour and ground cloves.
3. On a lightly floured board, roll out the pastry slightly larger than a 20cm pie dish and cut two 2.5cm wide strips long enough to go around the edge of the pie dish. Brush them with water and press onto the edge. Brush the tops of the strips with water.
4. Spoon the apples into the dish, cover with the remaining pastry and press the pastry edges firmly together to seal.
5. Trim away the excess pastry and crimp the edges by pinching with your fingers. Roll out the trimmings and cut decorative shapes for the top of the pie and secure them on with a little water.
6. Brush the whole top of the pie lightly with milk or water and sprinkle with sugar. Cut a few steam holes in the pastry.
7. Bake for 25 minutes or until the pastry is golden. Test with a skewer to see if the apple is soft and cooked. If not, reduce the oven temperature to 180°C and cook for a few more minutes until the apple is tender.

Apple Strudel

1½ HOURS   4 SERVES

Master the basic strudel and then let your imagination run wild with combinations of different fresh and dried fruit. You could even add nuts for extra crunch.

6 sheets Edmonds filo pastry, thawed
cooking oil spray
½ cup soft breadcrumbs
½ tsp lemon zest
3 Granny Smith apples, cored,
    peeled and sliced

1 tsp ground cinnamon
¼ cup brown sugar
½ cup sultanas
1 Tbsp butter, melted
icing sugar

1. Preheat the oven to 200°C. Grease a baking tray or line with baking paper.
2. Place the first filo sheet onto the prepared tray, spray lightly with cooking oil then place the next sheet on top and spray with oil. Continue layering the filo sheets in this way on the prepared tray.
3. Spread the breadcrumbs over the pastry. These will absorb any juices from the apples as they cook.
4. Mix lemon zest, apples, cinnamon, sugar and sultanas together. Do this just before you are going to assemble the strudel or the sugar will cause the liquid to come out of the apples and it will be messy to handle. Spread over the centre of the pastry to within 5cm of the short edges of the pastry.
5. Dampen pastry edges with water. Fold the pastry over the filling like you're wrapping a parcel and seal the edges. Place the strudel so the join is on the bottom then cut three slashes in the top of the pastry. Brush with the melted butter.
6. Bake for 30 minutes or until the pastry is golden. Dust with icing sugar and serve warm or cold.

Baked Apples

1½ HOURS   6 SERVES

A homely and simple pudding – made special by a fruity filling and whipped or runny cream.

2 Tbsp butter, softened
2 Tbsp brown sugar

¼ cup sultanas or currants
6 Granny Smith apples

1. Preheat the oven to 160°C.
2. Mix together the butter and sugar and add the sultanas or currants.
3. Peel the apples one third of the way down and remove the cores. Score the peeled apples with a fork.
4. Spoon the fruit mixture evenly into the cavities, place the apples in an ovenproof dish and add 2cm of water to the dish.
5. Bake the apples for about 1 hour or until they are tender. Serve with cream.

Baked Apple Dumplings

Baked apples enclosed in a scone-like pastry – think of individual apple pies.

2½ cups Edmonds standard flour
½ tsp salt
3 tsp Edmonds baking powder
75g butter
1 cup milk

4 small Granny Smith apples, peeled
 and cored
1 cup sugar
1 cup hot water

1. Preheat the oven to 190°C. Grease an ovenproof baking dish.
2. Sift the flour, salt and baking powder into a bowl and rub in the butter with your fingertips until the mixture resembles coarse breadcrumbs.
3. Add the milk, mix to a soft dough and divide the dough into four. On a lightly floured board, roll out each portion to a 20cm square and place an apple in the centre.
4. Dampen the edges with water, sprinkle each apple with 1 teaspoon of the sugar, then carefully wrap the dough around each apple, pressing the edges to seal well.
5. Place the apples in the prepared dish. Put the water and remaining sugar into a saucepan and heat gently, stirring constantly until the sugar has dissolved. Pour the hot syrup over the apples.
6. Bake for 45 minutes or until the pastry is golden and the apples are cooked when tested with a fine skewer. Serve with cream or custard.

Baked Custard

A very simple custard – pleasant and light to eat.

2 cups full-cream milk
3 eggs, beaten
¼ cup sugar

½ tsp vanilla essence
pinch of nutmeg

1. Preheat the oven to 150°C.
2. Heat the milk until almost boiling and whisk it into the beaten eggs with the sugar and vanilla. Pour the custard through a strainer into a 20cm pie dish.
3. Sprinkle the top with nutmeg and set the dish carefully in a shallow roasting pan. Pour enough hot water into the pan to come halfway up the sides of the pie dish. Slide the whole assembly carefully into the oven.
4. Bake for 1 hour or until set. Serve hot or cold.

Brandy Butter

The perfect accompaniment to a steamed Christmas pudding. Also known as hard sauce.

100g unsalted butter, softened
100g caster sugar

2–3 Tbsp brandy

1. Cream the butter until very soft and pale, then gradually add almost all the caster sugar, a spoonful at a time.

2. Mix in the brandy, then add the last of the sugar very slowly to ensure that the mixture does not curdle.
3. Pile into a serving bowl and chill until firm before using.

VARIATION
Rum Butter
If you prefer rum butter, replace the brandy with rum and use soft brown sugar rather than caster sugar.

Brandy or Rum Custard

Custard with a warming hit of brandy – pour it on a spongy fruit pudding.

2 Tbsp Edmonds Fielder's cornflour
2 Tbsp sugar
1½ cups full-cream milk

1 Tbsp butter
2 Tbsp brandy or rum
pinch of nutmeg

1. Put the cornflour, sugar and ¼ cup of the milk in a saucepan and mix to a smooth paste, then add the remaining milk.
2. Place over a medium heat and bring slowly to a simmer, stirring constantly. Cook for 2–3 minutes then remove from the heat and stir in the butter, brandy or rum and nutmeg.

Bread and Butter Pudding

How to turn leftover bread into cake – make this bread and butter pudding.

2 Tbsp butter, softened
6–8 thick slices stale bread
2 Tbsp currants
¼ cup sugar

2 tsp finely grated lemon zest
4 eggs
2 cups full-cream milk
icing sugar

1. Butter the slices of bread and cut them into triangles.
2. Arrange the slices in layers in an ovenproof dish interspersed with the currants, sugar and lemon zest.
3. Beat the eggs and milk together and pour over the bread. Set aside for about 30 minutes, pushing the bread back down into the milk occasionally.
4. Preheat the oven to 180°C.
5. Put the dish into a roasting pan filled with hot water and bake for about 45 minutes or until golden and set. Serve dusted with icing sugar.

VARIATION
Try spreading the bread with jam, add chocolate chips or use slices of stale brioche or raisin bread.

Spanish cream page 193, Flummery page 189

Lemon Tart page 191

Chocolate Custard

A very dark chocolate sauce, not too sweet.

1 Tbsp Edmonds Fielder's cornflour
¼ cup cocoa
1 cup milk

1–2 Tbsp sugar
1 Tbsp butter

1. Mix the cornflour, cocoa and ¼ cup of the milk to a smooth paste in a saucepan.
2. Add the remaining milk, the sugar and the butter and cook, stirring constantly for 2–3 minutes or until thick and smooth.

Chocolate Self-Saucing Pudding

A magic pudding trick in which sugar and cocoa on top of the pudding mixture are miraculously transformed into a smooth chocolate sauce underneath it. Always a favourite with children and adults alike.

SAUCE
½ cup brown sugar
4 Tbsp cocoa

1 Tbsp Edmonds Fielder's cornflour
2 cups boiling water

100g butter, softened
¾ cup sugar
1 egg
1 tsp vanilla essence

1¼ cups Edmonds standard flour
2 tsp Edmonds baking powder
2 Tbsp cocoa

1. Preheat the oven to 180°C. Grease an ovenproof dish that will hold about 6 cups.
2. Combine the brown sugar, cocoa and cornflour for the sauce.
3. Cream the butter, sugar, egg and vanilla together. Sift the dry ingredients together and fold into the creamed mixture.
4. Scoop the mixture into the dish and sprinkle with the dry sauce mixture, then carefully pour over the boiling water – hold a spoon upside down over the pudding and pour the water over it to stop splashing.
5. Bake for 35 minutes or until the pudding springs back when lightly touched.

Christmas Pudding

This recipe for a Rich Christmas Pudding first appeared in the Edmonds Cookery Book in the 1950s. It is a classic with many devoted followers and the best recipe to use if you want a thoroughly delicious, traditional, hot Christmas pudding.

50g Edmonds standard flour
125g soft breadcrumbs
125g soft brown sugar
125g shredded suet
125g apple, peeled and chopped
125g raisins
125g sultanas
125g currants

25g mixed peel
finely grated zest of 1 lemon
½ teaspoon nutmeg
½ teaspoon mixed spice
¼ teaspoon salt
2 large eggs, well beaten
juice of ½ lemon
2 tablespoons brandy or ale

1. Sift the flour, breadcrumbs, sugar and suet into a large mixing basin. Add the chopped apples, dried fruit, lemon zest and the spices and salt.

2. Mix together with your hands then tip in the eggs and the lemon juice. Mix thoroughly, then cover and leave overnight.

3. The next morning, generously grease an 8–10 cup capacity pudding basin and have ready a large saucepan half-filled with boiling water with a trivet or an upturned saucer in the base.

4. Add the brandy or ale to the pudding and combine well. Spoon the mixture into the prepared pudding basin. Cover with pleated greaseproof paper or tinfoil and secure with string around the rim of the basin, leaving a loop to lift out the pudding when it is cooked.

5. Carefully lower the pudding into the saucepan, making sure the water comes two-thirds of the way up the sides of the basin.

6. Cover and cook for 5 hours, making sure the water is constantly bubbling. Check the water level from time to time and top up with more boiling water. Keep for 2 weeks before serving.

Edmonds Custard

The perfect thing for pouring generously over hot puddings.

2 Tbsp Edmonds custard powder   *2 cups milk*
2 tsp sugar

1. In a saucepan mix the custard powder, sugar and ¼ cup of the milk to a smooth paste.

2. Add the remaining milk and heat gently, stirring constantly until the custard boils and thickens.

Fruit Betty

An old-fashioned layered bread and fruit pudding.

100g butter   *2 cups stewed fruit – e.g. apples,*
2 cups soft breadcrumbs   *plums, apricots*
½ cup sugar   *2 Tbsp brown sugar*

1. Preheat the oven to 190°C.

2. Melt the butter in a large frying pan and fry the breadcrumbs gently until they are crisp and golden. Mix in the first measure of sugar.

3. Fill a buttered ovenproof dish with alternate layers of stewed fruit, scattering each fruit layer with a little brown sugar and crisp breadcrumbs, finishing with breadcrumbs.

4. Bake for 30 minutes or until golden.

Fruit Crumble

1 HOUR   6 SERVES

Any baked fruit becomes a treat with a crunchy crumble topping. This is easy to make and a perennial family favourite.

2 cups stewed fruit – e.g. apples,
*   plums, apricots*
2 Tbsp brown sugar
¾ cup Edmonds standard flour

1 tsp Edmonds baking powder
100g butter
½ cup sugar

1. Preheat the oven to 190°C.
2. Place the stewed fruit in an ovenproof dish and sprinkle with the brown sugar.
3. Sift the flour and baking powder into a bowl and rub in the butter with your fingertips until the mixture resembles coarse breadcrumbs.
4. Stir in the sugar and spoon the crumble mixture evenly over the fruit.
5. Bake for 30 minutes or until pale golden. Serve with cream, yoghurt or custard.

VARIATIONS
Wholemeal Crumble
Replace the white flour with wholemeal flour.
Wholegrain Oat Crumble
Reduce the flour to ¼ cup. Stir in ½ cup wholegrain oats after the sugar.

Fruit Sponge

1 HOUR   6 SERVES

Make sure the fruit is hot or the sponge topping won't cook properly. Serve with plenty of cream.

2 cups hot stewed fruit – e.g. apples,
*   boysenberries, apricots*
125g butter
½ tsp vanilla essence
½ cup sugar

2 eggs
1 cup Edmonds standard flour
2 tsp Edmonds baking powder
2 Tbsp milk
icing sugar

1. Preheat the oven to 190°C.
2. Place the sweetened stewed fruit in an ovenproof dish, cover and keep hot while you make the sponge topping.
3. Put the butter, vanilla and sugar into a bowl and beat hard until pale and creamy.
4. Beat in the eggs one at a time, beating well after each addition. Sift on the flour and baking powder and fold into the mixture, followed by the milk. Spoon the sponge mixture over the fruit.
5. Bake for 40 minutes or until the sponge springs back when lightly touched. Serve hot dusted with icing sugar.

Lemon Delicious

1 HOUR   6 SERVES

A very light lemon sponge with creamy lemon custard underneath.

1 cup full-cream milk
½ cup sugar
finely grated zest and juice of 1 lemon

2 Tbsp Edmonds standard flour
1 Tbsp butter, melted
2 eggs, separated

1. Preheat the oven to 160°C. Grease a shallow 3-cup baking dish. Find another ovenproof dish into which it will fit neatly.
2. Put the milk, sugar, lemon zest and juice, flour, melted butter and egg yolks into the bowl of a blender or food processor. Whiz until smoothly blended then pour into a bowl.
3. Beat the egg whites until stiff and gently combine with the lemon mixture – don't over-mix.
4. Pour the mixture into the buttered dish. Place it inside the larger dish, and add enough hot water to come halfway up the sides of the pudding dish.
5. Cook for about 40 minutes until the pudding is risen and golden.

NOTE
To make by hand, use a whisk to combine all the ingredients before you add the egg whites, and fold them through with a few strokes of the whisk.

Lemon Meringue Pie

1 HOUR   6 SERVES

Crisp pastry, creamy lemon filling and gold-tipped meringue. A classic pudding for any occasion.

300g Sweet Shortcrust Pastry (page 103) or 2 sheets Edmonds sweet short
    pastry, thawed

FILLING
¼ cup Edmonds Fielder's cornflour
2 tsp finely grated lemon zest
½ cup lemon juice
¾ cup cold water

½ cup sugar
3 egg yolks
1 Tbsp butter

TOPPING
3 egg whites

½ cup caster sugar

1. Preheat the oven to 190°C.
2. On a lightly floured board, roll out the pastry or use a ready-rolled sheet. Line a 23cm flan ring or pie dish and trim away any excess pastry. Chill for 10 minutes.
3. Put a crumpled sheet of baking paper or tinfoil into the pastry case and fill it with dry chickpeas, rice or beans. Bake the pastry case for 15–20 minutes, and then remove it from the oven and carefully take out the paper and the beans. Return the case to the oven for 5 minutes to dry the pastry. The pastry must be thoroughly cooked and crisp.
4. While the pastry is cooking, make the filling and topping. Combine the cornflour, lemon zest and juice in a saucepan and mix until smooth, then add the cold water. Cook gently, stirring until the mixture boils and becomes thick and clear. Stir in the

sugar, egg yolks and butter and mix well. Take off the heat and set aside.

5. Beat the egg whites until stiff but not dry. Beat in the sugar a spoonful at a time, until very thick and glossy.

6. Pour the filling onto the cooked pastry base and spoon the meringue topping over the filling, taking it up to the pastry edge, but not over it. Swirl into points and tips.

7. Bake for 15–20 minutes or until the meringue is lightly golden. Serve warm or at room temperature.

VARIATION
Add the pulp of 2–3 passionfruit to the lemon filling.

Lemon Soufflé

Soufflés have a reputation for being difficult to get right, but that isn't really the case with this one. Give it a go and surprise yourself – it's a winner.

75g butter
3 Tbsp Edmonds standard flour
¾ cup milk
2 tsp finely grated lemon zest

2 Tbsp lemon juice
¼ cup sugar
4 eggs, separated

1. Preheat the oven to 190°C. Lightly grease a 4-cup soufflé dish.

2. Melt the butter in the top of a double boiler or a heatproof bowl set over a saucepan of simmering water. Remove from the heat and stir in the flour, mixing until smooth.

3. Add the milk, lemon zest and juice and mix well, then return to the heat and cook until the sauce is thick. Add the sugar, stirring until it dissolves. Remove from the heat and leave to cool for 5 minutes.

4. Whisk the egg yolks until pale and fluffy and stir into the sauce.

5. Beat the egg whites until soft peaks form. Fold half into the sauce mixture, followed by the rest. Pour the mixture carefully into the prepared dish.

6. Bake for 40 minutes or until the mixture is well risen and golden. Serve immediately.

VARIATION
Chocolate Soufflé
Increase the milk to 1 cup and leave out the lemon zest and juice. Add 150g grated dark chocolate to the sauce with the sugar and stir until the chocolate melts.

Moist Date Pudding

Sweet and sticky, with an irresistible caramel sauce.

1½ cups halved pitted dates
1½ cups water
1 tsp Edmonds baking soda
150g butter, softened
1 cup brown sugar
⅓ cup golden syrup

2 eggs
1 tsp vanilla essence
2 cups Edmonds standard flour
1 tsp Edmonds baking powder
Caramel Fudge Sauce (page 174)

1. Preheat the oven to 180°C. Grease a 22cm round cake tin and line the base with baking paper.

2. Combine the dates and water in a saucepan, bring to the boil then set aside to cool to lukewarm. Stir in the baking soda.

3. Beat the butter and sugar until light and creamy, then beat in the golden syrup.

4. Add the eggs one at a time, beating well after each addition, followed by the vanilla.

5. Sift on the flour and baking powder and fold through, then scoop the mixture into the prepared tin.

6. Bake for about 45 minutes or until the cake springs back when lightly touched. Stand for 2 minutes before turning out and cutting into wedges. Serve warm with Caramel Fudge Sauce.

Queen of Puddings

One of the best British puddings, this baked bread custard with meringue topping acquired its royal name during the reign of Queen Victoria. Although grand and majestic looking, it is easy to make – and to eat.

2 cups milk	½ tsp finely grated lemon zest
2 Tbsp butter	3 Tbsp raspberry jam
1 cup soft breadcrumbs or cake crumbs	¼ cup sugar
2 eggs, separated	
2 Tbsp sugar	

1. Preheat the oven to 180°C Grease a shallow 6-cup ovenproof dish or individual ovenproof dishes.

2. Bring the milk and butter almost to the boil, pour it over the breadcrumbs and leave to soak for about 10 minutes.

3. Add the beaten egg yolks. The first measure of sugar and the lemon zest to the milk mixture and combine well. Pour into the prepared dish.

4. Bake for about 30 minutes or until just firm. Remove from the oven.

5. Warm the jam a little and spread it carefully over the baked custard without breaking the surface. Then whisk the egg whites until stiff and whisk in the second measure of sugar a tablespoon at a time.

6. Pile the meringue on top of the jam layer, spread out and swirl the top decoratively – or you could pipe the meringue on with a forcing bag fitted with a star nozzle. Sprinkle with a little more sugar.

7. Bake for 10–15 minutes until the meringue is a golden brown. Serve hot.

Rice Pudding

Baked rice pudding, cooked very slowly until it is very creamy inside with a nice golden crust and slightly crisp edges.

5 Tbsp short grain rice	2–3 drops of vanilla essence
2 Tbsp sugar	1 Tbsp butter
3 cups full-cream milk	¼ tsp ground nutmeg

1. Preheat the oven to 150°C. Grease a 4-cup ovenproof dish.

2. Put the rice and sugar in the dish and add the milk and vanilla. Mix well and leave to soak for 30 minutes.
3. Add the butter in small pieces and sprinkle over the nutmeg.
4. Bake for 2–3 hours, stirring two to three times in the first hour.

VARIATION
Sago Pudding
Replace the rice with 3 tablespoons of sago.

Roly-Poly Pudding

1 HOUR 6 SERVES

A roll of jam-filled dough, cooked with a sweet sauce. A special winter treat and best after a light meal.

SYRUP
1 cup water
½ cup sugar
1 Tbsp golden syrup

1 Tbsp butter
2 Tbsp lemon juice

DOUGH
1½ cups Edmonds standard flour
2 tsp Edmonds baking powder
2 Tbsp butter
1 Tbsp sugar

2 tsp finely grated lemon zest
⅓ cup milk
½ cup warmed apricot, blackberry or
*   blackcurrant jam*

1. Preheat the oven to 190°C. Grease a large shallow baking dish.
2. Make the syrup by putting the water, sugar, golden syrup and butter into a saucepan and bring to the boil, stirring. Add the lemon juice and set aside.
3. Sift together the flour and baking powder and rub in the butter with your fingertips until the mixture forms fine crumbs. Add the sugar and lemon zest and then as much milk as you need to make a soft dough.
4. Roll out the dough on a floured board to a 25cm rough square and spread with warmed jam. Moisten the edges with milk, fold in the sides and then roll up gently, finishing with the join underneath the roll. Use two spatulas to lift the roll carefully into the prepared dish, then pour over the warm syrup.
5. Bake for about 30 minutes until golden brown and bubbling. Serve with cream or custard.

Steamed Sponge Pudding

2 HOURS 6 SERVES

In the days when coal ranges were common in New Zealand houses, steaming a pudding gently for several hours on top of the range was an easy matter. Today it is a less usual way of cooking puddings, and you could bake this one in the oven if you prefer, but do try steaming at least once.

½ cup sugar
2 eggs
115g butter, melted
½ cup apricot jam
1 cup Edmonds standard flour

1½ tsp Edmonds baking powder
⅛ tsp salt
½ tsp Edmonds baking soda
3 Tbsp full-cream milk

1. Grease a 4-cup heatproof pudding basin generously and have ready a large saucepan half-filled with simmering wate, with a trivet or an upturned saucer in the base.

2. Beat together the sugar and eggs until pale and fluffy, add the melted butter and beat again, then add the apricot jam.

3. Sift on the flour, baking powder and salt and fold through, followed by the baking soda dissolved in the milk. Stir to combine.

4. Pour the mixture into the pudding basin. Cover with pleated greaseproof paper or tinfoil and secure with string around the rim of the basin, leaving a loop to lift out the pudding when it is cooked. Carefully lower the pudding into the saucepan, making sure the water comes two-thirds of the way up the sides of the basin.

5. Steam for 1½ hours. Check the water level occasionally and top up with boiling water. Turn out and serve with cream or custard.

VARIATIONS

Golden Syrup Pudding
Place ½ cup golden syrup at the bottom of the pudding basin.

Apple Pudding
Add ½ cup stewed apple to the mixture.

Fig or Prune Pudding
Add ½ cup chopped figs or prunes to the mixture.

NOTE

If you want to cook this pudding in the oven, put the mixture into 6 small ramekins in a roasting pan half-filled with hot water and cover the whole dish with tinfoil. Bake at 180°C for about 30 minutes. The foil holds in the steam so the puddings stay very moist.

Upside-Down Pudding

1 HOUR   6 SERVES

Pineapple rings with cherries in the centre look glamorous and pears more homely, but both taste wonderful.

TOPPING
25g butter, melted
¼ cup brown sugar
1 tsp mixed spice

425g can pear halves, drained, or
*　6 pineapple rings, drained*
6 glacé cherries

PUDDING
125g butter, softened
½ cup sugar
2 eggs

1 cup Edmonds standard flour
2 tsp Edmonds baking powder
2 Tbsp milk

1. Preheat the oven to 180°C. Grease a 20cm round cake tin.

2. Combine the melted butter, brown sugar and mixed spice and spread over the base of the cake tin then arrange the pears or pineapple rings carefully on top. Put the cherries in the centre of the pineapple rings.

3. Cream the butter and sugar until light and fluffy and add the eggs one at a time, beating well after each addition.

4. Sift on the flour and baking powder and fold into the creamed mixture, followed by the milk. Scoop the cake mixture carefully on top of the fruit and spread out evenly.
5. Bake for 40 minutes or until the pudding springs back when lightly touched. Turn the pudding out onto a serving plate and serve warm with cream or custard.

Yoghurt Cream

Perfect with summer fruits or poached stone fruit.

200g natural unsweetened yoghurt
1 Tbsp icing sugar

2 tsp grated orange rind
2 Tbsp whipped cream

1. Combine all the ingredients, mix well and chill until ready to serve.

Desserts with Edmonds Mixes

Our Edmonds cake mixes are not only quick and easy but extremely versatile. Use them to re-create some classic desserts like fruit sponge and steamed pudding or to put a twist on trifle.

Apple Coconut Flan

The surface of this flan has a light crunchy crust tasting of toasted coconut, topping a beautifully airy sponge. Underneath is the tangy lemony apple.

1 packet Edmonds Golden Butter
   Cake Mix
1 cup coconut
125g butter, softened

2 cups stewed apple
1 tsp finely grated lemon zest
¼ cup lemon juice
1 cup water

1. Preheat oven to 180°C. Grease a large ovenproof dish.
2. Put the contents of the cake mix packet and coconut into a bowl or food processor. Process to combine. Process or rub in the butter with your fingertips until it resembles coarse breadcrumbs.
3. Combine the stewed apple and lemon zest.
4. Place the stewed apples in the bottom of the prepared dish. Spoon the crumble-like cake mixture evenly over the apples. Combine the lemon juice and water. Pour this over the cake mixture.
5. Bake for 50–55 minutes or until pale golden and firm to touch. Serve hot or cold with hokey pokey ice cream or whipped cream.

Black Forest Cheesecake

The texture of this dessert is more mousse-like rather than a heavy cheesecake. Best made the night before serving.

1 packet Edmonds Continental
   Cheesecake Mix
6 Tbsp butter, melted
1½ cups cold milk

½ cup chopped cherries
100g chocolate, melted
½ cup whipped cream
grated chocolate

1. Put the contents of the biscuit base sachet into a bowl. Mix in the melted butter. Press the crumbs firmly over the base and sides of a greased 20cm pie dish or over the base and 5cm up the sides of a springform tin. Chill.
2. Place the milk and the contents of the filling sachet in the bowl of an electric mixer. Beat on low speed until all the ingredients are moistened. Beat on medium speed for 3 minutes or until thick and creamy. Fold the cherries and chocolate through the cheesecake mixture.
3. Pour into the prepared crumb shell. Chill until firm.
4. Serve decorated with whipped cream and grated chocolate.

Mini Lemon Berry Cheesecakes

2 HOURS **8** MAKES

The presentation of these little cheesecakes is the key to success. Try mixing it up with different flavoured jellies.

1 packet Edmonds Continental
   Cheesecake Mix
1½ cups cold milk

finely grated zest of 2 lemons
1 packet lemon jelly
fresh berries

1. Sprinkle the contents of the biscuit base sachet evenly into 6–8 glasses.
2. Place the milk and the contents of the filling sachet in the bowl of an electric mixer. Beat on low speed until all the ingredients are moistened. Beat on medium speed for 3 minutes or until thick and creamy. Stir through the lemon zest.
3. Divide the filling evenly between the glasses. Place the glasses in the fridge for at least 1 hour.
4. Prepare the jelly according to the packet, and chill until cold but not set. Divide the jelly mix evenly between the glasses, and refrigerate until set. Serve with fresh berries on top.

Fruit Sponge

1 HOUR6 **6** SERVES

You can't beat a good fruit sponge. Throw in what you have in the fruit bowl. Use canned fruit or liberate some rhubarb from the garden if in season.

3 cups stewed fruit
1 packet Edmonds Golden Butter
   Cake Mix
2 eggs

¾ cup milk
60g butter, softened
icing sugar

1. Preheat the oven to 180°C. Grease a large ovenproof dish.
2. Put the stewed fruit into the bottom of the dish.
3. Put the cake mix, eggs, milk and butter into a medium mixing bowl. Using an electric mixer, beat on low speed for 30 seconds to combine. Increase the speed to medium and mix for 2 minutes. Scrape down the sides of the bowl occasionally.
4. Pour the mixture over the fruit.
5. Bake for 35–40 minutes or until the sponge springs back when lightly touched. Serve dusted with icing sugar.

Steamed Pudding

1½ MINS **6** SERVES

This makes a wonderfully light pudding.

2 Tbsp jam or ¼ cup currants
1 packet Edmonds Golden Butter
   Cake Mix
½ cup milk

2 eggs
50g butter, softened
Edmonds Custard to serve (page 202)

1. Spoon the jam or currants into the bottom of a greased 6-cup capacity pudding basin and have ready a large saucepan half filled with simmering water, and with a trivet or an upturned saucer in the base.
2. Put the cake mix, milk, eggs and butter into an electric mixer bowl. Mix at low speed until the ingredients are combined. Beat for 2 minutes at medium speed. Scrape down the sides of the bowl occasionally.
3. Spoon the mixture into the prepared basin. Cover with pleated greaseproof paper and secure with string. Carefully lower the pudding into the saucepan, making sure the water comes two-thirds of the way up the sides of the basin.
4. Steam for 1¼ hours or until the pudding feels firm to touch. Check the water level occasionally and top up with boiling water.
5. Unmold onto a serving plate. Serve hot with the Edmonds Custard.

Red Velvet Trifle

1½ MINS   12 SERVES

A modern twist on the classic trifle. You could even try making little individual versions in a collection of pretty glasses.

BASE
*1 packet Edmonds Red Velvet
   Cupcakes Mix*
½ cup milk

2 eggs
60g butter, softened

TOPPING
60g butter, softened
80g white chocolate, grated
4 tsp milk
300ml cream
2 punnets ripe strawberries, sliced
2 Tbsp icing sugar

4 Tbsp strawberry jam
*3 Tbsp strawberry schnapps or other
   sweet liqueur (optional)*
450g Edmonds Custard (page 202)
*berries and white chocolate curls to
   decorate*

1. Preheat the oven to 180°C. Grease and line a 20cm square shallow cake tin.
2. Put the cake mix, milk, eggs and butter into an electric mixer bowl. Mix at low speed until the ingredients are combined. Beat for 2 minutes at medium speed. Scrape down the sides of the bowl occasionally. Pour mixture into the prepared tin.
3. Bake for 25 minutes or until an inserted skewer comes out clean. Set aside to cool.
4. Place the red velvet frosting mix, butter, white chocolate and milk into a mixing bowl. Beat with an electric mixer on low for 30 seconds, then on high for 3 minutes, scraping down the sides of the bowl occasionally. Whip the cream to soft peaks then fold through the frosting mix. Cover and set aside.
5. Sprinkle the strawberries with icing sugar, toss and set aside for 30 minutes.
6. Now assemble the trifle. Once cool, cut the red velvet cake into two layers. Spread the bottom layer with strawberry jam, then sandwich the top layer back on. Cut into 2cm cubes and place in a layer in a large trifle bowl.
7. Drizzle with the liqueur if you wish and spoon over the sliced strawberries, including the juice.
8. Spread the custard over the fruit, and spoon the frosting mix on top. Decorate with fresh berries and white chocolate curls.

Sweets

Whether you're making them as a family treat or as an offering for the school fundraiser, these classic homemade sweets are sure to disappear quickly.

Hints for making sweets at home:

- Hot sugar syrup can be tricky to manage, and you will need to work quickly once the sugar reaches the correct temperature, so make sure you have all the ingredients and equipment ready before you start.
- Always use a large heavy-based saucepan since the sugar will rise up in the pan as it boils.
- Make sure that all the sugar is dissolved before you let the syrup come to the boil. A good way to test this is to dip a wooden chopstick into the syrup, then into a cup of cold water, then rub the syrup between wet fingertips to feel whether any sugar granules remain undissolved.
- Once the syrup boils it is best to stop stirring and shake the pan occasionally to keep the mixture moving.

Use a sugar thermometer to take the guesswork out of judging the correct temperature. If you have no thermometer, use the techniques below to test the syrup:

114°C Soft ball   Drop a small amount of syrup into very cold water. You should have a soft ball that flattens when you remove it.

118°C Firm ball   Drop a small amount of syrup into very cold water. You should have a firm ball that does not flatten when you remove it.

125°C Hard ball   Drop a small amount of syrup into very cold water. You should have a ball that is hard enough to hold its shape, yet plastic.

135°C Soft crack   Drop a small amount of syrup into very cold water. The syrup should form separate threads that are hard but not brittle.

150°C Hard crack   Drop a small amount of syrup into very cold water. The syrup should form separate threads that are hard and brittle.

Apricot Balls

1 HOUR   20 MAKES

Dried apricots simmered in orange juice are the stars of these not-too-sweet treats.

200g dried apricots, chopped
½ cup orange juice
¼ tsp citric acid
½ cup icing sugar

1 cup fine desiccated coconut
1 cup fine biscuit crumbs
½ cup coconut or 100g dark chocolate, melted

1. Put the apricots, orange juice and citric acid into a saucepan, cover and bring to the boil, then reduce the heat and simmer for 10 minutes. Set aside to cool.
2. Purée the apricot mixture in a food processor or blender and put it into a bowl.
3. Add the icing sugar, the first measure of coconut and the biscuit crumbs and mix well.
4. Scoop out tablespoonfuls of the mixture and roll them into balls, then roll in the second measure of coconut or dip in melted chocolate. Chill until set.

Bliss Balls

1 HOUR   16 MAKES

These are quickly made in the food processor from nuts and dried fruit with additional flavourings of your choice and are gluten free. Here are two variations:

Date and Ginger Bliss Balls
1 cup soft, pitted dates, roughly chopped
½ cup shredded coconut
¼ cup crystallised ginger, chopped

1 Tbsp honey
1 Tbsp cocoa
½ tsp ground ginger
2 Tbsp currants or raisins

Apricot and Cashew Bliss Balls
1½ cups cashew pieces
1½ cups dried apricots, roughly chopped
½ cup fine desiccated coconut

½ tsp ground cardamom
pinch of salt
finely grated zest of 1 orange

1. Combine all the ingredients in a food processor and pulse until the mixture comes together and can be pressed into a ball, but is still slightly lumpy. Add a little water 1 teaspoon at a time if the mixture seems too crumbly. Taste for flavour and adjust if you need to.
2. Roll into about 16 balls. If you wish you can now roll the balls in cocoa, grated chocolate, toasted coconut or finely chopped nuts.
3. Chill until firm and store in the fridge.

Brandy Balls

1 HOUR   20 MAKES

Currants and walnuts add spice and texture to these Brandy Balls.

250g packet vanilla wine biscuits
2 Tbsp currants
2 Tbsp chopped walnuts
1 egg, lightly beaten
¼ cup sugar

1 Tbsp cocoa
1½ Tbsp brandy or sherry
125g butter, melted
fine desiccated coconut
    or chocolate hail

1. Crush the biscuits finely in a food processor or with a rolling pin, and combine in a mixing bowl with the currants and walnuts.
2. In another bowl stir the beaten egg, sugar and cocoa together until thoroughly mixed.
3. Add the brandy or sherry to the egg mixture and pour this onto the crumbs, followed by the melted butter. Stir until well combined.
4. Scoop out tablespoonfuls of the mixture and shape into balls, then roll in coconut or chocolate hail. Chill until firm.

Chocolate Fudge

30 MINS   36 MAKES

Always popular at the school fair sweet stall.

2 cups sugar
2 Tbsp cocoa
25g butter

½ cup milk
½ tsp vanilla essence

1. Lightly grease a 20cm square tin.
2. Mix the sugar and cocoa in a saucepan and add the butter and milk.
3. Heat gently, stirring constantly until the butter has melted and the sugar dissolved, about 10 minutes.
4. Stop stirring, bring to the boil and simmer until the mixture reaches the soft ball stage (114°C on a sugar thermometer).
5. Immediately remove the pan from the heat, add the vanilla and let stand for 5 minutes.
6. Beat with a wooden spoon until the fudge begins to thicken, then quickly pour into the tin and mark into squares. Cut when cold.

Chocolate Truffles

2 HOURS   15 MAKES

Serve these after dinner, or make up a box of them for a festive gift. Chocolate heaven.

100g unsalted butter
100g dark chocolate
1 cup icing sugar, approximately

1 Tbsp rum
1 tsp cocoa
fine desiccated or shredded coconut

1. Put the butter and chocolate into a saucepan and heat gently, stirring until melted.
2. Add ½ cup of the icing sugar and stir until the mixture is thick, then add the rum and cocoa. Add enough of the remaining icing sugar to form a stiff mixture.
3. Scoop out tablespoonfuls of the mixture and shape into balls, then roll in the coconut and chill until firm.

Coconut Ice

1 HOUR   36 MAKES

Pale, pretty and moreish with that delicious coconut texture. Get creative and theme with different colours for your next gala offering.

3 cups icing sugar
½ cup milk
25g butter

¼ tsp salt
¾ cup fine desiccated coconut
few drops of red food colouring

1. Lightly grease a 20cm square tin.
2. Put the icing sugar, milk, butter and salt into a saucepan and heat gently, stirring constantly until the sugar dissolves, about 10 minutes.
3. Stop stirring, bring to the boil and simmer until the mixture reaches the soft ball stage (114°C on a sugar thermometer).
4. Remove from the heat, mix in the coconut, and cool for 10 minutes.
5. Pour half of the mixture into a bowl, add the food colouring and beat with a wooden spoon until the mixture starts to thicken.
6. Pour into the prepared tin, and then beat the white portion until it starts to thicken and spread it over the pink mixture. Cool, then cut into squares.

Florentine Caramels

2 HOURS   64 MAKES

Creamy morsels with a fudgy texture and a spicy hit of ginger.

2½ cups sugar
2 Tbsp fine desiccated coconut
1 tsp ground ginger
1 Tbsp golden syrup

25g butter
½ cup milk
1 tsp vanilla essence

1. Lightly grease a 20cm square tin.
2. Put the sugar, coconut and ground ginger into a heavy-based saucepan and mix to combine.
3. Add the golden syrup, butter and milk and heat gently, stirring constantly with a wooden spoon until the sugar dissolve, about 10 minutes.
4. Increase the heat, bring to the boil and stop stirring, but watch closely. Boil for about 5 minutes or until the mixture reaches the soft ball stage (114°C on a sugar thermometer).
5. Remove from the heat and place the saucepan in the sink filled with about 5cm of cold water. Add the vanilla and beat with a wooden spoon until the mixture thickens and becomes creamy.
6. Pour into the prepared tin, smooth the surface and mark into squares. Cut into pieces when cold.

Queen of Puddings page 206

Red Velvet Trifle page 212

Hokey Pokey

1 HOUR   25 MAKES

A school holiday favourite and very quickly made. Sweet and crunchy.

6 Tbsp sugar
4 Tbsp golden syrup

1 tsp Edmonds baking soda

1. Lightly grease a 20cm square tin.
2. Put the sugar and golden syrup into a saucepan. Heat gently, stirring constantly for about 6 minutes until the sugar dissolves.
3. Stop stirring, increase the heat and bring to the boil, then boil for 3 minutes.
4. Remove from heat and stir in the baking soda. When the mixture froths up – about 30 seconds – pour it into the tin. Leave until cold and hard and then break into pieces.

NOTE
Don't try to make hokey pokey on a rainy or humid day since it will remain sticky rather than crunchy.

Marshmallows

3 HOURS   60 MAKES

These are easy to make and always impress. Try rolling them in toasted coconut, or flavouring them with mixed spice for the festive season.

2 Tbsp gelatine
½ cup water
2 cups sugar
1 cup water

1 tsp vanilla, peppermint or
**   strawberry essence**
few drops of red or green food
**   colouring**
coconut or icing sugar

1. Line the base and two sides of a 20cm x 30cm shallow tin with baking paper. Splash the baking paper with water.
2. Sprinkle the gelatine onto the first measure of water and set aside to swell for 10 minutes.
3. Place the sugar and second measure of water in a large saucepan and heat gently, stirring constantly until the sugar dissolves, about 10 minutes.
4. Put the bowl with the swelled gelatine over a saucepan of simmering water until it dissolves. Pour onto the sugar mixture and bring to the boil.
5. Boil steadily for 15 minutes without stirring, then cool until lukewarm.
6. Using an electric beater, beat the mixture until white, thick and fluffy but still pourable. Beat in the essence and food colouring then pour the mixture into the prepared tin.
7. Chill until set then turn out of the tin, cut into squares and roll in coconut or icing sugar. Store in the refrigerator.

Nut Toffee

1½ HOURS 25 MAKES

A caramel-coloured toffee with added flavour from the chopped nuts – try toasted walnuts or salted peanuts.

2 cups sugar
½ cup cream

2 Tbsp butter
½ cup chopped nuts

1. Lightly grease a 20cm square tin or line with tinfoil.
2. Put the sugar, cream and butter into a heavy-based saucepan and heat gently, stirring constantly until the sugar dissolves, about 5 minutes.
3. Stop stirring, bring to the boil and simmer until the mixture reaches the soft crack stage (135˚C on a sugar thermometer).
4. Remove from the heat, stir in the nuts and pour quickly into the tin. After 2 minutes, mark the surface of the toffee into squares with a knife, then leave to cool and set completely.
5. Once the nut toffee is cold, remove it from the tin and cut or break it into rough squares. It will break easily and have a slightly honeycomb texture inside.

Russian Fudge

2 HOURS 36 MAKES

Caramel-coloured, creamy smooth fudge – not Russian at all, but a New Zealand classic.

3 cups sugar
½ cup milk
½ cup sweetened condensed milk
125g butter

⅛ tsp salt
1 Tbsp golden syrup
2 tsp vanilla essence

1. Lightly grease a 20cm square tin.
2. Put the sugar and milk into a saucepan and heat gently, stirring constantly until the sugar dissolves, about 10 minutes.
3. Add the sweetened condensed milk, butter, salt and golden syrup and stir until the butter has melted.
4. Bring to the boil and continue boiling for about 5 minutes or until it reaches the soft ball stage (114˚C on a sugar thermometer). Stir occasionally to prevent the mixture burning on the base of the pan.
5. Remove from the heat, add the vanilla and cool for 2–3 minutes.
6. Beat the fudge with a wooden spoon or electric beater for about 3 minutes until it is the consistency of thick custard. It should still level out when you remove the spoon, so check every 30 seconds or so.
7. Pour into the tin and mark into squares. Cut when cold.

If you want to add chopped walnuts to the fudge, stir them in just before you start beating.

Toffee

2 HOURS   25 MAKES

2 cups sugar
1 cup water

1 Tbsp white vinegar
1 Tbsp butter

1. Lightly grease a 20cm square tin.
2. Put all the ingredients into a saucepan and heat gently, stirring constantly until the sugar dissolves, about 10 minutes.
3. Stop stirring, bring to the boil and boil until the mixture reaches the hard crack stage (150°C on a sugar thermometer).
4. Pour quickly into the tin and mark into squares. Cut when cool.

Toffee Apples

1 HOURS   10 MAKES

Make sure the apples are crisp and not too big and these will steal the show.

8–10 small apples
8 wooden ice-block sticks or
*   wooden skewers*
3 cups sugar
1 Tbsp white vinegar

1 Tbsp butter
½ cup water
½ tsp cream of tartar
few drops of red food colouring

1. Line a baking tray with baking paper. Wipe the apples, push a wooden ice-block stick into each stem end and place them on the tray.
2. Put the sugar, vinegar, butter and water into a saucepan and heat gently, stirring constantly until the sugar dissolves, about 10 minutes.
3. Add the cream of tartar and the food colouring and bring to the boil without stirring, then boil until the mixture reaches the hard crack stage (150°C on a sugar thermometer).
4. Remove from the heat, put the base of the pan in a bowl of cold water, tilt the pan slightly and dip an apple into the toffee, turning to coat evenly. Place on the lined tray.
5. Repeat with the remaining apples, then leave until cold and set.

NOTE
If the toffee becomes too thick as you dip the apples, return it briefly to a low heat to liquify it.

Turkish Delight

OVERNIGHT HOURS MAKES

Rosy pink sweet perfection.

2 Tbsp gelatine
¾ cup water
2 cups sugar
1 cup boiling water
½ tsp tartaric acid

few drops of flavouring – e.g. rosewater
or lemon or crème de menthe
few drops of red food colouring
½ cup icing sugar
½ cup Edmonds Fielder's cornflour

1. Line a 20cm x 30cm shallow tin with baking paper and splash the paper with water.
2. Sprinkle the gelatine over the first measure of water in a saucepan and leave to swell for 10 minutes.
3. Add the sugar and boiling water and stir until the sugar and gelatine dissolve.
4. Heat gently, stirring until the mixture boils, then stop stirring and boil for 15 minutes, stirring occasionally.
5. Remove from the heat, add the tartaric acid, flavouring and food colouring and pour the mixture into the tin. Leave to set for 24 hours.
6. The next day sift together the icing sugar and cornflour and place in a shallow dish. Cut the Turkish Delight into squares and roll in the icing sugar mixture.

Jams & Jellies

The adage that nothing tastes better than homemade is undoubtedly the case with jams and jellies. It's a great way of making the most of bountiful seasonal fruit and a very satisfying thing to do. Homemade preserves also make great little gifts.

How to make delicious jam:

Getting ready

- Use fresh or frozen fruit to make jam – or a mixture of the two. Make sure that fresh fruit is ripe, but not over-ripe.
- Use granulated or caster sugar – about three-quarters of the weight of the fruit.
- Find jars that have well-fitting lids and prepare them by washing in hot, soapy water and rinsing well. Place the jars on a baking tray spread with a clean tea towel and dry in an oven heated to 120°C. By the time the jam is ready they will be dry and sterilised.
- Alternatively, if you have a microwave oven put the rinsed jars into the microwave on high power (100%) for 45 seconds.
- Put two saucers into the freezer. You will use them to test the jam for setting.

Cooking the jam

You will need a wide, heavy-based pan for jam making. It doesn't have to be enormous and it should not be too deep. Low sides encourage rapid evaporation so that jams taste fresh and have a good, bright colour. A 12–15cm deep pan will allow space for the jam to bubble up, but not bubble over. Make jam in small batches so that the pan is only one-third full – no more than 2kg of fruit, and preferably a bit less.

- Cook the fruit with a little water, or on its own until the fruit is soft. Once you add the sugar the fruit will not soften any more.
- Add the sugar slowly and stir until it dissolves.
- Bring the jam to a rapid boil and stir often with a wooden spoon. The stirring will help prevent the jam sticking to the bottom of the pan.

Testing for a set

Once the surface of the jam is covered with small bubbles, begin timing. After 5–6 minutes, remove the pan from the heat while you test the jam. (If you have a sugar thermometer look for a temperature of 105°C, at which most jams will set.) Spoon a little jam onto one of the chilled saucers and leave it for 2 minutes. Then run your finger through the jam. If small wrinkles appear on the surface the jam has reached setting point. If not, return to the heat, bring back to a rolling boil and test again in another 5 minutes. Once the jam reaches setting point, remove from the heat and drop in 1 teaspoon of butter. As it melts it will magically make any surface froth disappear.

Filling the jars

When the jam has reached setting point, take the sterilised jars out of the oven. Ladle or pour the jam into the jars (a wide-mouthed funnel is useful here) and fill them as full as possible. Put on the lids firmly, or use cellophane covers. Leave undisturbed overnight or until completely cold.

Storing

Keep your jams in a cool, dark, dry place – not in a hot cupboard. Most jams will keep for at least one year with no deterioration. If you find a little mould on top of a jar, just spoon it off.

Pectin and acid

You need both pectin and acid to make jam set. Some fruits are high in both and some are not. Increase the pectin in jam by adding some high-pectin fruit like sour apples, and increase the acid by adding lemon juice or tartaric acid.

FRUITS RICH IN PECTIN AND ACID

apples (sour varieties) — grapes (under-ripe)
crab-apples — grapefruit
boysenberries, loganberries — lemons
raspberries — oranges (sour varieties)
currants, red and black — plums
gooseberries — passion fruit

FRUITS WITH PECTIN BUT NEEDING ACID

feijoas — blackberries
melon — quinces
oranges (sweet varieties) — apples (sweet varieties)

FRUITS WITH ACID BUT NEEDING PECTIN

apricots — tamarillos
kiwifruit — guavas
pineapple

FRUITS LOW IN PECTIN AND ACID

cherries — peaches
figs — rhubarb
elderberries — pears
strawberries

How to make clear fruit jellies:

Jellies are delicate preserves which have a stained-glass loveliness when in the jars. They taste wonderful on bread and butter or with a creamy dessert or as a condiment with roasted or cold meats.

- Jellies are made from strained fruit juice boiled with sugar which sets to a clear jelly as it cools.
- There is no need to peel or core the fruit for a jelly, just chop it up and then simmer it very gently with water in a covered pan to extract as much flavour as possible.
- Ladle the fruit and juice into a jelly bag or a clean old cotton pillowcase and hang it from a hook over a bowl which will collect the juice.
- Leave the juice to slowly drip out overnight, but don't squeeze the bag or the jelly will be cloudy.
- Have ready some smallish jars, sterilised as for making jam.
- Boil the juice in a jam pan with caster sugar and skim off any scum as it appears. You will lose a little jelly in the process, but you don't want white froth suspended in the jars.
- Test for setting in the same way as for jam, then pour the jelly into the sterilised jars and cover tightly.

General directions
Good fruit for jelly making

SOFT   –   berries, strawberries, red currants, grapes, plums
FIRM   –   apples, guavas, crab-apples, pineapples, feijoas, tamarillos
HARD   –   oranges, grapefruit, quinces

For each 1.5kg of fruit you should use:

- 3 cups water for soft fruit
- 5 cups for firm fruit
- 10 cups for hard fruit

1. Mash small and soft fruit and chop or slice large fruit, leaving the pectin-rich cores in and skin on. Put them into the jam pan.
2. Add enough water just to cover, using the list above as a guide. For low-acid fruit like guavas, tamarillos and pineapple, add 2 tablespoons lemon juice or ½ teaspoon citric or tartaric acid.
3. Cover the pan and cook the fruit gently until it has become a pulp – at least 30 minutes for soft fruit and up to 1 hour for hard fruit like quinces.
4. Strain the pulp through a jelly bag or an old cotton pillowcase.
5. The next day, measure the juice and allow 1 cup sugar to 1 cup juice for hard fruits, or ¾ cup sugar to 1 cup juice for softer fruits.
6. Heat the juice to boiling point, remove from the heat and add the sugar, stirring until it has dissolved.
7. Return the pan to the heat and boil briskly until it reaches setting point – skimming off the scum as it rises. The boiling time is usually about 15 minutes.
8. Pour into sterilised jars, cover tightly and try not to move the jars until the jelly is cold and set.

Apricot Jam

1 HOUR   8 CUPS

Use the best and sweetest apricots you can find to make the best jam.

**1.5kg fresh apricots, halved
  and stoned
2 cups water**

**juice of 1 lemon
7 cups sugar
1 tsp butter**

1. Put the apricots and water into a preserving pan with the lemon juice and bring to a simmer, stirring. Cook for 10–15 minutes.
2. Add the sugar gradually and stir until it has dissolved. Bring the jam to a fast, rolling boil, stirring often, and boil for 5–6 minutes.
3. Remove from the heat and test the jam for a set. When the jam reaches setting point stir in the butter to remove any froth.
4. Pour the jam into sterilised jars and cover tightly.

Dried Apricot and Pineapple Jam

OVERNIGHT   13 HOURS   4 CUPS

A jam to make in the winter from dried apricots and tinned pineapple. It has a very good flavour and beautiful colour.

**250g dried apricots, roughly chopped
2¾ cups water
½ cup lemon juice**

**440g can unsweetened crushed
  pineapple
3½ cups sugar
1 tsp butter**

1. Soak the apricots in the water for 12 hours overnight, then put in a saucepan with the soaking liquid and bring to the boil. Simmer for 20 minutes or until tender.
2. Add the lemon juice and crushed pineapple and bring back to the boil, then add the sugar and stir until it has dissolved.
3. Bring the jam to a fast, rolling boil, stirring often, and boil for 5–6 minutes.
4. Remove from the heat and test the jam for a set. When the jam reaches setting point stir in the butter to remove any froth.
5. Pour the jam into sterilised jars and cover tightly.

Feijoa Jam

1 HOUR   2 CUPS

If you are lucky enough to have a feijoa tree then you'll be glad of this quickly made jam to help use up the harvest.

**1kg feijoas (unpeeled weight)
½ cup water
1 tsp grated fresh ginger**

**grated zest and juice of 1 lemon
1 cup sugar
1 tsp butter**

1. Scoop out the feijoa flesh and chop it roughly. Put into a jam pan with the water, ginger and lemon zest and juice, and simmer until the fruit is soft.
2. Add the sugar gradually and stir until it has dissolved. Bring the jam to a fast, rolling boil, stirring often, and boil for 5–6 minutes.

3. Remove from the heat and test the jam for a set. When the jam reaches setting point stir in the butter to remove any froth.

4. Pour the jam into sterilised jars and cover tightly.

NOTE

You could double this recipe if you have a glut of feijoas.

Grapefruit Marmalade

OVERNIGHT   HOURS   CUPS

A New Zealand home-style chunky marmalade.

4 large grapefruit, minced, chopped or
  thinly sliced
2 large lemons, minced, chopped or
  thinly sliced

water to cover
sugar
1 tsp butter

1. Cover the grapefruit and lemons with water and stand overnight.

2. The next day, boil the fruit for 45 minutes or until it is soft and pulpy, then allow it to cool a little.

3. Measure the pulp, return it to the jam pan and bring to the boil. For each cup of pulp, add 1 cup sugar. Add the sugar gradually and stir until it has dissolved.

4. Bring the jam to a fast, rolling boil, stirring occasionally, and boil for 5–6 minutes.

5. Remove from the heat and test the marmalade for a set. When the marmalade reaches setting point stir in the butter to remove any froth.

6. Pour the marmalade into sterilised jars and cover tightly.

Guava Jelly

HOUR   CUPS

A tart, spicy jelly which is a traditional accompaniment to roast lamb – along with mint sauce of course.

1½kg red guavas
4 cups water

1 lemon, sliced
caster sugar

1. Put the guavas into the jam pan with the water and the sliced lemon. Cover the pan and simmer for 30 minutes or until pulpy – you can use a potato masher to squash the fruit.

2. Strain the pulp through a jelly bag or old cotton pillowcase suspended over a bowl to catch the juice. Don't squeeze the bag.

3. Measure the juice and allow ¾ cup caster sugar for each cup of juice.

4. Stir the juice and sugar over a gentle heat until the sugar has dissolved, then bring to a rapid boil and boil hard until the jelly reaches setting point. Skim off any scum as it appears.

5. Pour the jelly into the sterilised jars and cover tightly. Don't move the jars until the jelly is cold and set.

Lemon Honey

45 MINS · 4 CUPS

Sometimes called lemon curd or lemon cheese, this rich, buttery spread is always a treat, and a small jar makes a simple gift. Because of the eggs this must be stored in the fridge and consumed within 2 weeks.

125g butter
2 cups sugar

zest and juice of 4 lemons
4 eggs, beaten

1. Put the butter into the top of a double boiler or a heatproof bowl set over a saucepan of simmering water. When the butter has melted, add the sugar and lemon juice and zest and stir until the sugar has dissolved.
2. Pour a little of this mixture onto the beaten eggs and mix well, then pour it all back into the double boiler or bowl and return to the heat.
3. Cook, stirring all the time until the mixture thickens. (It will thicken more as it cools.)
4. Pour the lemon honey through a sieve into a jug and then pour into sterilised jars and cover tightly. Allow to cool then store in the refrigerator.

Mint & Apple Jelly

1 HOUR · 2 CUPS

Since apples have a lot of pectin and acid, they are easy to make into a jelly. By adding a little vinegar and some chopped herbs like mint – or tarragon – you can make a savoury herb jelly to serve with meat.

1kg cooking apples, washed
**   and chopped**
water
caster sugar
zest and juice of 1 lemon

½ cup firmly packed mint leaves, finely
**   chopped (retain stalks)**
½ cup white wine vinegar
green food colouring (optional)

1. Put the chopped apples, including the peel and cores, into a jam pan with enough water to cover.
2. Cover the pan and simmer for 30 minutes or until the apples are completely pulpy.
3. Strain the pulp through a jelly bag or old cotton pillowcase suspended over a bowl to catch the juice. Don't squeeze the bag.
4. Measure the juice and allow 1 cup caster sugar for each cup of juice.
5. Put the juice and sugar into the jam pan. Put the lemon zest and mint stalks in a small piece of muslin and tie the ends. Add to the pan with the strained lemon juice and the wine vinegar.
6. Heat gently, stirring, until the sugar has dissolved then bring the jelly to the boil.
7. Add the chopped mint leaves and boil rapidly for about 5 minutes or until the jelly reaches setting point.
8. Remove the muslin bag and add a few drop of green food colouring if you wish.
9. Pour the jelly into sterilised jars, cover tightly and don't move the jars until the jelly is cold and set.

Plum Jam

1 HOUR 4 CUPS

Tart and dark and a wonderful colour, plum jam is a great standby for baking or desserts. Easy and quick to make.

1kg plums, halved and stoned
1 cup water

4 cups sugar
1 tsp butter

1. Put the plum halves into a jam pan with the water. Bring to a simmer and cook until the plums are soft.
2. Add the sugar gradually and stir until the sugar has dissolved. Bring to a fast rolling boil and boil for 5–6 minutes.
3. Remove from the heat and test the jam for a set. When the jam reaches setting point stir in the butter to remove any froth.
4. Pour the jam into sterilised jars and cover tightly.

Strawberry Jam

OVERNIGHT 1¼ HOUR 3 CUPS

Jam made with strawberries is unlikely to set firmly since strawberries are low in both pectin and acid. But this fresh-tasting, softly set jam – as long as it doesn't run right off your toast – is a summer delight. Try it with yoghurt, too.

500g strawberries, halved
2 cups sugar

1 tsp tartaric acid
1 tsp butter

1. Put the strawberries into a bowl with the sugar, cover and leave overnight. The sugar will draw the juice from the strawberries and you will not need to add any water to the jam.
2. The next day put the strawberries and sugar into the jam pan and stir until the sugar has dissolved. Bring to a fast rolling boil and boil for 5 minutes, then add the tartaric acid and boil for another 5 minutes.
3. Remove from the heat and test the jam for a set. When the jam reaches setting point stir in the butter to remove any froth.
4. Pour the jam into sterilised jars and cover tightly.

VARIATION
Try adding 250g frozen raspberries or boysenberries to the strawberries and use 3 cups sugar. The jams will have a darker colour and more complex flavours, with strawberry still predominant.

Fresh or frozen berries can be used to make jam.

Sweet Orange Marmalade

A clear marmalade with fine shreds of golden peel suspended in it.

1½kg sweet oranges
2 lemons
1.5L water

1kg sugar
1 tsp butter

1. Wash the fruit, remove the stem ends and cut into quarters. Put in a jam pan with the water, bring to a simmer, cover the pan and cook the fruit for 1 hour or until the peel is tender when pierced with a fork.
2. Drain the fruit and return the juice to the preserving pan. Once the fruit has cooled a little use a spoon to scrape the pulp away from the skins and add the pulp to the juice in the pan. Simmer for 10 minutes – this extracts the pectin from flesh and pips – while you cut the soft peel into fine strips.
3. Strain the liquid, discard the pulp and return the strips of peel to the pan. Bring this to a simmer and add the sugar gradually, stirring until the sugar has dissolved.
4. Bring the marmalade to a fast, rolling boil, stirring often, and boil for 5–6 minutes.
5. Remove from the heat and test the marmalade for a set. When the marmalade reaches setting point stir in the butter to remove any froth and let stand for 10 minutes. The marmalade will thicken a little as it cools and the strips of peel will not rise to the top.
6. Pour the marmalade into sterilised jars and cover tightly.

Tamarillo Jam

There are not so many tamarillo trees in backyards anymore but for those lucky enough to get a glut of fruit here is a way to keep the taste all year round.

600g tamarillos, blanched, skinned
    and chopped
250g cooking apples, peeled
    and chopped

1 cup water
sugar
4 Tbsp lemon juice
1 tsp butter

1. Put the tamarillos, apples and water into a preserving pan. Boil until pulpy. Cool a little. Measure pulp and return to pan. Bring back to the boil.
2. For each cup of pulp, add 1 cup sugar then add the lemon juice. Stir until sugar is dissolved.
3. Boil briskly for 20–25 minutes. Remove from the heat and test for set. When the jam reaches setting point stir in the butter to remove any froth.
4. Pour into sterilised jars and cover tightly.

Pickles, Chutneys & Sauces

Make the most of surplus seasonal fruits and vegetables and enjoy the satisfaction of making your own pickles and chutneys. You'll probably produce more than you can easily get through at home, but friends and family will always appreciate being given one of your extras.

How to make pickles, chutneys and sauces:
Ingredients
- Use ripe, but not over-ripe vegetables and fruit for making pickles, and fully ripe for chutney, relish and sauces.
- Cider vinegar is best for most preserves, but use malt vinegar for darker pickles. Vinegar must have 5% acetic acid – check the label. Vinegar is the preservative in pickles so always use the amount given in the recipe.
- Use white or brown sugar as you wish.
- Use whole spices tied in muslin for paler preserves, or ground spices for darker ones.
- Use iodised or non-iodised salt as you wish.

Techniques and methods
- Always wash, drain and dry vegetables and fruit before you begin.
- Chutneys, relishes and sauces need at least 1 hour of cooking to thicken them and achieve a warm, rounded flavour so make a good-sized batch or the mixture may catch and burn on the bottom of the pan.
- Use an aluminium or stainless steel preserving pan for this sort of preserve, not a copper pan.
- Always use hot sterilised jars or bottles and fill close to the top. Less air space means less likelihood of mould.
- You can leave chutneys and relishes to get cold in the jars, covered with a cloth, then cover with sterilised lids. Make sure metal lids are lined or the vinegar may make them rust.
- A food processor or blender is useful for making smooth sauces.
- Always label preserves and store them in a cool, dark place.
- Leave pickles, chutneys and sauces for at least a fortnight – and as long as two years – before using them. They improve and mellow with age.

Any Fruit Chutney

An excellent recipe for using up excess ripe fruit. This keeps extremely well.

2kg apples, plums or tamarillos, peeled,
   cored or stoned, then chopped
500g onions, chopped
2 cups raisins
1 clove garlic, crushed
4 cups brown sugar

2 tsp salt
1 tsp ground cloves or
   mixed spice
½ tsp cayenne pepper
4 cups malt vinegar,
   approximately

1. Put all ingredients except vinegar into a preserving pan. Add enough vinegar to almost cover the fruit.
2. Bring slowly to a simmer, stirring constantly until the sugar has dissolved.
3. Simmer gently for 2 hours, stirring frequently. The chutney will be thick and jam-like.
4. Pack into sterilised jars and cover tightly. Keep for at least 2 weeks before using.

Beetroot Chutney

A beautifully coloured chutney with a good, spicy flavour.

1kg beetroot
500g onions
2½ cups malt vinegar
1 Tbsp salt
2 cups sugar

1 tsp ground allspice
1 tsp white pepper
1 tsp ground ginger
½ cup Edmonds standard flour
½ cup malt vinegar

1. Steam or boil the unpeeled beetroot for 30 minutes or until tender.
2. When the beetroot have cooled a little, rub off the skins and finely chop the beetroot and onions – you can do this in a food processor.
3. Put the vegetables in a preserving pan with the first measure of vinegar and bring to a simmer. Cook until the onion is tender.
4. Add the salt, sugar, allspice, pepper and ginger and boil for 25 minutes, stirring occasionally.
5. Mix the flour to a smooth paste with the second measure of vinegar, add to the pan and bring to the boil, stirring. Simmer for 5 minutes.
6. Pack into sterilised jars and cover tightly. Keep for at least 2 weeks before using.

Mustard Pickle

OVERNIGHT — HOURS — CUPS

A yellow vegetable pickle, sometimes called piccalilli, which is the perfect condiment for cold meats or in a corned beef sandwich.

4 cups cauliflower florets
4 cups pickling onions
4 cups green tomatoes, diced
4 cups cucumber, diced
1¼ cups salt
2L water

1 cup Edmonds standard flour
4 tsp dry mustard
1½ Tbsp turmeric
½ tsp cayenne pepper
1 cup sugar
1L malt vinegar

1. Put the prepared vegetables into a large non-metallic bowl, then dissolve the salt in the water and pour over the vegetables.
2. Leave to stand for 24 hours covered with a cloth, then drain thoroughly.
3. Mix together the flour, mustard, turmeric, cayenne pepper and sugar and stir in a little of the vinegar to make a smooth paste. Gradually add the remaining vinegar and put the liquid into a preserving pan.
4. Bring gradually to the boil, stirring until the mixture thickens. Add the drained vegetables and boil for 5 minutes or until the vegetables are heated through.
5. Pack into sterilised jars and cover tightly. Keep for at least 2 weeks before using.

Peach Chutney

HOURS — CUPS

Fruit chutneys like this one make very good accompaniments for meat or vegetable curries.

2.25kg peaches, peeled, stoned and
    chopped
500g onions, chopped
2 cups raisins
1 cup mixed peel
½ cup crystallised ginger, chopped

2 cups brown sugar
1 Tbsp salt
1 Tbsp curry powder
½ tsp cayenne pepper
3½ cups malt vinegar

1. Put all the ingredients into a preserving pan and heat gently, stirring until the sugar has dissolved.
2. Boil steadily for 1 hour, stirring frequently until the mixture is thick and jam-like.
3. Pack into sterilised jars and cover tightly. Keep for at least 2 weeks before using.

Pickled Onions

OVERNIGHT — HOUR — LITRES

This recipe has no sugar at all, so the onions will be sharp and strong.

1.5kg pickling onions
½ cup salt
water to cover

3 dried chillies, approximately
6 peppercorns, approximately
malt or white vinegar

1. Peel the onions by putting them into a large bowl and covering with boiling water. Leave for just 20 seconds, then drain and cover with cold water. Peel away the skins.
2. Put the onions in a non-metallic bowl and sprinkle with the salt, then add cold water to cover and let stand for 24 hours.
3. Drain the onions and rinse them in cold water then pack them into sterilised jars. Add 1 chilli and 2 peppercorns to each jar, then pour in enough vinegar to cover the onions.
4. Seal with non-metallic lids and keep for 4–6 weeks before using.

VARIATION
Sweet Pickled Onions
These are crisp and sharp and just slightly sweet. Try them in a corned beef sandwich or with cheese. Add 1 cup sugar for each 3 cups vinegar. Heat the sugar and the vinegar and stir to dissolve, then pour over the onions. Makes 2 litres.

Pickled Vegetables

OVERNIGHT HOURS LITRE

Colourful, crisp and tasty, these are a great accompaniment for any cold meats, cheese, or even in a salad.

12 shallots or pickling onions, peeled
1 cucumber, peeled and diced
1 cup sliced celery
1 cup sliced green beans
2 cups cauliflower florets

1 red capsicum, sliced
6 Tbsp salt
500ml Spiced Vinegar,
*   approximately (page 237)*

1. Prepare the vegetables so that the pieces are a similar size. Put the onion, cucumber and celery into one non-metallic bowl, the beans and cauliflower into another and the red capsicum in a third.
2. Sprinkle the capsicum with 1 tablespoon of the salt and divide the remaining salt between the other two bowls. Cover and let stand for 12 hours or overnight.
3. The next day drain off the liquid and rinse the vegetables in cold water. Drain again.
4. Drop the cauliflower and beans into boiling water and cook for 2 minutes, then remove.
5. Mix all the vegetables together, pack into sterilised jars and pour over enough spiced vinegar to cover.
6. Seal the jars with non-metallic lids and keep for at least 3 weeks before using.

Plum Sauce

HOURS LITRES

Plum sauce can be used as a general relish in the same way as tomato sauce and is an excellent addition to a marinade for barbecued meats.

2.75kg plums, halved and stoned
1.5L malt vinegar
3 cups brown sugar
50g garlic, peeled
2 tsp ground black pepper

2 tsp ground cloves
2 tsp ground ginger
1 tsp ground mace
½ tsp cayenne pepper
1 Tbsp salt

Florentine Caramels page 216
Bliss Balls page 214

Mint Jelly

Mustard Pickle page 233, Mint & Apple Jelly page 228, Tomato Relish page 238

1. Put all the ingredients into a preserving pan and bring slowly to the boil, stirring until the sugar has dissolved.
2. Boil steadily until the mixture is pulpy, then purée in a blender or food processor – work in small batches to avoid spills.
3. Return the sauce to the pan and bring back to the boil. Simmer for 2–3 minutes.
4. Pour into sterilised bottles and seal. Keep for at least 2 weeks before using.

Spiced Vinegar

40 MINS   2 LITRES

Make this in advance and use it for Pickled Vegetables (page 234). It keeps indefinitely.

2L malt or cider vinegar
1 cup sugar
2 Tbsp black peppercorns
2 Tbsp whole cloves
1 Tbsp whole allspice

4cm piece of fresh ginger
2 Tbsp salt
1 Tbsp mustard seeds
2 tsp crushed nutmeg pieces

1. Put all the ingredients into a large saucepan and bring to a simmer, stirring to dissolve the sugar.
2. Simmer gently for 10 minutes, then either strain out the spices and use immediately, or leave the spices in for 2–3 days and then strain them out – this gives a spicier flavour.
3. Bottle and store in a dark place.

Sweet Pickled Gherkins

OVERNIGHT   1 HOUR   4½ LITRES

4kg gherkins
½ cup salt
6 cups water
2.25L malt vinegar

5 cups brown sugar
25g whole mixed pickling spice
10cm piece of cinnamon stick
1 tsp whole cloves

1. Wash the gherkins and scrub lightly with a coarse cloth to remove any roughness. Mix the salt and water in a non-metallic bowl, add the gherkins and let stand for 24 hours.
2. The next day, put the vinegar, sugar, pickling spice, cinnamon and cloves into a saucepan, bring to the boil, stirring to dissolve the sugar, and simmer for 5 minutes.
3. Drain the gherkins, put in a bowl and pour over enough boiling water to cover them. Pour off the boiling water immediately and, while they are hot, pack the gherkins into sterilised jars.
4. Pour the hot vinegar mixture over the gherkins to cover them and seal at once with non-metallic lids. Keep for at least 3 weeks before using.

NOTE
You can buy pickling spices ready mixed or make your own. Combine 1 tablespoon each of black peppercorns, mustard seeds, whole allspice and dried chillies; 1 teaspoon each of coriander seeds and whole cloves, 1 bay leaf and 1 cinnamon stick, both broken up, and 2 blades of mace. Keep in an airtight jar.

Tomato Relish

OVERNIGHT · 2½ HOURS · 1½ LITRES

A fairly thick and chunky relish to serve with cold meats and cheese. For a finer result, cut the tomatoes and onions into smaller pieces.

1.5kg tomatoes, blanched, skinned
   and quartered
4 onions, quartered
2 Tbsp salt
2 cups brown sugar
2¼ cups malt vinegar

3 fresh or dried red chillies
1 Tbsp mustard powder
1 Tbsp curry powder
2 Tbsp Edmonds standard flour
¼ cup malt vinegar

1. Put the tomatoes and onions into a non-metallic bowl, sprinkle with the salt and let stand for 12 hours then drain well.
2. Put the vegetables, sugar, first measure of vinegar and chillies into a preserving pan, bring to the boil slowly, then simmer for 1½ hours, stirring frequently.
3. Mix the mustard, curry powder, flour and the second measure of vinegar to a smooth paste and stir it into the relish. Simmer for 5 more minutes.
4. Pack into sterilised jars. Keep for at least 2 weeks before using.

Tomato Sauce

2½ HOURS · 7 CUPS

The classic sauce. Good with just about everything

3.5kg tomatoes, chopped
1kg apples, peeled and chopped
6 onions, chopped
3 cups sugar
4 cups malt vinegar

2 Tbsp salt
½–1 tsp cayenne pepper
1 tsp black peppercorns
1 tsp whole allspice
2 tsp whole cloves

1. Put the tomatoes, apples, onions, sugar, vinegar, salt and cayenne pepper into a preserving pan. Tie the peppercorns, allspice and cloves in a piece of muslin and add to the pan.
2. Bring slowly to the boil, stirring until the sugar dissolves, then simmer gently for about 2 hours or until completely pulpy.
3. Remove the spice bag and either press the sauce through a coarse sieve, or purée in a blender or food processor. Work in small batches to avoid splashes and spills.
4. Return the sauce to the pan and bring back to the boil and simmer for 2 minutes.
5. Pour into sterilised bottles and seal tightly. Keep for at least 3 weeks before using.

To skin tomatoes, cut a small cross through the skin at the base of each tomato
and drop them into a saucepan of boiling water for 30 seconds. Remove and
plunge them into a bowl of cold water, then peel.

Index

Notes

Notes

Notes

De Luxe Edition		Printings	De Luxe Edition		Printings
1st	1955	120,000	36th	1994	27,000
2nd	1956	120,000	37th	1994	30,000
3rd	1957	120,000	38th	1995	20,000
4th	1959	120,000	39th	1996	30,000
5th	1962	80,000	40th	1996	30,000
6th	1964	80,000	41st	1997	30,000
7th	1966	80,000	42nd	1998	30,000
8th	1967	80,000	43rd	1998	15,000
9th	1968	80,000	44th	1998	35,000
10th	1969	80,000	45th	1999	35,000
11th	1971	80,000	46th	1999	35,000
12th	1972	100,000	47th	2000	35,000
13th	1973	80,000	48th	2001	35,000
14th	1974	100,000	49th	2001	35,000
15th	1976	200,000	50th	2002	35,000
16th	1978	200,000	51st	2003	35,000
17th	1980	100,000	52nd	2003	35,000
18th	1982	50,000	53rd	2004	35,000
19th	1983	100,000	54th	2005	35,000
20th	1985	30,000	55th	2005	35,000
21st	1985	54,000	56th	2006	35,000
22nd	1986	54,000	57th	2006	35,000
23rd	1986	50,000	58th	2007	35,000
24th	1987	50,000	59th	2007	35,000
25th	1988	30,000	60th	2008	10,000
26th	1989	30,000	61st	2008	50,000
27th	1990	30,000	62nd	2009	35,000
28th	1990	30,000	63rd	2010	35,000
29th	1990	30,000	64th	2011	35,000
30th	1991	16,000	65th	2011	35,000
31st	1991	19,000	66th	2012	35,000
32nd	1992	35,000	67th	2013	35,000
33rd	1992	27,000	68th	2015	35,000
34th	1993	27,000	69th	2016	35,000
35th	1993	27,000			

Published by Goodman Fielder New Zealand Limited, 2/8 Nelson Street, Auckland 1010
Distributed by Goodman Fielder New Zealand Limited and Hachette New Zealand Ltd,
Level 2, 23 O'Connell St, Auckland 1010.

ISBN 978-1-86971-342-3
Recipes developed by Goodman Fielder New Zealand Limited and Alexa Johnston
Photography by Melanie Jenkins, Cover Illustration by Evan Purdie.